# Mentoring at Work

# Mentoring *at* Work

*Developmental Relationships in*
*Organizational Life*

Kathy E. Kram
Boston University

UNIVERSITY
PRESS OF
AMERICA

Lanham • New York • London

**Library of Congress Cataloging-in-Publication Data**

Kram, Kathy E., 1950–
Mentoring at work : developmental relationships in organizational life /
Kathy E. Kram.
p.   cm.
Reprint. Originally published: Glenview, Ill. : Scott Foresman, ©1985. (Organizational
behavior and psychology series) Bibliography: p. Includes index.
1. Success in business. 2. Mentors in business. 3. Mentors in the professions.
4. Interpersonal relations. 5. Organizational behavior. I. Title.
[HF5386.K78 1988]      303.3'4—dc19      87–31593 CIP
ISBN 0–8191–6755–X (pbk. : alk. paper)

88594

# PREFACE

*Mentoring at Work* is about relationships in organizations that enhance individuals' development in the early, middle, and later career years. What began as a study of mentor relationships between junior and senior managers in one corporate setting evolved into a program of research designed to clarify the nature of a variety of relationships between junior and senior colleagues, or between peers, who provide mentoring functions. The primary purpose is to present an intricate and realistic view of mentoring, to delineate its potential benefits and limitations, and to illustrate the various forms of developmental relationships that can exist in work settings.

I have brought an open systems perspective to this project. This means that I assume that relationships are significantly affected by the context in which they evolve and by the expectations, needs, and skills that individuals bring to them. Thus, I set out to understand how individuals' career histories and current situations, as well as the surrounding organizational circumstances, have jointly shaped the essential characteristics and evolution of their relationships with mentors, proteges, and peers.

Throughout this book I address three distinct audiences. First, for individuals at every career stage, I discuss a perspective on mentoring that I hope will discourage the "search for the right mentor" and encourage systematic self-diagnosis of relationship needs as well as strategies for building relationships that provide relevant developmental functions. Second, for practicing managers, I outline the major forces that must be taken into account when creating a context that stimulates an effective mentoring process. Finally, for human resource specialists and organizational researchers, I consolidate the available research to date and outline strategies for intervention and further research that will help improve the quality of worklife and organizational effectiveness.

At this point I'd like to add a stylistic note about the book. In order to avoid both sexism and consistently awkward phrasing, I have tried to balance my examples between the third person male and female managers. Some examples refer to the individuals in question as "he," others as "she." "He or she" could be freely interpreted into most of these examples. When gender was an important attribute, I referred to individuals as either a male manager or female manager.

Many people have made significant contributions to this book. My teachers at M.I.T., including Professors Dick Beckhard, Irv Rubin, and

Ed Schein introduced me to the field of Organizational Behavior and initially provided encouragement and guidance. My teachers at Yale University, including Professors Clay Alderfer, David Berg, Richard Hackman, Madeline Heilman, Rosabeth Kanter, and Dan Levinson, provided tremendous intellectual stimulation as well as constructive feedback and support. In particular, Clay Alderfer created a context in which my professional and personal growth flourished; I am most grateful to have had him as a mentor. In addition, Dan Levinson first sparked my interest in mentoring and continued to nurture it over the years in a manner that has significantly influenced my program of research on adult relationships in organizations. All of these individuals, and my doctoral student colleagues, significantly supported my early efforts to become a scholar.

My colleagues at Boston University, including Tim Hall, Dave Brown, Lloyd Baird, Max Bazerman, Marty Charns, Gerry Leader, Meryl Louis, Phil Mirvis, Don Pease, Zeba Hyder, and Kathy Fink have since helped me create an exciting intellectual climate in which to do my work. Tim Hall, in particular, provided ongoing guidance and conceptual input that improved the quality of the final manuscript. Others at the university, including Kathy Padwater, Leslie Lomasson, Vince Mahler, and Kathleen Kemmer, helped me get through the inevitable red tape of manuscript production.

Two individuals were directly involved in one of the major studies that is reported in this book. Lynn Isabella and Manny Berger, both doctoral students at Boston University at the time the research was conducted, were collaborators with me on the study of peer relationships at successive career stages. I greatly appreciate their insights, their hard work, and their colleagueship. Several other colleagues and friends, including Andrea Sigetich, Stephanie Zehnder, Gil Williams, Peter Gustavson, Dave Stevenson, Barry Seltser, Andy Souerwine, Carol Schreiber, Vickie Zelin, Norma Reiss, Bill Sackett, Ann Lewis, and Gene Dalton were wonderful sounding boards along the way. Finally, all of the individuals who participated in interviews with me or my colleagues shared invaluable parts of themselves that greatly contributed to the emergent perspective on mentoring that is reflected in the following pages.

The first major study was funded by the Columbia University Center for Research on Careers, and the second major study was funded by the Boston University School of Management. I am grateful to have received both the financial support and the endorsement for the work that I set out to do. The *Academy of Mangement Journal* willingly gave permission for Scott, Foresman to publish parts of articles that appear in the December 1983 and March 1985 issues. I am also quite indebted to John Nolan and Andrea Coens at Scott, Foresman, who managed the editing process and final production of this book so effectively.

I want to thank my mentors and peers for enabling me to learn about developmental relationships from my own experience. Also, I want to thank my family who have always provided the most important and consistent source of love, stimulation, and support. Finally, a most special thank you goes to my best friend, critic, advisor, and love, Peter Yeager, who was there at all hours of the day and night to help me see this book through to its completion.

Kathy E. Kram

# CONTENTS

# Relationships
# at Work

When asked to reflect on their major satisfactions and frustrations at work, people consistently mention others who influenced them. Relationships with superiors, peers, subordinates, friends, and family members are essential sources of support both during periods of major transition and throughout the ongoing process of career development.

Relationships that support career development enable an individual to address the challenges encountered moving through adulthood and through an organizational career. For example, the young adult who strives to launch a successful managerial career benefits from the coaching, counseling, and sponsorship of a more experienced senior manager. The middle-aged individual who reaches a plateau in terms of future advancement opportunity learns how to adjust to his organizational fate by sharing his experience with a peer who has encountered a similar dilemma. The female professional who forges a career in a nontraditional occupation finds support in talking with other women who are further along and more experienced. Finally, the impending retiree gains satisfaction and integrity from passing on knowledge and experience to younger, less experienced organizational members.

What do these relationships have in common? First, they allow individuals to address concerns about self, career, and family by providing opportunities to gain knowledge, skills, and competence, and to address personal and professional dilemmas. Second, they benefit both individuals; these relationships thrive precisely because they respond to current needs and concerns of the two people involved. Third, they occur in an organizational context that greatly influences when and how they unfold. Finally, these kinds of relationships are not readily available to most people in organizations; they remain a greatly needed but relatively rare occurrence in most work settings.

This book clarifies the nature of relationships that enhance career development. For students of management or practicing managers, the book defines the essential characteristics of these developmental relationships and suggests ways to build them at work. For management and organizational development specialists, the book provides a thorough understanding of the psychological and organizational factors which facilitate supportive relationships and suggests specific strategies for enhancing the quality of worklife and career development practices of their organization. For those engaged in related research, the book consolidates available theories and empirical studies on the role of mentoring (and other significant relationships) in career development.

## THE MENTOR RELATIONSHIP

The prototype of a relationship that enhances career development is the mentor relationship. Recently, both academic and business circles have focused a great deal of attention on this relationship. Derived from Greek mythology, the name implies a relationship between a young adult and an older, more experienced adult that helps the younger individual learn to navigate in the adult world and the world of work. A mentor supports, guides, and counsels the young adult as he or she accomplishes this important task.

Levinson et al. (1978), in their study of adult males suggest that a mentor relationship is the most important relationship in young adulthood. They emphasize the importance of the mentor in the young adult's development.

> In the usual course, a young man initially experiences himself as a novice or apprentice to a more advanced, expert, and authoritative adult. As the relationship evolves, he gains a fuller sense of his own authority and his capability for autonomous and responsible action. The young man increasingly has the experience of "I am" as an adult, and the relationship becomes more mutual . . . [p. 99].

> He [the mentor] may act as a teacher to enhance the young man's skills and intellectual development. Serving as sponsor, he may use his influence to facilitate the young man's entry and advancement. He may be a host and

guide, welcoming the initiate into a new occupational and social world and acquainting him with its values, customs, resources, and cast of characters. Through his own virtues, achievements and way of living, the mentor may be an exemplar that the protege can admire and seek to emulate. He may provide counsel and moral support in times of stress . . . [p. 98].

This kind of relationship benefits the mentor as well (Levinson et al., 1978; Dalton et al., 1977; Clawson, 1980; Kram, 1980). The reappraisal of one's past is a central developmental task at midlife. While helping a young adult establish a place in the adult world of work, an individual benefits from providing support and guidance. Through helping others, a mentor gains internal satisfaction, respect for his or her capabilities as teacher and advisor, and reviews and reappraises the past by participating in a young adult's attempts to face the challenges of early career years.

A number of research studies focus on understanding the nature of mentoring in organizational settings. These studies, done by individuals of varying perspectives, produced many descriptions of the nature of relationships between less experienced and more experienced adults in a work context. Kanter's (1977) notion of the sponsor relationship emphasizes the instrumental nature of a relationship between a junior and a senior manager; she suggests that the senior manager, by virtue of his or her formal position and organizational clout, empowers the young manager striving to climb the corporate ladder. Dalton et al. (1977), in a study of professional engineers and scientists, describes the necessity of a stage in career development when an individual expands his or her role to include the development of subordinates by providing the variety of functions outlined by both Kanter and Levinson. Clawson (1979), in his study of superior-subordinate relationships, describes how learning occurs in those relationships where many developmental functions are present.

Relationships between younger and older adults that contribute to career development are alternatively referred to as mentor relationships (Levinson et al., 1978; Dalton et al., 1977), sponsor relationships (Kanter, 1977), patron relationships (Shapiro et al., 1978), godfather relationships (Kanter, 1977), or as a relationship between good friends. Each of these suggests a slightly different picture of the relationship. While there is agreement about the potential value, there are differences in perceptions about the range of developmental functions provided, the intensity of the relationship, and the exclusivity of the relationship.

Levinson et al. (1978) suggest that the mentor relationship, as they describe it, is rare in organizational settings. Institutional constraints make it difficult for individuals to provide mentoring by discouraging supportive behavior in a highly competitive and bottom-line-results climate. Also, individuals are often limited in their capacities to nurture others because of their own personal dilemmas and concerns. Other less involving, exclusive, and intricate forms, like the sponsor relationship, are likely to be more available to more individuals. Each of these can be considered a developmental relationship because it contributes to individual growth and career advancement. Rather than limit our discussion to the classic mentor relationship, which is hard to come by in most organizational settings, we will consider the range of possible adult working relationships that can provide developmental functions for career development.

The popular press has done a disservice by implying that the key to career success is finding a mentor. This is an oversimplification of a complex web of work relationships that could be made available to individuals in organizational settings. The popular and academic literature several years ago suggested that further study of mentoring would show which developmental functions are needed by individuals at successive career stages, the range of developmental functions that can be provided by relationships at work, the potential positive and negative consequences of relationships that influence career development, and how the organizational context shapes the course of these relationships over time. Understanding the nature of the mentor relationship is the place to start.

## DEVELOPMENTAL RELATIONSHIPS

In order to investigate the nature of mentoring in organizations, I conducted an in-depth interview study of relationships between younger and older managers in a corporate setting. As I talked with members of a public utility organization of 15,000 employees (4,000 of whom were managers) about mentoring, it became apparent that the word *mentor* had a variety of connotations, and that from a research point of view it would be best not to use it. This decision allowed the more general concept of developmental relationships to become the focus of inquiry.

The managers talked about their career histories and, in particular, about relationships with more experienced managers that they viewed as contributing to their development. Thirty young managers between the ages of 25 and 35 were interviewed at length about their career histories in a two hour interview that enabled them to review their experiences and to reflect on significant relationships. When individuals identified one or more relationships with senior managers who had taken a personal interest in them, I arranged a second interview to explore either one or two developmental relationships in depth.

In order to complete the picture, the senior managers participated in a parallel sequence of interviews about the relationship and about their career histories. In the first random sample of fifteen young managers, only three were able to identify relationships with senior managers that had positively contributed to their development (indicating the relative unavailability of enhancing relationships with senior managers). In order to obtain enough relationship pairs to complete a thorough study, internal personnel staff were asked to suggest individuals who appeared to have mentors, sponsors, or the like. Eighteen relationship pairs were studied in detail, and they are our primary sources (see Table 1-1). I developed a comprehensive understanding of developmental relationships between junior and senior colleagues by researching fifteen young managers who reportedly had no enhancing relationships with more experienced senior managers, eighteen relationship pairs of young managers and senior managers, and ten top executives of the corporation who agreed to participate in retrospective interviews about their career histories and relationships that had significantly influenced their development.

The demographic characteristics of the research participant group are interesting for several reasons. First, at the outset of the study it was not clear whether age or hierarchical level was more important in shaping the nature of a developmental relationship; thus, both were studied by choosing a defined age group for young managers at second or third level management. Senior managers identified by these individuals were always older (though in one instance by only four years), and at third, fourth, or fifth level management. The effects of age and organizational rank are clarified by looking at the variation across relationships studied.

Second, by design, half of the young managers in the research sample of relationship pairs were female. However, only one of the senior managers and one of the officers were female, reflecting the general demographics of the organization. While cross-gender dynamics are discussed at length in Chapter 5, it was necessary to look toward other sources for additional insight. There was only one female mentor in the study, and no male managers identified female senior managers as their mentor.

Finally, there were no instances in this sample of the senior managers being younger than the junior managers. With more and more individuals changing careers or launching careers at midlife, we can expect to see more developmental relationships where the less experienced "junior" member is older than his or her mentor. These complexities become the focus of speculation throughout the book as we examine the effects of life and career stages on relationships at work.

From this first study I learned that relationships with peers frequently provide an important alternative to the primary developmental relationship with a senior manager. In a second study I interviewed individuals at three different career stages in order to explore how

**Table 1–1.**   Demographic characteristics of the primary research
participants in the study of mentor relationships.

| Relationship[a] | Junior Manager | | | Senior Manager | | | Relationship | |
|:---:|:---:|:---:|:---:|:---:|:---:|:---:|:---:|:---:|
| | Age | Sex | Level | Age | Sex | Level | Age difference | Level difference |
| 1 | 33 | M | 3 | 44 | M | 4 | 11 | 1 |
| 2[b] | 32 | M | 3 | 49 | M | 4 | 17 | 1 |
| 3[b] | 32 | M | 3 | 46 | M | 4 | 14 | 1 |
| 4 | 34 | M | 3 | 39 | M | 4 | 5 | 1 |
| 5[b] | 33 | M | 3 | 45 | M | 5 | 12 | 2 |
| 6[b] | 33 | M | 3 | 55 | M | 5 | 20 | 2 |
| 7 | 33 | M | 2 | 46 | M | 3 | 13 | 1 |
| 8 | 31 | M | 3 | 44[c] | M | 4 | 13 | 1 |
| 9 | 33 | M | 3 | 48[c] | M | 4 | 15 | 1 |
| 10 | 33 | M | 3 | 63 | M | Retired | 30 | 2 |
| 11[b] | 32 | F | 3 | 41 | M | 3 | 9 | 0 |
| 12[b] | 32 | F | 3 | 44 | M | 4 | 12 | 1 |
| 13 | 30 | F | 2 | 44 | M | 4 | 14 | 2 |
| 14 | 31 | F | 2 | 44[c] | M | 4 | 13 | 2 |
| 15 | 26 | F | 3 | 48[c] | M | 4 | 22 | 1 |
| 16 | 28 | F | 2 | 47 | M | 3 | 19 | 1 |
| 17 | 31 | F | 2 | 55 | M | 4 | 24 | 2 |
| 18 | 30 | F | 2 | 42 | F | Left company | 12 | 2 |

[a]In the research sample, relationships varied from less than two years to eleven years. At the time of the research study, only one relationship had clearly ended, five relationships were in the cultivation phase, and the remainder had been through one or more phases of separation created by structural job changes and/or significant changes within one or both individuals. The four phases vary in length, and in some instances, recycling through the cultivation and separation phases occurs several times.

[b]Three junior managers had two developmental relationships that were studied. Relationships 2 and 3, 5 and 6, and 11 and 12 each have a junior manager in common. Thus, there are fifteen different junior managers in the sample.

[c]Two senior managers were twice identified as significant others. Relationships 8 and 14, and 9 and 15 each have a senior manager in common. Thus, there are 16 different senior managers in the sample.

relationships with peers might be affected by unique developmental concerns that become salient in early, middle, or late career stages.

In this study of peer relationships, individuals in three different career stages in a large, traditional manufacturing organization were interviewed about their career histories and were asked to identify relationships with colleagues or peers that they felt supported their career development. During a second interview, two relationships were explored in depth in order to understand how these relationships developed over time and the relationships' essential characteristics. Then we conducted a parallel interview sequence with the significant others that were identified. The final research sample consisted of twenty-five relationship pairs (see Table 1–2).

Both of these major studies of relationships provided the basis for understanding the range of relationships between peers, and between junior and senior colleagues, that provide mentoring functions. The conceptual framework presented throughout this book is a direct outcome of systematic analysis of the interview transcripts, as well as extensive discussions about the data with professional colleagues and clients. Individuals' personal accounts not only offered insights into the essential characteristics of these developmental relationships, but also enhanced understanding of the complexities of cross-gender relationships, and how the organizational context shapes relationships.

The relationships between younger and older managers did not always replicate the prototype of the mentor relationship. Often, both provided important developmental functions that helped the young adult enter the world of work and helped the senior adult pass on experience to the next generation of managers. At the same time, however, there were some obvious and subtle variations among the relationships that are key to understanding what forces contribute to effective developmental relationships. The following examples point out the range of possibilities that exist and why.

## A Mutually Enhancing Relationship

The first example concerns a relationship that benefits both individuals. The young female manager met her sponsor, as she called him, after she had been working for the organization for one year as a first level manager in the department where he was a fourth level manager. Although they had never had a direct reporting relationship, they had interacted on a frequent basis for nine years. Since the first six months of their relationship, Anne had a sense that Norman was taking an interest in her career, and Norman had decided to support her movement up the corporate ladder.

The relationship supported both of them. It enabled Anne to develop a sense of competence and self-worth in the managerial role, and it provided opportunities for her continued advancement in the organization. At the same time, it enabled Norman to develop a sense of competence and self-worth, at a time in his career when his own rate of advancement began to decline, by passing on his wisdom and experience to

**Table 1–2.** Demographic characteristics of the research participants in the study of peer relationships.

| | Focal Person Organizational Level* | Age | Sex | Sex | Age | Significant Others Organizational Level* |
|---|---|---|---|---|---|---|
| **E** | Sub-section manager | 32 | F | F | 35 | Sub-section manager |
| **a** | | | | M | 55 | Unit manager |
| **r** | Unit manager | 32 | M | M | 36 | Individual contributor |
| **l** | | | | M | 32 | Individual contributor |
| **y** | Unit manager | 32 | M | M | 32 | Sub-section manager |
| **C** | | | | M | 40 | Section manager |
| **a** | Individual contributor | 31 | F | M | 38 | Individual contributor |
| **r** | Individual contributor | 29 | F | F | 34 | Sub-unit manager |
| **e** | | | | M | 29 | Individual contributor |
| **e** | Individual contributor | 27 | M | M | 36 | Individual contributor |
| **r** | | | | M | 32 | Individual contributor |
| **M** | Section manager | 45 | M | M | 48 | Sub-section manager |
| **i** | | | | M | 52 | Section manager |
| **d** | Section manager | 43 | M | M | 38 | Section manager |
| **d** | | | | M | 39 | Section manager |
| **l** | Unit manager | 43 | F | | | None |
| **e** | Unit manager | 36 | M | M | 42 | Sub-section manager |
| **C** | | | | M | 34 | Unit manager |
| **a** | Individual contributor | 42 | F | F | 55 | Unit manager |
| **r** | | | | | | |
| **e** | | | | | | |
| **e** | | | | | | |
| **r** | | | | | | |
| **L** | Section manager | 58 | F | F | 42 | Sub-section manager |
| **a** | | | | M | 53 | Sub-section manager |
| **t** | Sub-section manager | 61 | M | M | 59 | Sub-section manager |
| **e** | Unit manager | 63 | M | M | 63 | Individual contributor |
| **C** | | | | M | 57 | Unit manager |
| **a** | Individual contributor | 55 | F | F | 57 | Individual contributor |
| **r** | | | | M | 63 | Individual contributor |
| **e** | | | | | | |
| **e** | | | | | | |
| **r** | | | | | | |

*Organizational hierarchy progresses from individual contributor to unit manager to sub-section manager to section manager.

someone who could benefit from his interest and support. Anne's ongoing development was proof of Norman's ability to develop young
managerial talent.

During the first four years of their relationship, Norman sponsored
Anne for two significant promotions, coached her on organizational
politics, and protected her or intervened when she was criticized by
peers and immediate supervisors. In addition, he served as a role model
for Anne as one who had successfully battled the organization enroute
to senior management.

> Norm had an influence on what happened in my career; he kind of looked
> out for where I went and what kind of jobs I got. I always knew that he
> would be willing to take me back into his department at any time because I
> had done well before.

> I never worked directly for him . . . and yet he is the only person I have really
> felt a relationship with to some degree. When he supported me, it was like he
> knew who I was; if he saw me coming down the hall, he would know me.

Both personal and organizational factors stimulated changes in the
relationship during the last four years. When Anne was promoted out
of Norman's department into middle management, they had less contact, and their relationship began to evolve into a more peerlike friendship. A year before the interviews Norman lost the last opportunity for
promotion and a personal crisis of esteem began as he confronted his
aging and increasing obsolescence and the prospect of no further
advancement. During this period he was no longer psychologically
available to coach Anne, and organizationally he had lost considerable
power to sponsor and promote. These changes in Norman's situation
occurred while Anne was experiencing greater self-confidence and
autonomy. Anne had moved from being a novice to becoming a successful middle manager who was now more committed to an organizational career in which she felt increasingly competent. Simultaneously,
Norman had moved from being an organizational climber and
developer of young talent, through a crisis of blocked opportunity, into
a period of reassessment and redirection.

This relationship, like most work relationships that enhance development, provided functions that contributed to both career advancement
and personal development of each individual. Functions that enhance
career advancement, like sponsorship, coaching, and exposure-and-
visibility, are common to all developmental relationships between
younger and older adults in a work setting. Those that enhance personal development and an increasing sense of competence and self-
worth, like role modeling, counseling, or friendship, are common to

those relationships characterized by considerable interpersonal intimacy. Frequently, these latter functions are less available because of individual and organizational circumstances that interfere with forming a strong interpersonal bond. Anne and Norman's relationship took on considerable meaning and significance for both individuals. Norman used a parental analogy to describe the personal satisfaction he derived from the relationship.

> Maybe if I could say this without sounding corny . . . I kind of look at Anne, and she could be . . . , like my child, and that as a parent, I would want my children to be able to stand on their own two feet. I would like to think as a father that I had some contribution to what they stood for, what they believed in, and what they wanted to aspire to.

> If I thought, at some point, I could measure that what a child of mine was doing was the best thing in the world that they could possibly do, no matter what level it was or anything else, then I would feel I had made some contribution to that — a tremendous sense of satisfaction. I feel that way about Anne, although I don't think of her as a child. . . . I think of Anne as almost a peer, and hell, I was just 55 and she is about 30.

A supportive relationship between a younger and older adult in a work context can enhance the younger individual's development. This example demonstrates the reciprocal nature of the relationship and the mutual benefits to be had by both individuals. By coaching, counseling, and guiding a younger individual in challenges of early career years, the senior manager receives recognition and respect from peers and superiors for contributing to the development of young managerial talent. In addition, the senior manager, like Norman, receives confirmation and support from the young adult who emulates him and seeks his counsel. Finally, he experiences internal satisfaction in helping a less experienced adult learn how to navigate successfully in the world of work.

## A Destructive Relationship

The second example concerns a relationship that was mutually beneficial but is now unsatisfactory and frustrating for both individuals. Like the relationship between Anne and Norman, it had, for several years, provided developmental functions that aided the young manager's sense of competence and his advancement opportunities in the organization. In addition, like Norman, the more experienced manager had derived technical support, respect from peers, and internal satisfaction in providing mentoring functions.

This example deviates from the first in that after several years of mutual satisfaction, both Jack and Bill found the relationship problematic, noting that their interaction is now cumbersome and ineffective. After a structural separation of three years, Jack, at age 33 and now in a middle management position, has returned to a direct reporting relationship with Bill who, at 45, has just received his first promotion to senior management. Each has gone through significant changes during the period of separation and the trust, respect, and mutual value of the relationship is hampered by considerable frustration, anger, and guilt.

From Jack's perspective the relationship is more difficult because he now occupies the position that Bill previously held. He describes Bill as being unwilling to let him do the job he thinks ought to be done. In contrast to earlier years, Jack finds himself arguing frequently and feeling guilt and resentment about doing so. Jack now holds stronger convictions which developed during the three years that they did not work together, and has returned to Bill's department with more self-confidence. With this struggle for control, Jack experiences considerable guilt and anger that threatens his new-found sense of himself as a competent middle manager.

> We've had disagreements on what machinery to buy — but that's not the crux of it. From my end he's not listening to me and not letting me do the job the way I think it should be done. He's not supporting me anymore. From his side of it he probably feels that I'm not being a supportive subordinate. I honestly don't know what I am doing wrong — I've never encountered this problem before.

Jack's transition to middle management occurred after he completed his first job with Bill. When he returned to a direct reporting relationship, his self-confidence, his identity as a manager, and his career aspirations had altered considerably. These changes affected the degree to which he was willing to accommodate Bill's direction and control. In his new job he was responsible for the organization that Bill had recently managed. These factors contributed to the mounting tension and dissatisfaction in the relationship. During this same period, Bill also went through significant changes that influenced what he brought to the relationship after their structural separation.

After waiting years for a promotion to fourth level, having experienced disappointment and rejection each time he was "passed over," Bill finally reached the new position shortly before Jack returned to his department. The transition to fourth level and senior management had been a difficult one. He had faced the tasks of developing new peer relationships and learning how to operate effectively at this higher level. Undoubtedly, the transition affected his responses to Jack.

Holding on to his old responsibilities was the only way for him to maintain pride in the midst of the confusion and loneliness that he experienced in the new role. While Jack was feeling a high degree of self-confidence and ambition, Bill was struggling to get his feet on the ground in the role of senior manager.

Bill's self-doubts at work are compounded by changes in his family that threatened his sense of competence in the parenting role. Six years earlier, when Jack and Bill began working together, Bill was anticipating a bright future, both professionally and personally. At that earlier time, far more energy was available to coach, guide, and counsel someone like Jack. The self-doubts, competitive feelings with peers and subordinates, and the anxiety experienced during the transition, combined with Jack's newfound autonomy and strength in the middle-manager role, contributed to an increasingly strained relationship. Like Jack, Bill now feels some guilt and responsibility for the nature of their relationship.

> I don't feel as though I am using people near me as resources as best I could. I feel like I am directing too much. I am imposing my own thoughts on Jack too much. I guess . . . that's probably what he would say. . . .

> I can't even do as much for him as I could before—I've got my own concerns. At this level and at his level you are more on your own. I can do less for him now. . . . He will have to get support from others, not from me. . . .

In contrast to earlier years of their relationship, Jack and Bill now have needs and concerns that conflict; as a consequence, neither individual responds to the other. The current dissatisfaction and non-complementarity of the relationship is related to the transition that each individual experienced during the previous three years. The nature of the new reporting relationship, as well as new personal concerns, has pushed the relationship to a point where it now detracts from each individual's self-worth and continued development.

Thus, a previously enhancing developmental relationship can become dissatisfying and destructive as individual needs and/or organizational circumstances change. Like the relationship between Anne and Norman, this one went through phases. Different from the former, this relationship is no longer mutually enhancing. This difference highlights the fact that relationships at work are dynamic and changing and that their mutually enhancing value is limited by personal and organizational factors.

The similarities and differences reflected in these two cases highlight several important characteristics of developmental relationships. First, they provide a range of functions that enhance career advancement and psychosocial development of both individuals. Second, relationships are dynamic and changing; while enhancing at one time, a relationship can become less satisfying and even destructive. Third, the developmental functions that characterize a particular relationship and the phases that characterize its changes are shaped by individual needs and organizational circumstances. Given these characteristics, it is essential to understand how particular life and career concerns and the organizational context influence relationships.

## HOW LIFE AND CAREER STAGES AFFECT RELATIONSHIPS

Every individual brings a unique set of needs and concerns to relationships at work. These needs and concerns are shaped by all the events, experiences, and relationships that encompass one's life. When relationships allow one to address important needs and concerns, they are enhancing and valued. When relationships interfere with one's capacity to address these needs and concerns, they are dissatisfying and potentially destructive.

Research on adult development and career development has established that, at each stage of life and a career, individuals face a predictable set of needs and concerns which are characteristic of their particular age and career history (Levinson et al., 1978; Gould, 1978; Hall, 1976; Schein, 1976). These predictable patterns are reflected in concerns about self, concerns about one's career, and concerns about one's family. A particular set of concerns determine what an individual brings to and seeks from relationships at work.

Young adults who are launching new careers, for example, are concerned about competence and whether they will succeed in establishing viable and successful careers. Not only do they question their skills and abilities, but they search for occupational identities and a sense of who they can become in a new role and work context. Because they are new to the organization, they have many questions about how committed to become to this chosen career and organization, and whether or not advancement is desirable, given other personal sacrifices that may be required in order to compete for positions of responsibility and authority.

In the early stage of a career, and the early stage of adulthood, concerns about self and career may be accompanied by concerns about family life as well. Most individuals in their twenties are exploring intimate relationships and searching for an appropriate family structure apart from the family of origin. Defining one's role as spouse, lover, and/or parent are critical concerns. Finding the appropriate structure and the appropriate balance with one's work life are critical challenges that are part of what one brings to relationships at work.

Young adults seek out relationships that enable them to work on these developmental concerns. For example, since feedback on performance is needed to build a sense of competence and confidence, a relationship with a more experienced boss or colleague can satisfy concerns about competence and identity. Since this individual is new to the organization, she will need guidance, coaching, and support in learning the ropes. A more experienced boss or senior colleague who wants to teach and develop others is, again, a likely candidate for an enhancing relationship. This occurred in both of the earlier examples. These young managers, in the process of launching new careers, were able to address concerns about self and career in their relationships with more experienced senior managers.

A look at an individual further along in an organizational career is a useful contrast to the individual who is entering the adult world and the world of work. While the latter is in a period of initiation and exploration, the individual at midcareer is likely to be in a period of reassessment, reflection, and redirection. Still, with the difference in age and career history, this individual has concerns about self, career, and family.

The individual in midcareer is no longer establishing competence and defining an occupational identity. Instead, he is adjusting self-views now that he is no longer a novice but older with more experience. Questions about one's competence in relationship to peers and subordinates surface. For the individual who has advanced to a senior position in terms of organizational status, there are new questions about what it means to be a "senior" adult rather than a newcomer. There may also be questions about what lies ahead, given that advancement and growth opportunities are limited as the organizational pyramid narrows. For those who are satisfied with their accomplishments, it may be a time of shifting creative energies away from advancement concerns to concerns about leisure time, family commitments, or developing younger colleagues in the work context. Alternately, for those who are dissatisfied with their accomplishments, it may be a time of self-doubt and a sense of urgency as one realizes that life is half over, and one's career has been fairly well-determined (Levinson et al., 1978; Sofer, 1970; Jacques, 1965).

Coinciding with these concerns about self and career are concerns about one's role in the family as well. For many at midcareer and midlife, children are leaving home, and the complexion of the family is changing radically. In addition, as concerns about one's career shift, the family is needed for greater meaning and involvement. Each sphere of life is changing, and the primary concerns, while not ones of initiation, are likely to be ones of redirection and redefinition.

Individuals at midcareer bring these concerns about self, career, and family to relationships at work. Providing coaching, counseling, and support to younger adults at work may be essential to their sense of well-being and continued growth. It helps them redirect creative energies when career advancement is no longer a primary concern, and it allows them to review past decisions as they relive the same decisions with a less experienced colleague. So, as in the case described earlier, Norman derived great satisfaction in helping Anne develop her career. He found a new source of confirmation and identity in becoming a guide, sponsor, and mentor for someone in his organization.

There are numerous predictable patterns of needs and concerns that are possible at each stage of life and career. For those who launch careers at midlife, a unique set of concerns will surface as one faces dilemmas of early career years at a later age. For women who launch careers in male-dominated professions, there are concerns about identity, competence, and commitment to the occupation that relate to participation in a non-traditional career. For individuals who anticipate retirement, the impending loss of a work identity and organizational membership raises still other concerns. Whatever the particular dilemmas, questions, and concerns, they are the driving force behind significant relationships.

Any two individuals involved in a relationship bring a unique set of needs and concerns that are shaped by their respective life histories. We must examine what these are in order to understand why the relationship evolves, how it develops over time, and how it contributes to, or interferes with, continued growth and development. When individuals can address their concerns, as in the case where a young adult seeks guidance as he launches a new managerial career and a middle age manager seeks to develop younger talent, the relationship is an enhancing one. It thrives because the two individuals have complementary needs. Alternately, when one individual seeks aid in advancing his career and another is plagued with self-doubts and resentful of those who may surpass him, the relationship is likely to be dissatisfying since neither finds support in relating to the other. Finally, as was the case with Bill and Jack described in the last section, relationships may begin as mutually enhancing, and then later become less so as individual concerns change with movement to a new career stage.

## HOW THE ORGANIZATIONAL CONTEXT AFFECTS RELATIONSHIPS

Relationships at work are situated in an organizational context. Features of the organization, including its culture, the reward system, task design, and performance management systems, affect relationships by shaping individuals' behavior. It is essential to understand how an organization's structures and processes influence behavior in order to maintain those features that encourage supportive relationships and to modify those that impede them.

The multiple levels of authority and position that characterize hierarchical organizations create different responsibilities and perspectives which shape relationships at work. First, these multiple levels create needs at lower levels for support, guidance, and sponsorship. Frequently, developmental relationships between junior and senior managers provide the coaching, sponsorship, and visibility that is essential for career advancement. In addition, each time an individual moves to a higher level in the organization, the necessity to learn the ropes reappears, and more experienced colleagues become a critical resource for meeting this challenge. People at higher levels can offer important developmental functions to a less experienced individual, both upon entry into the system, and as he or she moves to each higher level of responsibility.

Multiple levels create peer and superior-subordinate relationships. While relationships with superiors are essential for developmental opportunities like sponsorship, coaching, and visibility, they are frequently viewed by individuals at lower levels as inaccessible, uncomfortably evaluative, or to be approached with caution. The unequal distribution of power in the hierarchical structure interferes with the formation of supportive relationships by creating the belief that initiating relationships with higher level managers is in violation of organizational norms. A culture that encourages frequent and open communication across hierarchical levels encourages the formation of enhancing developmental relationships more effectively than one in which communication across levels is rigid and discouraged (Deal & Kennedy, 1982).

Hierarchical organizations are characterized by a narrowing pyramid, which makes competition for promotion more severe as one advances. The potential for collaborative peer relationships is affected by this fact of organizational life, particularly when the reward system recognizes and encourages individual effort over collaborative effort at all costs. When opportunities are limited and individuals compete with their peers for those opportunities, relationship dynamics become strained and potentially destructive.

A limited opportunity structure creates perceptions of opportunity for advancement and growth that affect individual satisfaction, productivity, and behavior at work. Kanter (1977) suggests that individuals who have optimistic perceptions for their futures engage more positively in their work than those who perceive low opportunity or hold less power. The latter become withdrawn and depressed in their work context. For example, the senior manager who is plagued with depression, anger, and decreasing self-esteem as a result of blocked opportunity is likely to be unable to contribute positively to younger managers' development. Thus, perceptions of opportunity, created by the narrowing pyramid in particular and the opportunity structure in general, affect the extent to which people are willing and able to engage in supportive relationships.

The nature of task design influences productivity and satisfaction at work (Hackman, 1977; Hackman & Oldham, 1980). Jobs that provide skill variety and opportunities for feedback and growth can influence relationships by helping managers provide critical developmental functions. Most importantly, assignments that legitimize interaction across hierarchical levels encourage individuals at different career stages to interact with each other. This particular kind of task design encourages more experienced managers to teach, guide, coach, and provide feedback, and allows young managers to interact with, learn from, and gain exposure to potential sponsors and mentors. In contrast, highly individualized task design offers less opportunity for interaction and makes it less likely that individuals who have the potential to engage in mutually beneficial relationships will find each other.

The reward structure of an organization affects behavior in relationships through individuals' expectations (Lawler, 1977). If, for example, managers are encouraged and rewarded for developing subordinate managers, it is more likely that they will provide developmental functions than if their objectives stress only the importance of bottom-line results. Similarly, if individuals are rewarded for collaborative efforts in their immediate organizations or departments, they are more likely to form enhancing relationships with peers and superiors than if they are rewarded only for individual effort. An organization can perpetuate competitive dynamics, lack of trust and openness, and alienation among organizational members through a system of rewards that discourages attention to relationship-building activities and only recognizes bottom-line results.

Advancement to higher levels of an organization is a measure of career success. Since movement to higher levels brings increased status, financial benefits, responsibility, and authority, most individuals want to advance. While individuals may question this measure of success when they experience either significant costs associated with advancement or blocked opportunity, it is rare for one to remain free of the pressures to advance up the organization ladder. The promotional system, as a consequence, significantly influences relationships at work. It governs who assumes which positions, who makes critical career decisions, and what the requirements for success are.

For example, if sponsorship through a committee process is required for promotion, young managers are encouraged to secure this in relationships with more senior managers. At the same time, if senior managers are evaluated by superiors and peers by their efforts to develop younger talent, they will be careful to select and provide developmental opportunity to those who have high potential. In addition, as a result of Affirmative Action policies and fast-track programs, some individuals have greater access to coaching and support from higher level managers than others. The promotional system determines, to some extent, what developmental functions are needed by younger managers, and the accessibility of developmental relationships for individuals favored by particular organizational practices.

Frequently, job rotation is a requirement for promotion into higher managerial ranks. This requirement can both encourage and interfere with supportive relationships at work. Periodic movement facilitates exposure to individuals who can aid one's development. At the same time, if movement is required on an untimely basis, a significant relationship may be disrupted prematurely, and both individuals may suffer from the imposed separation. Job rotation policies, while an essential part of the human resource planning efforts of an organization, may impede relationships that are supportive of career development.

Effective performance management systems affect the quality and availability of developmental relationships by creating opportunities for managers and supervisors to coach, counsel, and support their subordinates' growth and advancement (Meyer, Kay & French, 1965; Beer, 1980; Levinson, 1976). *Performance appraisal systems* can offer feedback on individuals' competence and potential. *Management by objectives* systems offer a context in which relevant and realistic goals can be defined in order to increase the congruence between individuals' efforts and organizational goals. Finally, a *development planning* system can offer career counseling and advice on future opportunities. When these systems are absent or ineffective because organization members do not perceive them as relevant or because they lack the knowledge to implement them effectively, few discussions that provide developmental functions and solidify relationships occur.

A systematic diagnosis of how organizational structures, norms, and processes influence behavior in relationships with peers, superiors, and subordinates is a critical first step toward identifying the factors that encourage or impede effective relationship-building activities. In addition to modifications in promotional system practices, in the design of work, or in the design of a reward system, individuals can develop relationships through educational intervention that increases self-awareness and interpersonal skills. If organizational conditions are right, and if individuals are aware of their needs at successive career and life stages and have relationship skills, there are many opportunities for alliances. Often, these opportunities are untapped.

## CHALLENGES AND OPPORTUNITIES

The complexities of developmental relationships in organizations are quite apparent. An *open systems perspective* insures that a realistic and intricate view of the conditions that create or interfere with effective mentoring is achieved (see Figure 1-1). This perspective suggests that developmental relationships (with mentors and peers) are embedded in a larger system—the organization. Through its structures, systems, and processes, the organization influences which developmental functions

**Figure 1–1.**   An Open Systems Perspective on Mentoring. Individual attributes and organizational circumstances shape relationship dynamics. This model also applies to peer relationships.

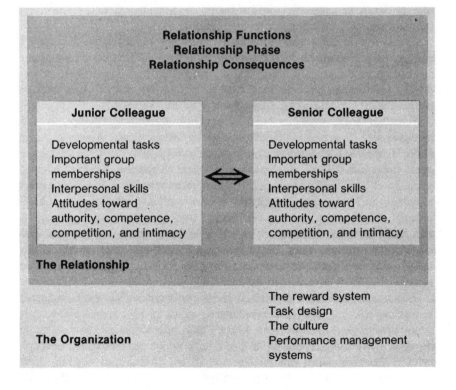

are provided and how relationships unfold (see Chapter 7). In addition, relationships are comprised of two smaller systems—two individuals who bring attitudes, skills, and concerns about self, career, and family to relationships (see pp. 39–42). These also influence which functions are provided and how relationships unfold (see Chapter 3). However, due to predictable changes in individuals' needs over the course of lives and careers, relationships will change, and they are limited in their duration and mutual value (see Chapter 4). The interaction of these individual and organizational forces creates relationship dynamics that significantly enhance or interfere with individual development.

Relationships that positively contribute to both individuals' professional and personal growth are essential from several perspectives. They ensure a high quality of worklife that allows individual growth and self-improvement. In addition, they increase organizational effectiveness by supporting the competence and professional development of an organization's membership. Finally, since work influences the quality of life in general, enhancing relationships contribute to an overall sense of well-being. These relationships are difficult to come by in most organizations, suggesting a need to create conditions that encourage individuals to form relationships. Individuals, organizations, and researchers face considerable challenge and opportunity.

There are at least two general avenues for exploration. Education can provide individuals with the knowledge and skills needed to manage relationships effectively. In addition, organizational structures, procedures, and norms can be modified to encourage rather than impede positive interaction among individuals who can benefit.

Whether in university or business settings, educational programs that increase self-awareness, understanding of relationship dynamics, and skills in building and maintaining relationships in a work context have great potential. Often, relationships are left to chance rather than consciously chosen and managed. By understanding how life and career histories and the organizational context affect relationships, individuals will develop greater sensitivity, awareness of self and others, and the diagnostic skills to make self-enhancing choices about relationship opportunities. Then, with training in critical relationship skills, individuals can scan the opportunities in a work context with positive action.

Education, however, is limited in its potential value. First, whether or not individuals can learn relationship skills in an educational setting is uncertain; perhaps previous history and relationships have more to do with individual capacities to build supportive relationships. Second, even if essential skills can be learned in an educational setting, their usefulness is limited by the organizational context in which individuals work. Organizational structures, processes, and norms can encourage or inhibit the use of effective relationship skills. Significant modifications in reward systems, task design, organizational culture, and performance management practices are needed before educational efforts are successful and individuals can form supportive relationships at work.

Several avenues for research warrant further exploration as well (Hunt & Michael, 1983). Educational efforts should be evaluated to assess whether relationship dynamics, self-awareness, awareness of others, and relationship skills can be developed in these bounded learning sessions. In addition, comparative organizational studies are needed to define the conditions under which enhancing relationships are available to more individuals in work settings and how to create these conditions. Finally, given the changing work force, further study of cross-gender and interracial dynamics in relationships at work is essential. Most research to date focuses on understanding the life stages and career development of men who followed traditional career advancement patterns. Both theory and intervention will be enriched by studying individuals with different backgrounds and aspirations in a variety of contexts. It is critical to consider not only interracial and cross-gender dynamics, but also the relationship experiences of adults at midlife who are launching new organizational careers.

This book provides the foundation for students, practicing managers, human resource specialists, and organizational researchers to pursue the challenges and opportunities outlined. Chapters 2, 3, and 4 discuss the characteristics of mentoring relationships, how they unfold over time, and how they contribute to development at different stages of managers' careers. Chapters 5, 6, and 7 address concerns of special interest, including the complexities of cross-gender mentoring, the alternatives to the classic mentor relationship found in peer alliances, and the organizational change strategies that can enhance the quality and frequency of supportive relationships.

The concluding chapter summarizes a new perspective on mentoring which emphasizes the value of considering a range of developmental relationships at each life and career stage. This perspective highlights both the benefits and the potential destructiveness of relationships. The book ends with specific implications for those concerned with the quality of relationships at work and their critical role in development.

# Mentoring Functions

Mentoring functions are those aspects of a developmental relationship that enhance both individuals' growth and advancement. These functions are the essential characteristics that differentiate developmental relationships from other work relationships. A number of research studies on relationships between junior and senior managers have identified a range of mentoring functions or mentoring roles (Levinson et al., 1978; Schein, 1978; Davis & Garrison, 1979; Phillips, 1982; Missirian, 1982; Clawson, 1979; Kram, 1980) that enhance development in unique ways. Some functions are observed more frequently than others, and a given developmental relationship may provide few or many of the possible mentoring functions.

Among the studies completed, a set of functions converges. These functions can be summarized in two broad categories. *Career functions* are those aspects of the relationship that enhance learning the ropes and preparing for advancement in an organization. *Psychosocial functions* are those aspects of a relationship that enhance a sense of competence, clarity of identity, and effectiveness in a professional role (see Figure 2-1). While career functions serve, primarily, to aid advancement up the hierachy of an organization, psychosocial functions affect each

**Figure 2–1.** Mentoring Functions. When a hierarchical relationship provides all of these functions, it best approximates the prototype of a mentor relationship.

| Career Functions[a] | Psychosocial Functions[b] |
|---|---|
| Sponsorship | Role Modeling |
| Exposure-and-Visibility | Acceptance-and-Confirmation |
| Coaching | Counseling |
| Protection | Friendship |
| Challenging Assignments | |

[a]**Career Functions** are those aspects of the relationship that enhance career advancement.

[b]**Psychosocial Functions** are those aspects of the relationship that enhance sense of competence, identity, and effectiveness in a professional role.

individual on a personal level by building self-worth both inside and outside the organization. Together these functions enable individuals to address the challenges of each career stage.

Career functions are possible because of the senior person's experience, organizational rank, and influence in the organizational context. It is this structural role relationship that enables him or her to provide sponsorship, coaching, and exposure-and-visibility to help a junior colleague navigate effectively in the organizational world. The senior colleague thus develops support among subordinates and respect among peers and superiors for developing talent for the organization. Both individuals benefit from these functions in increasing their position of influence through the relationship.

In contrast to career functions, psychosocial functions are possible because of an interpersonal relationship that fosters mutual trust and increasing intimacy. The quality of this interpersonal bond enables the younger to identify with the older and to find a model whom the younger would like to become. In addition to providing a role model, the senior colleague counsels the younger one on dilemmas that surface as the novice launches a career. Each individual experiences acceptance and confirmation through interaction with the other; mutual liking and respect support the young adult's views of self in the new work role, and simultaneously support the senior adult's views of self as someone with valuable wisdom and experience to share.

The range of career functions and psychosocial functions in relationships varies. In a study of managers in a corporate setting (Kram, 1980), all of the eighteen relationships provided career functions, and three of the relationships did not provide any psychosocial functions.

Relationships that provide both kinds of functions are characterized by greater intimacy and strength of interpersonal bond and are viewed as more indispensable, more critical to development, and more unique than other relationships in the manager's life at work. Relationships that provide only career functions are characterized by less intimacy and are valued primarily for the instrumental ends that they serve in the organizational context.

In her study of female managers, Phillips (1982) made a distinction between primary mentors and secondary mentors. Primary mentors are individuals who are labeled as mentors and who are considered unselfish, altruistic, and caring. Secondary mentors are individuals who are part of a more businesslike relationship where an exchange benefits both individuals' career advancement. Phillips noted that primary mentors are more scarce and are described with greater indebtedness by female managers, while secondary mentors are easier to come by; a manager might have several during a particular period of a career. Primary mentors provide both career and psychosocial functions, whereas secondary mentors provide only career functions.

Shapiro et al. (1978) describe a continuum of advisory/support relationships at work that ranges from mentor to sponsor to guide to peer pal. This continuum suggests that, on the mentor end, relationships are highly exclusive, characterized by a hierarchical or parental role relationship, and are high in emotional intensity. As one moves toward the other end of the continuum, relationships become more available and less exclusive, less parental, and less emotionally involving. These dimensions paralleled the variations found in the previously mentioned mentoring studies. Primary mentors are those who provide both career and psychosocial functions and are relatively scarce, exclusive, parental, and intense. Secondary mentors are those who provide only career functions and on the continuum would be sponsors or guides.

Clawson (1979) offers two dimensions for distinguishing developmental relationships that parallel the continuum, the primary and secondary classification, and the career and psychosocial functions categorization. In his study of effective boss-subordinate relationships he delineated (1) comprehensiveness of influence, that is, how many different aspects of an individual's life a relationship affects; and (2) mutuality of individual commitment to the relationship where high commitment on the part of both individuals characterizes the primary mentor relationship.

## CAREER FUNCTIONS

Career functions are those aspects of a relationship that enhance advancement in an organization. These functions include sponsorship, exposure-and-visibility, coaching, protection, and challenging work assignments. These functions have three common characteristics. They are possible because of the senior person's position, experience, and organizational influence. In addition, they serve career-related ends of the junior person by helping him or her learn the ropes of organizational life, gain exposure, and obtain promotions. Finally, they serve career-related ends of the senior person by helping him or her build respect by developing younger talent and develop support among people who work in his or her area of responsibility and who are likely to be in positions to reciprocate support.

## Sponsorship

Sponsorship is the most frequently observed career function. A senior individual's public support of a young individual launching a career is critical for advancement in an organization. Sponsorship involves actively nominating an individual for desirable lateral moves and promotions. Opportunities for advancement through the hierarchy are made possible in one-on-one conversations as well as in formal promotional decision meetings. Without sponsorship, an individual is likely to be overlooked for promotions regardless of his or her competence and performance.

> I would tell people on the committee that I felt she was the best candidate for the job. I didn't say to them that she was the only candidate, but I let them know very strongly that I would be happy if they found Anne was the person they wanted to fill the job. The way it works is that the committee would have a job opening, and they would all argue for people they were supporting, and then a selection would be made.

Sponsorship occurs at formal committee meetings as well as in informal discussions with peers, superiors, and subordinates who participate in promotion decisions. Movement to a new department or to a higher level in the organization depends on how much good press concerning the potential and competence of an individual is communicated. This communication can range from direct verbal support in a promotion meeting discussion (as previously illustrated) to indirect support through association. Kanter (1977) suggests that individuals gain "reflected power" from their sponsors. It is not only what a sponsor says about an individual, but the knowledge that he or she is a sponsor that empowers the less experienced person and creates opportunities for movement and advancement.

To rely on one individual for sponsorship is a high-risk strategy in most organizational settings. If a sponsor leaves the organization or loses credibility with colleagues, an individual's career may suffer. In addition, since sponsorship depends on interpersonal and political processes, the more who favor a particular individual, the more likely it is that such processes will work in his or her favor.

Sponsorship from several individuals strengthens the credibility of the positive recommendations offered. Even if a sponsor continues to be powerful and active in the promotional decision process, there is the risk that others will question to what extent the younger individual can thrive on his or her own without a particular senior's support. Not only might questions about favoritism be raised, but doubts about the individual's merit and performance potential apart from the sponsor may surface.

> When I put in an evaluation on Dick and recommended him for certain positions, people would say, they aren't too sure Dick's all that good. When you're the only one he has worked for for a few years, they feel maybe that you're getting biased. As I began to sense that more and more in the first year or two that we worked together, I realized that he had to get away from me into a different job so that he would be exposed to different people.

During the early stage of an organizational career, sponsorship helps a newcomer build a reputation, become known, and obtain job opportunities that prepare him or her for higher level positions. Later in a career, sponsorship is a deciding factor in obtaining a promotion that might otherwise go to an experienced and well-regarded peer. The political processes inherent in promotion decisions are pervasive; as one climbs the organizational ladder, competition for promotions increases and sponsorship becomes more essential.

At first glance, sponsorship appears to benefit only the recipient. However, successful sponsorship benefits the sponsor as well. By sponsoring someone who advances and performs well, upper management views a senior as having excellent judgment. Credibility is enhanced as a reputation for finding and developing younger talent is confirmed. In addition, sponsorship recipients reciprocate support in the future through continued good performance and other avenues as they, too, reach senior status. In contrast, the individual who sponsors someone who later fails risks poor judgment by his or her peers and superiors. In this situation, the senior is viewed as indiscriminately supporting a friend, as having poor skills in assessing potential and developing talent, or as not looking out for the best interests of the organization.

Senior managers describe their success at sponsorship with pride; it is a measure of their good judgment and strong influence in the organization. Alternately, the inability to effectively sponsor a junior person for a promotion reflects poorly on the senior's credibility and influence. In the long run, sponsorship results in personal advancement and organizational recognition for both individuals. The sponsorship function creates opportunities for advancement for the junior person, and, at the same time, it is a measure of the senior person's credibility and organizational clout.

## Exposure-and-Visibility

The opportunity to demonstrate competence and performance is created by a senior manager's decision to give a junior person responsibilities that require written and personal contact with other senior managers. The exposure-and-visibility function involves assigning responsibilities that allow a lower-level manager to develop relationships with key figures in the organization who may judge his or her potential for further advancement.

> One of the things we talked about was getting him more direct exposure to the officers while he was still on this job, not wait until he goes to a new job. So there have been a number of cases just in the last couple of months where if the officer calls me I give it to Jerry and basically say, "close it out with so-and-so."

These assignments also allow a junior manager to learn about parts of the organization that he aspires to enter. Contact with people at higher levels or in different parts of the organization helps him learn about organizational life at middle or senior levels of management. The exposure-and-visibility function not only makes an individual *visible* to others who may influence his organizational fate, but it also *exposes* the individual to future opportunities.

> In terms of job experience, I feel that he benefited from his tour with me. It broadened his perspective and got him some experience and exposure in an area that he otherwise wouldn't have had. . . . I'd like to think that, through the discussions we had about his performance in this new area, he became more effective. All the time I tried to let him know what others thought of him as candidly as I could.

Exposure-and-visibility serves as a socializing force; it prepares an individual for positions of greater responsibility and authority, and it introduces her to others so that she becomes a viable candidate. At each stage of a career, the function supports movement in an organization by providing critical learning experiences and by ensuring that such experiences demonstrate competence and potential to key organization members.

A senior manager may be reluctant to provide this career function. The risk involved in providing exposure is similar to that in providing sponsorship; it can enhance or detract from the senior manager's reputation. For example, if a junior manager fails on a task that involves interaction with other senior managers, it can reflect badly on the senior who put him forward. Alternately, a senior may be more concerned with enhancing his own career. He may be uncertain about his own reputation in higher organizational ranks, and he may choose to hold on to high visibility tasks.

Exposure-and-visibility facilitates a young manager's entry into higher ranks of an organization. At the same time it reflects well on the senior person's choices about who to support when highly visible tasks are effectively completed.

## Coaching

This career function enhances the junior person's knowledge and understanding of how to navigate effectively in the corporate world. Much like an athletic coach, the senior colleague suggests specific strategies for accomplishing work objectives, for achieving recognition, and for achieving career aspirations. In early career stages, a senior manager helps a junior manager by providing advice on the requirements of the new position in the organization hierarchy. The senior colleague has an experienced perspective to share with the junior colleague who has the status, and limited knowledge, of a newcomer.

> At the end of the first week on this job, he called me to his office and gave me a list of things he expected of me. Very clear, what this coach guy wanted out of me in order of priority. He spent a couple of hours with me reviewing it all. And he asked me, "What do you want from this job? What do you want to get out of your tenure here? What do you want from me? Give me a list." So I gave him a list. I came back after a week and gee, it was so comfortable working with him since then. It was a different level of interest than other bosses have shown in me and it worked out very well in terms of knowing where you are. . . .

At later career stages, coaching continues to be important. While a person is no longer a novice, he or she continues to need access to information available only through connections with more senior managers.

> I try to inform him, I have an understanding of how I perceive what is going on up at the top of the business and how Congress is impacting our company. I don't want to limit topics in any way, but that to the best that I can understand it myself, that I can give him an appreciation for what the pressures are as perceived by the top people in the business. Not because he will then do anything directly because of that knowledge, but in effect that his work life, and all the little decisions that he makes as he goes along, will be done in the context of having that understanding.

Frequently, coaching involves sharing ideas on how to make a presentation to senior management in order to insure positive reception of a work product. It involves feedback after such critical events on the individual's style of operation. Often, coaching involves sharing a senior person's understanding of the important players—who can be trusted, who has the power, and who is likely to support or attack in a particular situation.

> In the last year things are moving in a different direction. We are starting to talk about my career, how we see people and how you handle things. General conversations of, well, he has experienced that and he knows this and understands certain relationships that are in the company and who knows who and how they interact—kind of passing that knowledge along. This is additional information that is helpful to me.

The individual without an interested coach is at a disadvantage in relating to the organization because of insufficient knowledge of the informal and political process. At the same time, however, the individual with an interested coach is significantly influenced by one particular perspective on the world; this may or may not be a perspective that ultimately enhances his or her ability to navigate in the organization. The information and advice gained through coaching is essential to career advancement; those who have several coaches at various career stages are most fortunate.

A senior manager is enhanced by providing the coaching function. Passing on useful knowledge and perspectives to a junior colleague confirms the value of one's experience. This sharing also helps create the next generation of managers who hold a similar perspective, thus insuring that one's views are carried on into the future. Finally, being a coach allows the individual at midcareer or beyond to feel effective at developing younger talent for the organization. Like sponsorship, successful coaching gains respect from one's peers and superiors.

## Protection

This function shields the junior person from untimely or potentially damaging contact with other senior officials. There may be times when visibility is not in the best interest of the individual. If a particular work task has not proceeded on schedule, or if the individual is new to an area and has yet to learn how to navigate appropriately, the senior manager may choose to take responsibility for contact with relevant senior officials until such time when exposure will benefit the junior colleague's reputation. Because of his or her previous track record, the senior person can afford the attention in tough situations and in doing so, protect the other from negative publicity. Protection involves taking credit and blame in controversial situations, as well as intervening in situations where the junior colleague is ill-equipped to achieve satisfactory resolution.

I tried to protect him from the outside world until I felt he was ready to be seen. I had spent an awful lot of time in that area and when I went back, I knew the environment—the likes and dislikes of my superiors and the general inner workings of the department. Inner relationships of various people, too, who could be trusted and who couldn't be trusted and stuff like that. So I pretty much kept Dick under wraps in terms of other people seeing him for several months, until I, from my own relationship with him, I could judge that he had picked up enough knowledge and could handle himself well enough.

Protection is a career function that can support or smother the individual. It supports career advancement by reducing unnecessary risks that can threaten an emerging reputation as a potential manager. It smothers the individual when it prevents exposure-and-visibility in high risk situations that can enhance the junior manager's reputation. A senior manager's decision to intervene and to provide protection is a critical one that can significantly enhance or interfere with future advancement opportunities.

We had a talk when I left his division and I had made a comment to him about how it was amazing to me that I still survived with all the trouble that I had gotten into. His remark to me was, well at least you were right! He said, "I backed you up on a lot of things but only because you were right." So that indicated to me that the reasons I didn't get into a lot of trouble on some of the things I had gotten into was because he had run interference.

In cross-gender relationships, the protection function is often perceived as inappropriate. Either a young female feels as though she is being deprived of important developmental opportunities, or the senior colleague notes that he has a tendency to protect a young female subordinate more than he would her male counterpart. Excessive protection reflects a basic discomfort with the unfamiliarity of working closely with a manager of the opposite sex. While a senior manager may have good intentions of supporting the young female manager, his response in tough situations may prevent her from learning to navigate independently. His desire to protect her stems from the real difficulties for women in the corporate world, as well as from stereotypical patterns of relating in male/female relationships. In contrast to excessive protection, there are times, especially in tough situations, when a young female manager feels abandoned and senses that a senior manager's intervention and support are needed but not available. The appropriate balance of this function appears to be more difficult to achieve in cross-gender relationships.

Providing this function also contributes to a senior's reputation by demonstrating his ability to develop junior talent for the organization.

Protection that shields a junior person from unnecessary risk or criticism confirms the senior's ability to positively intervene in a situation where he can use his status and clout in supportive actions for others. As with exposure-and-visibility, the protection function can be self-serving if it is offered in order to build one's own reputation at the expense of a junior colleague's growth and development.

## Challenging Assignments

This function characterizes effective boss-subordinate relationships. It relates to the immediate work of the department. The assignment of challenging work, supported with technical training and ongoing performance feedback, enables the junior manager to develop specific competencies and to experience a sense of accomplishment in a professional role. This job-related function is more limited in its direct impact on career advancement; however, it is critical in preparing the young manager to perform well on difficult tasks so that she can move forward. Often a senior manager is referred to as a teacher because of the technical knowledge and useful feedback provided in challenging work assignments.

> He's given me the respect or confidence to let me run pretty much on my own. I tend to go to him less for signouts on things and just assume that it's OK, and inform him of decisions I make. It's worked out well. This is different than I've ever had in my whole career. . . .
>
> I see him like a teacher—totally impressive in terms of knowing all the fundamentals, but also knowing them because he has experienced them—and sharing them with you and bringing you along. . . . The kind of teacher everybody would want to get into his class because you know he cares about you as an individual. He is one of a kind.

Through this function an individual develops essential technical and managerial skills through work that encourages learning. The senior person has a critical role in designing this kind of assignment. First, the ongoing support and feedback on performance enable the junior person to meet the challenges presented. Without critical feedback and support, the junior person might feel overwhelmed by the degree of complexity of assignments or angry for being asked to do so much at this point.

Challenging work assignments not only provide important learning opportunities for the young manager, but also relieve the senior manager of specific technical responsibilities. Thus, in providing this function, the senior manager receives technical support that enhances his or her ability to attend to other responsibilities.

> I think I completely trust him today. I trust him to know what is going on in his operations, to take care of things . . . I have no qualms in terms of confidentiality, I have no qualms about him badmouthing me, in running me upstairs. And I've had very good feedback from my peers on his performance.

> He has made my work life more enjoyable . . . He really has made it easier for me to do other things or to do things I think need doing because I don't have to spend an inordinate amount of time with him.

Without this function, a junior person remains unprepared for positions of greater responsibility and authority. While sponsorship, exposure-and-visibility, coaching, and protection open avenues for advancement, challenging work assignments equip the individual with the skills to take advantage of these opportunities.

The timing of a relationship in each individual's career, as well as the formal role relationship between the two managers, influence which career functions are likely to be provided. For example, a relationship involving a direct reporting situation that evolves at the beginnning of a young manager's career may emphasize coaching and teaching through challenging work assignments. Alternately, a relationship involving a structural separation of several management levels that occurs several years into a young manager's career may emphasize sponsorship; the frequency of interaction prohibits daily coaching, training, or teaching, and previous learning reduces the need for these functions.

## PSYCHOSOCIAL FUNCTIONS

Psychosocial functions are those aspects of a relationship that enhance an individual's sense of competence, identity, and effectiveness in a professional role. These functions include role modeling, acceptance-and-confirmation, counseling, and friendship. The junior person finds support for who he or she is becoming in a new work role that increases a sense of competence, effectiveness, and self-worth. The senior person can satisfy important needs at midlife that increase a sense of competence, effectiveness, and self-worth. Psychosocial functions affect each manager on a more personal level than career functions; their benefits extend beyond organizational advancement and generally carry over to other spheres of life.

While career functions depend on the senior person's position and influence in the organization, psychosocial functions depend more on the quality of the interpersonal relationship. The role relationship is not as crucial as the emotional bond that underlies the relationship. Career functions affect the individual's relationship to the organization while psychosocial functions affect the individual's relationship with self and with significant others both within and outside the organization.

## Role Modeling

Role modeling is the most frequently reported psychosocial function. A senior colleague's attitudes, values, and behavior provide a model for the junior colleague to emulate. The latter finds in the senior a particular image of who he can become. As he aspires to positions of greater authority and responsibility, he imagines himself in these roles by identifying with the senior manager. To the extent that the junior colleague sees parts of his current and idealized self, the senior colleague serves as an object of admiration, emulation, and respect.

> Alan was very influential. I respected him as being pretty sharp and pretty astute. He had a lot of guts to tackle the problems that existed in the area and that was the union-management business. I was really identifying with him in terms of what and how you run something, how you manage something. You would sit down and talk about or debate how you do certain things, what should we do in this kind of situation. We would be right in line. I think it was the way I came at a problem; it might be similar to the way he would come at a problem.

> I also respected him as an individual that I saw as very articulate, smart, sharp and the kind of boss that you would respect, at least from where I was. Maybe a good way to say it would be that he was a good role model for me.

Role modeling involves the senior person setting a desirable example, and the junior person identifying with it. It is both a conscious and an unconscious process; a senior person may be unaware of the example she is providing for a less experienced colleague, and a junior person may be unaware of the strength of identification. At the same time, interaction around business tasks, common organizational concerns, and larger career issues is a conscious modeling process; through such dialogue the junior person learns approaches, attitudes, and values held by his model, and the senior person has the opportunity to articulate central parts of her self-image in the work role.

The identification process is complex. The junior person may emulate certain aspects of the senior person's style and may reject others. Over time, he differentiates himself from the admired object by incorporating some aspects and by choosing to be different in other respects. As this differentiation process occurs, the junior person develops a clearer sense of who he is and what has been incorporated from a senior manager who has provided a role model. The model shapes his style, personal values, and professional identity.

For example, a young manager learns to manage work groups, relate to peers and superiors, manage work/family tensions, and assume positions of greater responsibility by observing how a senior manager approaches these tasks. Fundamental respect and admiration for the senior manager make the young manager open to learning through observation. The senior manager legitimizes growing parts of the young manager's self-image as he or she demonstrates that particular attributes are effective in the managerial world.

> I came to work for Michael about a year and a half ago. He is just a super guy. I've never met anybody like him before in the company. . . . I think what he does most for me is—just by his example. He's a model that you watch and see how he works. He is just an interesting guy. I'm learning a higher order of organizational skills that I will take with me where I go.

> He is a neat guy to work for. Well, I've tried to emulate a lot of things he does. After working for him I've had more meetings with my subordinates to develop a team effort which I know if I didn't work for him I wouldn't be doing. So, I've become more democratic about the way I operate because of him. I think I've taken greater interest in my subordinates and their livelihoods and wants and needs and desires than I ever did before. I have also taken a greater interest in my own development than I ever had before.

Role modeling succeeds because of the emotional attachment that is formed. Often, transferential feelings occur in the relationship. For example, a young male manager likens a senior manager to his father by using the same words and feelings to describe both figures. In addition, a senior manager likens a young manager to his or her children while watching the young manager develop an identity that incorporates parts of the senior manager's self-image. Both individuals feel attachment, protection, ambivalence, and rebellion that parallel experiences in earlier relationships.

The identification and transference that underly the role modeling function are more complex in cross-gender relationships (see Chapter 5). Young female managers are more ambivalent and confused about whether to, and how to, emulate senior male managers. They frequently wish for a senior female manager who has confronted similar experiences unique to women at work, since a senior male manager acts in ways that may be inappropriate or ineffective for the female manager. The limitations of a cross-gender relationship are most apparent in this function; not only does the female manager lack an adequate model in the senior manager, but the male senior manager is less likely to identify and to see parts of himself in the young woman.

However, in any junior/senior work relationship, both individuals benefit from role modeling. The junior person discovers valued parts of self by identifying with the senior person, and the senior person rediscovers valued parts of self in observing the extent to which these parts are incorporated by his or her junior colleague.

## Acceptance-and-Confirmation _____

Through this function both individuals derive a sense of self from the positive regard conveyed by the other. As the junior person develops competence in the work world, the senior person's acceptance-and-confirmation provide support and encouragement. Similarly, as the senior person strives to feel useful and creative in later career years when advancement and recognition are less frequent, a junior colleague's acceptance-and-confirmation provide support for the wisdom and experience offered the next generation of managers. Positive feedback on performance, mutual liking, and mutual respect help both individuals. A relationship provides psychological nurturance through this function.

> He has always been interested in me, and he always respected me — even when I had gotten into a lot of trouble when I was in my second level assignment. I used to have a propensity for pissing off people and got into a lot of battles. Norm would stick up for me. When I left his department he would still drop by and just ask me how things were going. He never stopped supporting me. . . .

Acceptance-and-confirmation enables a junior person to experiment with new behaviors. A relationship that provides this function has a basic trust that encourages the young adult to take risks and to venture into unfamiliar ways of relating to the world of work. This basic trust makes such risk-taking less awesome than for others who are not as convinced that mistakes while learning will not result in rejection.

The junior colleague who experiences acceptance-and-confirmation becomes more willing to disagree and start conflict in the relationship. The relationship that provides this function tolerates differences and thus allows self-differentiation. Conformity is more likely when a junior person does not experience acceptance-and-confirmation; in such instances, he spends more energy trying to please and win acceptance and less energy exploring who he wants to become in the organizational world.

> I trust him completely; I would have no fear of telling him anything. It's really nice. If I have problems with my boss or one of my people, I would go and bounce it off of him frequently. . . .

> He would bounce things off of me, too. That began to make me feel good, too. He trusts me as well and he would do that. If he had a problem, he would ask me what I thought about it. It has been a really nice relationship — whereas with some people you trust them to a certain extent, but you feel that you don't know them as well or you wouldn't want something to get around.

A senior person benefits from the acceptance-and-confirmation offered by his or her junior colleague in several ways. In the face of disconfirmation conveyed by blocked opportunity for advancement, the younger person provides an important source of respect and support that counteracts potential loss of self-esteem. In addition, as the senior manager confronts aging and possible obsolescence, the junior manager provides support and appreciation that enable the senior manager to find value in what he or she still has to offer to younger individuals and to the organization.

## Counseling

Counseling is a psychosocial function that enables an individual to explore personal concerns that may interfere with a positive sense of self in the organization. Internal conflicts that put him or her at odds with self become the focus of discussion in the relationship. In this context an individual finds a forum in which to talk openly about anxieties, fears, and ambivalence that detract from productive work. The more experienced senior colleague provides a sounding board for this self-exploration, offers personal experience as an alternative perspective, and helps resolve problems through feedback and active listening. Through this process the junior colleague is able to cope with personal concerns more effectively.

> Well, we might be getting into things, such as, do you really want to put up with this shit to be a manager? That type of thing. It is worth it? Look what happens if you continue to be the workaholic type and all this other stuff, what is it going to get you? Is it going to be worth it? Are you going to be satisfied with yourself? Do you see what it has done to some of these other people? Is that really what you want to be? It was that kind of thing. What I respect is, that it was the kind of a boss/subordinate—no, I really didn't view it as a boss/subordinate thing, it has got to be hard for a boss to say that to a subordinate, but he did. We would talk about it, and I didn't even have to initiate it.

Personal concerns in the early stage of a career fall into three major areas: how an individual can develop competence and potential while also feeling productive and satisfied in a newly chosen career; how an individual can relate to peers and superiors without compromising personal values and individuality; and how he or she can incorporate growing responsibilities and commitments at work with other areas of life. These developmental tasks involve clarifying one's relationship with self, with the organization, and with other spheres of life. The counseling function is important in accomplishing these tasks.

At each successive career stage an individual will have personal concerns about self, career, and family that can detract from effective work. In early years, important questions arise about competence, commitment to the organization and to advancement, work/family balance and relationships with peers and superiors. Other questions arise in later years. Exploring these concerns with a trusted other who empathizes because of similar experiences is desirable throughout one's career.While the concerns shift with age and experience, the need for a sounding board never disappears.

Both the content and the process of interaction are important to examine in order to understand the nature of the counseling function. A young manager may, for example, feel ambivalent about advancing in the organization because of the perception that important values must be compromised as one climbs the corporate ladder. In a counseling context, this concern may be discussed, but not necessarily resolved. It is the process of exchange when one's senior manager conveys acceptance, support, and empathy that enables the young manager to tolerate the ambivalence and address it. Without such an opportunity, the junior manager may leave the organization, withdraw psychologically from the organization, or relate falsely to others in order to hide the conflict. Any of these responses reduces the young manager's potential to effectively engage and produce in the world of work.

In providing counseling, the senior manager becomes a confidant for the young manager. As a confidant, he again provides an important function that enables him to feel helpful and productive. In the counseling context he not only aids the young manager, but also relives and reworks similar personal dilemmas encountered earlier in his career by helping the young manager work on these concerns.

> I was the same totally committed work type person for a number of years as Dick was. And I saw him going the same road where I had been. When I developed more perspective myself, I changed and I guess I was trying to explain to him that he probably will change too, and why doesn't he start thinking now about it — he might gain three or four years that I lost.

What is shared in the relationship goes beyond the boundaries of most hierarchical relationships. The young adult derives comfort in discovering that he can share doubts and concerns without risking exposure to others in the organization. He can also address conflicts that could otherwise interfere with effectiveness and self-worth. The senior adult satisfies important needs by enabling a younger colleague to successfully manage personal dilemmas. And by sharing his own experiences and self-insights, he remembers previous points of decision during earlier career stages. The alliance formed through the counseling function counteracts the organizational force that can contribute to alienation and a decline in self-worth.

## Friendship

This function is characterized by social interaction that results in mutual liking and understanding and enjoyable informal exchanges about work and outside work experiences. Both individuals are pleased with the friendship function since it enhances experiences at work. Each finds in the relationship someone she can enjoy sharing personal experiences with, eating lunch with, or at times, someone to escape from the pressures of work with. The social interaction of the friendship function enhances work on the difficult tasks of early and middle career years.

> I, with all the bosses I ever had, I am more personal with him. I had times of sharing about what do you think, what concerns do you have . . . and times of just relaxing and having fun. We share a lot of confidence and respect for each other and feel very comfortable working together. . . .

> There are lots of things that cause you to chew your fingernails, and it is nice to be able to emote and talk about them, get them off your chest, and then relax. . . .

The friendship function allows the young adult to begin to feel like a peer with a more senior adult. Whereas relationships with authority figures are generally more distant, evaluative, and parental, a developmental relationship that provides this function combines elements of a teacher, a parent, and a good friend. As the friendship function emerges, the young adult experiences increasing mutuality in the relationship. This facilitates movement into the upper level as she discovers colleagueship and informality in relating to someone who is more experienced and older. Over time the novice feels more like an experienced peer, and she can then interact more easily with others in authority.

The friendship function provides a special opportunity for the older adult as well. Through informal interaction with a younger adult, she can maintain connection with the youthful parts of herself. Fears of growing older and becoming obsolete are reduced as enjoyable interaction with a younger colleague demonstrates her ability to stay in touch and relate easily with a younger generation. The social interaction provided by the friendship function enables an individual at or beyond midcareer to maintain a sense of vitality.

In cross-gender relationships this function is more limited because of the anxiety about one-on-one informal encounters, as well as by the external scrutiny of the relationships by other organization members. In these relationships, individuals often avoid those informal settings where enjoyable interaction might occur. As a consequence, potential colleagueship is threatened.

I would never do those things with her that I did with the men — go out to lunch, one-on-one, stop for a drink, or many other things of the nature that you would do with people of your own sex. I just completely avoid one-on-one situations other than those that are completely work-related.

The reactions others might have if you're seen with a younger subordinate of the opposite sex — what they might think if you happened to be going out for lunch other than in the cafeteria, or seen after hours . . . what are they thinking? So I prefer to avoid those situations that make other people talk or suspect.

In general there are limits to the friendship function. Most individuals choose to contain informal social interaction to the work context in order to minimize the conflicts created in being both boss and friend. Thus a senior manager manages the boundaries of the friendship so that she can also evaluate and judge the young manager without feeling guilty or ambivalent. While friendship adds spontaneity and enjoyment to each manager's life at work, it is limited by other relationship functions and cross-gender dynamics that cause each individual to maintain a comfortable distance.

Psychosocial functions are important because they enhance each individual's sense of competence, identity, and effectiveness in his or her work role. Through these functions, a young adult launching a career clarifies personal values, develops confidence in a unique style, and can address dilemmas that surface during early adulthood. At the same time, the senior adult addresses critical tasks of middle adulthood. In the younger colleague, he or she finds someone to influence and help in ways that satisfy important needs of midlife. In providing a role model, counseling, acceptance-and-confirmation, and friendship, the more experienced adult relives the past; if the younger adult grows as a result of these efforts, the older adult experiences that growth as his or her own.

## WHICH FUNCTIONS ARE LIKELY TO BE PROVIDED?

Career and psychosocial functions are not entirely distinct; supporting career advancement may also enhance an individual's sense of competence and effectiveness in the managerial role. So, for example, a senior manager's sponsorship provides acceptance-and-confirmation to a younger colleague. Similarly, counseling involving discussion of a personal problem may also provide coaching on how to navigate effectively in the corporate world. Any interaction in a relationship may combine elements of a number of career and psychosocial functions. This interaction effect increases the potency and benefits of a relationship that provides a range of functions.

There are several factors that influence which functions are provided in a relationship. First, the developmental tasks of each individual shape what needs are brought to the relationship; individuals' important needs will affect what functions are sought out and offered in the relationship. Second, the interpersonal skills brought to the relationship influence how the relationship gets started, how it unfolds over time, and the range of possible functions. Finally, the organizational context shapes the range of functions by affecting the formal role relationship, the opportunities for interaction, and the extent to which individuals are encouraged to participate in mentoring activities.

Developmental tasks are reflected in concerns about self, career, and family (Levinson et al., 1978; Schein, 1978; Hall, 1976; Super, 1957). Each individual brings a particular set of concerns to a developmental relationship. Indeed, the opportunity to address concerns by relating to the other person is what frequently sets a relationship in motion. For example, a young adult who is launching a career may have concerns about how to establish a niche in the organizational world and may have questions about competence and potential for advancement. The individual who provides role modeling, coaching, and acceptance-and-confirmation will respond to this young adult. The senior adult who wants to coach and who embodies some of what the young adult wishes to become will provide both career and psychosocial functions.

It is, perhaps, less obvious how a senior manager's developmental tasks influence which functions occur in a given relationship. A senior manager's willingness to provide career and psychosocial functions is shaped by his or her own concerns about self, career, and family. The individual with generativity needs is more likely to want to coach and counsel than the individual who is still involved in developing his or her own sense of competence and possibilities for advancement. Similarly, the individual who is content with his or her own accomplishments is more likely to provide sponsorship, coaching, and acceptance-and-confirmation than the individual who is dissatisfied with blocked opportunities and career plateaus.

A developmental relationship begins because the developmental tasks of both individuals are complementary; both can fulfill important needs through the relationship. The career and psychosocial functions are shaped by what each seeks and offers. Over time, the range of functions will change as individual needs change; a young manager may come to need less coaching and more sponsorship, or a senior manager may be more motivated to coach and counsel.

The range of functions provided in a relationship is affected by the interpersonal skills and capacities of each individual. For example, a new relationship is nurtured when the younger individual knows how to ask for guidance, and the older individual knows how to offer counseling and coaching. In addition, skills in active listening and giving and receiving feedback affect the extent to which counseling, coaching, and acceptance-and-confirmation are provided. Frequently, coaching is provided and counseling is not; the former function involves advice-giving and direction whereas the latter involves active listening and acting as a sounding board rather than an expert.

Most career and psychosocial functions require effective communication skills; however, some do more so than others, as the examples of counseling and coaching indicate. If both individuals have effective skills in listening, giving and receiving feedback, managing conflict and disagreement, and managing competition and collaboration, there are no limits to the range of functions in a given relationship. Building rapport and increasing trust are the prerequisites for increasing the range of functions. After about six months to a year, sharing intimate career concerns through counseling and friendship functions can occur.

Interpersonal skills that support a wide range of career and psychosocial functions are affected by more subtle attitudes toward authority, toward one's own competence, and toward conflict, competition, and intimacy. The individual who has negative feelings toward those in authority is less likely to welcome some mentoring functions than the individual who has positive views. The individual who questions his or her own competence is less likely to provide mentoring functions than the individual who is self-assured. Those who can tolerate conflict and manage competitive feelings are more likely to seek out and offer a wide range of mentoring functions. These attitudes are substantially shaped by life experiences and relationships (Levinson, 1976). At the same time, they do change with movement through the life cycle as individuals address self, career, and family concerns and as they experience different adult relationships at work.

Attitudes toward the opposite sex also influence interpersonal styles and, consequently, the nature of a developmental relationship. Men in authority positions with the experience, position, and inclination to provide mentoring functions may be limited in their relationships with younger female colleagues; concerns about increasing intimacy, over-protectiveness, and sex-role stereotyping can narrow the range of functions. Similarly, women may find inadequate role models, may play the role of helpless maiden, or may fear the potential for increasing intimacy as well. And in the relatively rare instances where women are the mentors and men the junior colleagues, other potential barriers created by cross-gender dynamics are likely to ensue. In general, the counseling and friendship functions are threatening because of the intimacy that may develop, because the public image of the relationship cautions against frequent interaction and overt sponsorship, and because the role modeling function may be inadequate (see Chapter 5).

An individual's actions in a relationship are influenced by his or her other relationships. Thus, if an individual has supportive relationships with peers and superiors, it is likely that each will provide some of the mentoring functions. In contrast, the individual who is new to a job setting, with few supportive relationships, seeks a wide range of career and psychosocial functions in a relationship that offers that potential. Senior managers are also affected by the constellation of relationships in their work lives; managers without one or more subordinates to coach may provide mentoring functions if their own needs for growth are important. In contrast, managers who have a cadre of junior people may be less available to provide more than occasional coaching, exposure, or sponsorship to another junior colleague. One's willingness and capacity to undertake and build developmental relationships are affected by relationships already in place.

The organizational context also affects which functions are provided in a relationship. Many career functions are not possible without a particular role relationship and formal position in the organizational hierarchy. So, for example, sponsorship depends on the senior manager's position and influence in the organization. Similarly, exposure, coaching, and protection depend on the senior person's greater organizational experience. A senior's perceived status, relative to the junior's and to his or her peers, affects which career functions can be provided. In addition, the level difference between junior and senior parties in a relationship affects the range of functions possible. The smaller the level difference, the greater the opportunities to provide daily coaching, challenging assignments, counseling, and friendship. The greater the level difference, the greater the opportunities to provide sponsorship, exposure, and protection.

Other features of an organization affect which functions are provided in a relationship. The reward system influences which functions lead to advancement and the degree to which senior managers are rewarded for providing them. In some settings sponsorship is essential for advancement, and senior managers are expected to choose those they will actively support in promotional decisions. In other settings active sponsorship is considered favoritism and is not explicitly recommended, though it may occur informally. When mentoring functions are perceived as part of a manager's job, they are more likely to be provided.

The design of work also influences which functions can be provided. Daily coaching is more possible when interdependent work opportunities are available. More specifically, when the design of work encourages managers at different levels to work together, a range of mentoring functions will probably be provided, since frequent interaction is more likely. Collaborative tasks allow not only for coaching, friendship, and challenging assignments, but also for modeling, exposure, and protection.

Organizational norms and practices can influence which functions are provided in a relationship in ways beyond those concerning the reward system and the design of work. Practices concerning job rotation, promotion, performance management, and communication procedures all either support or interfere with particular career and psychosocial functions. It is necessary to consider these multiple influences on individual behavior in an organizational context to fully appreciate how the context limits or expands the range of career and psychosocial functions provided.

## IMPLICATIONS

The range of mentoring functions possible suggests that developmental relationships vary in the ways they support individual development. To assess whether a particular relationship is a mentoring relationship or not is not as worthwhile a task as to assess which career and psychosocial functions are evident. Some relationships provide the full range of functions (and therefore approximate the "classic" mentoring relationship), while many others provide only a subset of the possibilities.

Individuals are more likely to build supportive relationships at work if they consider what their needs are, which career and psychosocial functions would respond to those needs, and who in the organization might be available and capable of providing those mentoring functions. After a systematic diagnosis of this kind, it is possible to outline with whom to initiate and build a relationship. Such strategy enables an individual to assume responsibility for relationships at work and to direct one's energy in positive directions. Those who feel isolated or "disconnected" from the organization will feel empowered as they build relationships that support their career advancement and personal development.

Many junior managers assume that mentors and sponsors choose whom they want to support and that they have no control over whether they will be chosen. They fail to recognize the extent to which they can influence relationships. For example, the young manager who remains in his office hoping that someone will notice his work and competence is less likely to receive coaching, sponsorship, and other mentoring functions than the individual who seeks out advice and feedback while informing senior colleagues of his interests, skills, and activities.

It is equally important to recognize the potential reciprocity of a developmental relationship. When a manager at midcareer, for example, provides sponsorship, coaching, counseling, and friendship, she not only furthers a junior colleague's growth and development but her own as well. By offering career and psychosocial functions, the midcareer manager satisfies generative needs, stays in touch with a younger generation, and, if the junior colleague advances, receives recognition and respect from peers and superiors for developing younger talent.

Individuals who are aware of their own needs and who have the understanding and empathic skills to sense the needs of others are better prepared to focus on relationships with potential. It makes little sense, for example, for a junior manager to seek a relationship with a senior colleague who appears to be either immersed in advancing his own career or consumed with a personal crisis of esteem; these individuals are unlikely to support others. Similarly, the senior manager who wants to mentor and coach is wise to center his attention on those who want to learn and grow, rather than those who have little interest in their own development or in the organization.

Organizations can encourage supportive developmental relationships in two ways: educational intervention and structural intervention. The first allows individuals to learn concepts, skills, and attitudes that form supportive relationships at work. The second creates systems and practices that encourage mentoring functions and eliminates those systems that interfere or inhibit them.

Educational interventions increase self-awareness and awareness of others in similar and different career stages. In an educational context, individuals explore their own concerns about self, career, and family, and discover that they are not alone in their experiences of particular dilemmas. Through interaction with peers, they develop greater self-insight and legitimize the discussion of personal experiences, preparing them to build necessary relationships in their work settings. In workshops or seminars with peers, individuals find confirmation, empathy, and legitimization. In workshops or seminars with people at dissimilar career stages, individuals develop understanding for those with whom they may later want to build a mutually beneficial relationship.

Educational interventions also build skills that help form developmental relationships. While self-awareness is essential to defining what one needs, skills in listening, managing conflict and intimacy, giving and receiving feedback, and others are essential for building a mutually enhancing relationship. It is striking to observe how frequently opportunities to listen and counsel are lost and how often individuals do not reach out to each other for want of knowing how to do so. Through experiential learning methods, individuals practice overcoming obstacles to building the kinds of relationships they desire.

Educational intervention of this kind has little positive value if the organizational context does not support classroom experiences. Organizations can examine their reward systems to insure that managers are encouraged to provide mentoring functions to younger colleagues. They can examine the nature of work design, the procedures and practices of job rotation and promotion, and the general climate to see whether or not these factors encourage frequent and quality interaction across hierarchical levels (see Chapter 7).

Organizational researchers should investigate how various organization structures and processes affect relationships at work, since many features can encourage or interfere with mentoring functions. For example, frequent job rotation (as a prerequisite for advancement) provides wide exposure to departments and people; however, it can interfere with the formation of a developmental relationship that provides both career and psychosocial functions by disrupting continued and frequent interaction on the job. Systematic comparisons of how different organizations handle these and other practices, and how these practices affect the quality of such relationships, will lend further insight into the conditions that support mentoring functions.

There is also a need to evaluate the possibilities in the educational arena. To what extent can individuals learn to provide mentoring functions? What skills enable individuals to initiate and build supportive relationships at work, and can they be learned in the context of adult education in the work setting? Are some individuals more available than others for these kinds of relationships, and, therefore, should educational efforts be geared toward a particular population? What are the appropriate educational interventions, if useful skills in mentoring processes can be acquired?

Finally, while we have come far in understanding the nature of mentoring and how career and psychosocial functions support individual development in early and middle career years, a complete understanding of a variety of adult relationship types is lacking. There is a need to further explore how relationships that provide only some of the mentoring functions differ in their impacts, and how multiple relationships with senior colleagues and peers (in contrast to one classic mentor relationship) can support development (see Chapter 6). Mentoring functions are important because of the age-related and career stage-related concerns that individuals have which can be addressed through developmental relationships (see Chapter 4). Researchers interested in the role of relationships in career development will make significant contributions by delineating the constellations of relationships that are possible (and desirable) at each successive career stage.

# Phases of
# a Mentor
# Relationship

The most essential characteristics of a developmental relationship are found by noting the mentoring functions that the relationship provides. Through sponsorship, coaching, protection, exposure-and-visibility, or challenging work, the junior colleague learns the ropes of organizational life and prepares for advancement opportunities. Through role-modeling, acceptance-and-confirmation, counseling, or friendship, he or she develops a sense of competence, confidence, and effectiveness in the managerial role. By providing a range of career and psychosocial functions, the senior colleague gains recognition and respect from peers and superiors for developing young talent, receives support from the junior colleague who seeks counsel, and experiences satisfaction by helping a less experienced adult navigate effectively in the world of work.

A description that includes only these mentoring functions is, however, static and incomplete. Developmental relationships between junior and senior colleagues are characterized by an evolutionary process; the

An earlier version of this chapter appeared in article form in the *Academy of Management Journal,* December 1983.

functions provided, individual experiences, and the quality of interactions vary with time (Levinson et al., 1978; Clawson, 1979; Missirian, 1982; Phillips, 1977). This dynamic perspective illuminates how and why essential relationship characteristics change and the impact that this change has on each individual's development.

Most researchers' descriptions of phases of mentor relationships converge. For example, Levinson et al. (1978) acknowledge that mentor relationships generally begin with a sense of excitement and strong mutual attraction and, after several years, often end with ambivalence, anger, gratitude, and/or resentment. They suggest that, much like a love relationship, a battle occurs at the end. This battle enables mentor and protege to separate and to move in to new relationships that are appropriate for their current developmental needs.

In their studies of female managers, Missirian (1979; 1982) and Phillips (1977; 1982) outline specific phases of the mentor relationship. The former defined phases of initiation, development, and termination, and the latter defined phases of mutual admiration, development, disillusionment, parting, and transformation. In substance, these descriptive models are quite similar. At the same time, both of these models were derived from retrospective accounts of managers who described relationships from earlier in their careers, presenting the possibility of distorted data due to faulty recall. Second, they were derived from one perspective of the relationship, rather than from personal accounts of both parties in the relationships. Thus, they do not clearly delineate how the relationship benefits the mentor, but only how it benefits the junior colleague. Third, these phase models are based solely on interviews with female managers, limiting the findings to a population that does not include the many mentor relationships that involve men. Finally, and perhaps most importantly, these studies, while illuminating what generally occurs in the mentor relationship, did not identify the factors that cause movement from one phase to the next.

In this chapter, four predictable phases of a mentor relationship are described. These phases were derived from interviews with eighteen pairs of managers who were involved in hierarchical developmental relationships that provided a range of mentoring functions (see Table 1-1). The phases include an *initiation phase*, when the relationship is started, a *cultivation phase*, when the range of functions provided expands to a maximum, a *separation phase*, when the nature of the relationship is altered by structural changes in the organizational context and/or by psychological changes within one or both individuals, and a *redefinition phase*, when the relationship either evolves into a completely new form or ends entirely.

These phases suggest that mentor relationships are limited in their

**Figure 3–1.** Phases of the Mentor Relationship.

| Phase | Definition | Turning Points* |
|---|---|---|
| Initiation | A period of six months to a year when the relationship begins and becomes important to both managers. | Fantasies become concrete expectations. Expectations are met; senior manager provides coaching, challenging work, visibility; junior manager provides technical assistance, respect, and desire to be coached. There are opportunities for interaction around work tasks. |
| Cultivation | A period of two to five years when the maximum range of career and psychosocial functions are provided. | Both individuals continue to benefit from the relationship. Opportunities for meaningful and more frequent interaction increase. Emotional bond deepens and intimacy increases. |
| Separation | A period of six months to two years after a significant change in the structural role relationship and/or in the emotional experience of the relationship. | Junior manager no longer wants guidance but rather the opportunity to work more autonomously. Senior manager faces midlife crisis and is less available to provide mentoring functions. Job rotation or promotion limits opportunities for continued interaction; career and psychosocial functions can no longer be provided. Blocked opportunity creates resentment and hostility that disrupt positive interaction. |
| Redefinition | An indefinite period after the separation phase when the relationship ends or takes on significantly different characteristics, making it a more peerlike friendship. | Stresses of separation diminish, and new relationships are formed. The mentor relationship is no longer needed in its previous form. Resentment and anger diminish; gratitude and appreciation increase. Peer status is achieved. |

*Examples of the most frequently observed psychological and organizational factors that cause movement into the current phase.

duration and that they can become destructive for one or both individuals if they are maintained beyond the time when individuals' needs are complementary. Such mentor relationships must end so that young adults have the opportunity to establish autonomy and peer status in relation to their mentors.

Two kinds of forces act on a relationship to cause it to move to a new phase. First, the developmental tasks or personal and professional concerns of both individuals influence how each responds to the other and, therefore, which mentoring functions are sought out and provided. Second, the organizational context influences the amount and quality of interaction between the two individuals through systems and practices that shape behavior in the relationship. So, for example, as a young manager develops a sense of competence and confidence and desires to operate more autonomously, he or she may no longer seek counseling or coaching functions. Or a promotional decision that is unrelated to a developmental relationship may force a structural separation that decreases opportunity for interaction and continued critical career and psychosocial functions. These individual and organizational changes shape the functions provided, the affective experience of the relationship, and the quality of interaction. Combinations of individual and organizational forces can push a relationship to a new phase.

The tone of individuals' personal accounts suggests distinctions in the quality of relationships in their first year compared with that of three or four years later. For example, the initiation phase is often described with excitement and strong positive feelings. In contrast, the separation phase is often described with a sense of loss, confusion, or anxiety. These emotional cues suggest important differences in how a mentor relationship is experienced at various points.

Finally, there is variation in the current phase of the relationships. It is possible to learn about the different phases by comparing, for example, personal accounts of those individuals who are in relationships that began within the last two years with accounts of those individuals with relationships of more than five years. Managers starting out in a developmental relationship view the initiation phase differently from those who have moved through a separation phase. These comparisons provide insight into the subtle, but important differences reflected in relationship phases.

## RELATIONSHIP PHASES

At the time the research was conducted, one mentor relationship had clearly ended, five relationships were in the cultivation phase, and the remaining twelve had been through one or more phases of separation. Separations were created by structural job changes and/or emotional distancing that resulted from significant changes in one or both individuals' needs. While these developmental relationships varied in length (averaging five years), they all proceeded through the four predictable, yet not entirely distinct phases (see Figure 3-1). In the discussion of each phase, several relationships are illustrated in order to highlight important variations that can occur within that particular phase.

## Initiation

During the first six to twelve months of the relationship, both individuals' strong positive thoughts result in behavior which encourages an ongoing and significant relationship. While the formal role relationship varies from a direct reporting relationship to an indirect reporting relationship to no formal role relationship at all, experiences during the initiation phase have much in common. Each individual gains valuable experiences through interaction with the other.

Young managers' recollections of the first six to twelve months of the relationship suggest that a fantasy emerges in which the senior manager is admired and respected for his competence and capacity to provide support and guidance. In this fantasy, the senior manager embodies an object for positive identification and is viewed as someone who will support the young manager's attempts to operate effectively in the organizational world. With time, the senior manager's behavior lends credence to these initial fantasies and becomes inviting and supportive. The young manager feels cared for, supported, and respected by someone who is admired and who can provide important career and psychosocial functions.

> I think being a first job in my career, there were a lot of transitions I was making, and a lot of them were hard. . . . You know—realizing that you were at the bottom—there were thousands of others like you, and you didn't know everything to start with—wanting to know and not knowing . . . and wanting challenging work and not getting it. . . .

> Yet John, three levels of management away from me—he hired me—and I guess I had the feeling that he believed in me and that even though I didn't have the right degree, I could still do it. . . . I had the feeling that, in fact, there was someone who recognized what I was going through and who had faith in me to make the right decisions. . . . I was able to do a lot of different projects, work with others, and really get in the know because of him. . . .

Senior managers' recollections of this period suggest that the young manager quickly represents someone with potential, someone who is "coachable," and someone who is enjoyable to work with. A fantasy evolves of someone who can become an object for the transmission of the senior manager's values and perspectives on the world. The young manager is viewed as someone who can provide technical assistance and who can benefit from the senior manager's advice and counsel. Thus the possibility of contributing to the young manager's growth and success motivates the relationship.

> Karen was the second or third person that came in. I interviewed her and I was completely impressed with her. My assessment of her was that she was a real comer — I tried to give her some advice of sorts as I got to know her — you know, understanding what the company is about . . . taking her to meetings and giving her the opportunity to present her ideas. . . .

> I guess I really get an inner pride, particularly in being someone getting all that respect so fast from other people. It is kind of challenging to help them succeed. The accomplishment is not that I hired them, but that over time other people recognize them as well. That really puffs out your chest a bit. That other people agree with your assessment and judgments. . . . It's like being in a hall of fame, when they succeed because of your help — maybe you don't get all the applause, but you did a tremendous job!

Fantasies of the other individual combine with confirming events to help an important relationship grow. A mutual attraction develops and as time passes, both individuals develop positive expectations for the relationship based on those early encounters which suggest that fantasy will become reality. These positive expectations encourage both managers to seek out and to nurture the new relationship.

Initial interactions that create and support positive expectations occur in many ways, including a direct hire interview, an informal interaction around common work tasks, a direct reporting relationship created by unrelated promotional decisions, or through peer recommendations that encourage the senior manager to seek out the young manager as a potential subordinate. Work on common business tasks, recommendations from significant others, and discussions of performance or departmental concerns cause each to develop positive expectations of the value of relating to the other. In most cases there is a balance of initiative on both sides; the young manager begins to look toward the senior manager for support and guidance, and the senior manager begins to provide developmental opportunities.

The events of the first year transform initial fantasies into concrete positive expectations. For example, an opportunity to work on a high visibility project is interpreted by the young manager as proof of the senior manager's caring, interest, and respect. Alternately, a request for assistance or a volunteered criticism of the department is interpreted by the senior manager as proof of the young manager's assertiveness and competence. These interpretations set the relationship in motion and help move it to a new phase.

Fantasies are more powerful than concrete events during the initiation phase than at any other point in the relationship. The young manager's wish for someone to guide, counsel, confirm, and support and the senior manager's wish to pass on knowledge and experience and build loyal and competent fellowship are the most potent forces which push the relationship to a new phase.

## Cultivation

During the cultivation phase, which lasts from two to five years, the positive expectations that emerged during the initiation phase are continuously tested against reality. As the relationship continues to unfold, each individual discovers the real value of relating to the other. The range of career functions and psychosocial functions that characterize a mentor relationship peaks during this phase.

Generally, career functions emerge first as the senior manager provides challenging work, coaching, exposure-and-visibility, protection, and/or sponsorship. As the interpersonal bond strengthens with time, psychosocial functions emerge. Sometimes they include, primarily, modeling and acceptance-and-confirmation. In instances of greater intimacy they include counseling and friendship as well. While career functions depend on the senior manager's organizational rank, tenure, and experience, psychosocial functions depend on the degree of trust, mutuality, and intimacy that characterize the relationship.

Variation in the range of functions provided during the cultivation phase is due to differences in individual developmental needs, individual capacities to engage in trusting relationships, mutuality, and intimacy, as well as organizational features that may limit both frequency and quality of interaction. In addition, during this phase, the relationship shifts from a one-way helping relationship toward one of greater mutual exchange. As the young manager develops a sense of competence, self-worth, and mastery in the professional role, and the senior manager begins to trust the younger manager to continue to perform well, both encourage greater reciprocity. The young manager feels increasingly able to give to the senior manager, and the senior manager takes pride in seeing the effects of his or her efforts in the relationship. This shift toward greater mutual exchange reflects the individual growth that occurs as a result of the developmental relationship.

A young manager, after two years in a developmental relationship, noted how challenging work assignments, coaching, role modeling, and acceptance-and-confirmation contributed to his sense of competence and enabled him to navigate more effectively in his organization.

> It is a hard thing to put your finger on, but it is reinforcing. He has given me an awful lot of confidence in myself that I lacked before. I had almost begun to feel that I was not really of much value. . . . Now I feel that I am being pushed, advised, growing. He has given me a lot of self-confidence that has made me much stronger and more valuable a person to the company. . . . I never enjoyed speaking before groups and that sort of thing before and now it doesn't bother me. I have a certain confidence that I feel that he has given me, because he forced me into a lot of situations of speaking before a group, before superiors . . . running a meeting . . . he has given me this self-confidence.

For a senior manager, this phase of the relationship produced substantial satisfaction in knowing that he had positively influenced a younger individual's development. The young manager received a promotion into middle management and had recently left the department.

> I can tell you that the biggest satisfaction that I get is seeing someone that you have some faith in really go beyond where you expect and really seeing them get recognized for that. . . . To see them do an excellent job and see them get recognized for it is probably the most gratifying thing, like seeing your son graduate from college, like seeing your mother get a degree when she's 45 years old — it's that kind of pride that you take. You know you had faith in these people, you've helped them along, but you haven't told them what to do . . . it's like raising children . . . when you see those people get promoted and you're really pleased. And you say, "You know, I've had something to do with that."

Another senior manager described his experience of the cultivation phase by noting how the young manager has grown to provide technical and psychological support. Thus he has benefited from the relationship by enabling a younger individual to make his life at work easier and more enjoyable.

> He really has made it easier for me to do things that I think need doing, because I don't have to spend much time with him. With a less talented person, the other person would be taking another five to ten percent of my time — so I'd be spending my time assisting that person in his operation, when I could be doing something else.

> So my work life is a lot more pleasurable. He is also enjoyable to watch and to think about. . . . I enjoy thinking about him and his career. . . . I think he will make a major contribution to the company.

Finally, a young female manager discovered the limitations of her developmental relationship two and a half years after it began. She found coaching, exposure-and-visibility, counseling, and friendship.

However, she yearned for someone to model and to identify with in ways she could not with her mentor.

> I have yet to meet someone that I work for directly that I really want to emulate. That bothers me a lot. Jerry is close to it, but he does a lot of things that just aren't right for me. . . . He will get on my case, he will say I am a pussycat . . . but he just doesn't fully understand that women, just by being women, can't do exactly the same things that a man will do. It is almost like I need another woman to be in that job, where I can see her style and really try it her way.

The cultivation phase is generally described positively. It is typically the period least fraught with conflict or uncertainty. The young manager derives a sense of accomplishment as well as a sense of security as he becomes competent and feels increasingly confirmed and respected. The senior manager derives support and satisfaction in seeing the young manager realize the potential identified during the initiation phase.

The combined effects of psychosocial and career functions are complex, and each individual is changed in some obvious and some subtle ways. The young manager generally becomes more self-confident and optimistic about the future. By identifying with the senior manager, parts of himself are brought out through modeling and incorporating new attitudes, values, and styles of operation. Through the relationship, the young manager not only acquires critical technical skills and learns the ropes of organizational life, but also has the opportunity to experience confirmation and support for whom he is becoming.

The overriding benefit for the senior manager is greater power. He can support and nurture and, in doing so, can note the extent to which he has influence in the organizational world. Not only can the senior manager open doors, but he is also able to transmit values and skills that enhance the young manager's capabilities. These activities give rise to personal satisfaction and provide a unique avenue for expressing oneself through the next generation of managers.

The cultivation phase ends when changes in individual needs and organizational circumstances disrupt the equilibrium which characterizes this period of the relationship. For example, a young manager's growth and changes in developmental needs are often the catalysts for movement to the next relationship phase. As early fantasies are replaced with reality and the young manager no longer needs active guidance and support, she feels the need to move away from the senior manager. A more critical and realistic view of the senior manager emerges with the young manager's increasing competence, self-confidence, and sense of autonomy. Alternately, a senior manager's needs may change as psychosocial tasks of midlife become more important. The period of reappraisal and reassessment may cause some withdrawal and greater self-absorption; these make the individual less available to provide functions of the developmental relationship. Changes in either individual can cause the relationship to become non-complementary, as either manager begins to feel resentful, rivalrous, less trusting, or more at odds with the other.

Changes in organizational circumstances may also serve as a catalyst for movement to the separation phase of the relationship. For example, a job rotation or a promotion can place greater distance between the two individuals, making it more difficult to continue to provide the same range of career and psychosocial functions. Alternately, limited opportunity for advancement can create anger, resentment, or rivalry as the senior manager encounters blocked opportunity or the younger manager threatens to surpass his or her mentor in organizational accomplishments.

During the cultivation phase the boundaries of the relationship are clarified, and the uncertainty of what it might become during the initiation phase is no longer present. Some managers are disappointed when they discover that the relationship cannot meet important developmental needs, as with the young female manager who wanted someone whom she could emulate more fully. For others, the relationship is far richer than anticipated, and the interpersonal bond is far more intimate and meaningful.

## Separation

After about two to five years, a mentor relationship moves into the third phase—separation. This phase is marked by significant changes in the functions provided by the relationship and in the experiences of both individuals. Some turmoil, anxiety, and feelings of loss generally characterize this period as the equilibrium of the cultivation phase is disrupted. It is also a time when the young manager experiences new independence and autonomy, and both managers reassess the value of the relationship as it becomes a less central part of each individual's life at work.

Separation occurs both structurally and psychologically. If a structural separation is timely, it stimulates an emotional separation that enables the young manager to test his or her ability to function effectively without close guidance and support. If a structural separation occurs prematurely, anxiety may result as the young manager is forced to operate independently of his or her mentor before feeling ready to do so. Finally, if a structural separation occurs later than an emotional separation, either manager is likely to resent the other as the relationship becomes unresponsive to individuals' changing needs and concerns. In all instances, this phase is a period of adjustment because career and psychosocial functions can no longer continue in their previous form; the loss of some functions, and the modification of others, ultimately lead to a redefinition of the relationship.

Separation involves loss. The senior manager loses direct influence over the young manager's career and personal development, as well as the technical and psychological support of someone valued for high performance and potential. The young manager loses the security of having someone looking out for his or her career by providing developmental functions that enhance one's self-image and ability to navigate in the organization. The primary psychological work of the separation phase is to come to terms with these losses. Each individual has the opportunity to develop new relationships and to experience a period of operating without a primary developmental relationship. Until an individual comes to accept these losses, he or she yearns to return to the past, has little energy to form new relationships, and thus continues to feel significantly deprived.

The separation phase is a period of loss but it can be a period of excitement as well. If the separation is timely, the senior manager takes pride in seeing someone she helped move on to positions of greater responsibility. Great satisfaction comes from knowing that she helped a young manager learn critical skills, develop self-confidence, and advance in the organization. Similarly, the young manager feels a personal accomplishment in moving on and a positive challenge in operating effectively without the senior manager's close guidance. However, if the separation is untimely for either individual, feelings of abandonment, anger, or resentment dominate the experience during this phase.

Three years after a structural separation created by a promotion, a young manager describes the anxiety and turmoil of the first year apart from her mentor.

> I used to cry at home! What I did was much harder than ever, and the end of the first year, I said, "I made it! I must be O.K.!" The first year after I left was probably the hardest that I ever had in my life in terms of being emotionally trying. Proving myself, you know, having to prove myself more to me than to others, as it turns out.

This young manager struggled with the temptation to return to her mentor for help. The structural separation urged her to complete an emotional separation as well. Over time she developed self-confidence and a sense of autonomy.

> Part of the refusal to go back to him was that I really didn't want others to think that he was the reason I got my new job and that he was a crutch. I had to prove to myself and to everybody that it was me, that I could stand alone and that I no longer needed his support. . . .

My needs have changed now, in the growing up process, because I think I'm a lot more mature than I was. . . . I would hate to think that I am now like I used to be . . . but maybe he met the needs I had then and my needs are different now. . . . Things are different now—if I have a problem, I don't think of going to him with it and maybe it's because I like to think of myself as self-reliant.

This young manager's mentor had a less stressful experience of the separation phase; as with other young managers in whom he had taken a strong interest, his dominant feelings were pride and satisfaction in seeing her move on. While he missed having her around, he accepted the separation. He continues to keep track of her performance, he continues to provide acceptance-and-confirmation, and to whatever extent possible, he will sponsor her in the future at a distance.

I thought it was a good opportunity for her to have. I felt that she had a lot of potential, this was a promotion for her, and that she could best exercise her talent at the higher level. . . .

It is different though . . . after they leave you, you kind of keep up with them and try to follow them along, and you take great pleasure in seeing them move along in the business. That's the fun of it all. It's amazing sometimes—the nicest thing is when you talk to a peer and find out she's doing really well. . . .

There are other senior managers who anticipate such loss that they resist the separation by blocking promotional moves. Managers' comfort with their own positions seems to affect the extent to which they are willing to let their subordinates grow, separate, and move away or beyond them in organizational rank. For example, one senior manager, who recently learned that he would advance no further in the corporation, has predicted no further movement for a young manager who is ready to move on.

I don't think he will ever move out of this area, even though he wants to. That's my candid opinion. I think he's at the level where, if he were to move out of the group, he should have done it several years ago at a lower level. Lateral movement within a large corporation should occur at a lower level. The higher up someone goes, the more this movement slows down. I think he's right at that point now. He wants to be considered for a promotion out—I think he's locked in here.

Senior managers who shared this perspective on their young managers' potential for growth all had a dim view of their own opportunities for growth and advancement. It appears that organizational conditions which create blocked opportunity affect the extent to which a senior manager will encourage the separation phase. When a senior manager sees limited opportunity for personal advancement, he resents and therefore delays a structural separation that enables a young manager to advance and grow.

When structural separation is imposed prematurely, the young manager feels abandoned and unprepared to meet new challenges. The loss of critical career and psychosocial functions can be traumatic. At the same time, organizational norms and practices limit continued frequent contact. In one instance pressure was exerted to move a young manager to a new department. Both managers felt that the move was premature, and both felt that they had no choice but to accommodate the request. Two years later the young manager's performance had dropped considerably and the senior manager was angry and disappointed. The young manager had become an extension of the senior manager and thus her failure was his own.

> I cautioned against the move but my peers and my boss were extremely unsympathetic. They said it's where the business needs her and the needs of the business are more important than her feelings or my feelings. . . .

> Now her poorer performance reflects on me. I was the person who got her promoted to the third level, and I was her earliest supporter. . . . So my judgment is reflected upon now. When you see one of your stars rising, and you promoted or evaluated that individual, or affected that person's career, it is very satisfying. . . . If they begin to go the other way, and you were a strong supporter, you feel disappointed and frustrated.

It is possible that the immediate trauma of the premature separation will subside and that each will someday look back on this period with a new perspective. Whatever the long-term consequences of this separation, the current experience is disruptive to both individuals.

The separation phase is a transitional period in the relationship, and it is uncertain how each individual will relate to the other in the future. Changes in individual needs and organizational circumstances indicate that the relationship will not return to its previous form but rather evolve into something quite different.

> Things changed in the relationship. The contacts with him during the past year and a half have been so few and of such short duration that I sense when I see him it's kind of chilly. I'm glad to see him and I think he is too, but you realize that you have nothing to talk about and it is just kind of inane — you know — "nice day today, how are things going" type of thing, and you realize that "gee — I've lost something there" and it would take quite a while to build that back again. That's when I have these sentimental feelings — we really ought to go out to lunch or talk for a few hours to reestablish things which have obviously diminished — you can sense it.

My own personal view is that I got to know him well enough, and worked with him long enough, that he's one man I will always respect and admire in life. I will enjoy being with him if, and hopefully at some point, we'd actually get back into a working relationship.

Both young managers and senior managers anticipate the next phase of the relationship with enthusiasm and uncertainty. The anticipation of becoming peers creates some ambivalence; competitive feelings may become more pronounced, but the opportunity to establish a more mutual and equal relationship is appealing. In addition, peer status can be threatening to the senior manager if he or she is at odds with personal accomplishments, or it can be threatening to the young manager who fails to achieve a sense of autonomy and independence. For those who reestablish contact, the relationships become more peerlike and the developmental needs of the past are no longer as important. For others, the relationship never resumes in an active sense; the memories of its past value are treasured but the separation has resulted in a parting of ways.

The functions provided by the developmental relationship shift during this phase for two reasons. First, the formal role relationship prohibits certain career functions from continuing; a senior manager is no longer able to coach, counsel, or sponsor to the same degree because of the physical distance and a decrease in authority over the young manager's career. Similarly, the young manager now faces new responsibilities that consume energy which might otherwise be directed toward the senior manager. The demands of the new structural arrangement reduce the energy available for the developmental relationship.

Secondly, during separation, the psychological work involves emotional separation that significantly alters the identification and modeling processes of the previous phase. After a while the young manager feels more self-reliant and independent of the senior manager; while he or she may have incorporated aspects of the senior manager's style and values, the conscious attempt to emulate is no longer there. One young manager describes the separation phase as a time when the senior manager is still present "in spirit," suggesting that psychosocial functions have enabled the young manager to incorporate aspects of the admired senior manager while moving on to new experiences and new relationships.

The separation phase is critical to development. It allows the young manager to demonstrate essential job skills while operating without support from a mentor. At the same time, it enables the senior manager to demonstrate to himself and to peers and superiors that he has succeeded in developing new managerial talent. The end of this phase occurs when both managers recognize that the relationship is no longer needed in its previous form.

## Redefinition

After several years of separation, a developmental relationship evolves a new form. For some, the developmental relationship of the past is never replaced with a new one. For others, new relationships take on more importance and provide career and psychosocial functions that are more responsive to current developmental tasks. In either case, as the stress of the separation phase diminishes, the central relationship of the past takes on new meaning and a new role in each individual's current worklife.

Of the eight relationships that reached the redefinition phase, the dominant pattern is one in which the relationship becomes a friendship. Both individuals have contact on an informal basis in order to continue the mutual support created in earlier years. While the career and psychosocial functions are less evident, sponsorship from a distance, occasional counseling and coaching, and ongoing friendship continue. The senior manager continues to be a supporter of the young manager and takes pride in the junior colleague's accomplishments. The young manager, operating independently of the senior manager, now enters the relationship on more equal footing. With gratitude and appreciation for earlier guidance, the young manager is now content to continue the relationship for the friendship it provides.

While the senior manager is, to some degree, removed from a pedestal in the young manager's eyes, the young manager still feels indebted. The excitement of the first two phases of the relationship is replaced with gratitude and realism about the relationship's contribution to the young manager's learning and advancement. For the senior manager, the young manager is proof of effectiveness in passing on important values, knowledge, and skills; there is pride in seeing the young manager move on to greater responsibility and career advancement. Both individuals acknowledge that what was no longer is; they also recognize a new bond that is more responsive to their current needs.

> We can now talk about common problems, which I would have had some reservations talking to her about during the period when she was a subordinate. I guess I view it as I'm supportive of her and she's supportive of me—it's great—we have a mutual support system!

While two individuals may achieve peer status, there is frequently ambivalence and discomfort as both adjust to the new role relationship. This may reflect the young manager's wish to continue to see the senior manager as all-knowing, or the senior manager's fear of being surpassed in some fundamental sense.

> Well, to me he will always be the boss. Like, I don't really see myself so much as his peer because he was the boss for so long. I will probably always

look toward him for advice because I have a lot of respect for him. . . . We are peers now, but to me he will always have a part as the boss—even if I were to get promoted and he weren't.

In one relationship, the redefinition phase is characterized by almost no interpersonal contact. While the young manager is grateful and the senior manager is proud, neither has tried to maintain contact. This pattern may emerge in those relationships where psychosocial functions (e.g., counseling, friendship) are relatively absent. The attachment formed during earlier phases of the relationship was such that, without work-related reasons to get together, separation led to a natural parting. In this variation of a developmental relationship, there is little reason to foster contact after a structural separation has occurred.

Another relationship that entered a redefinition phase is characterized by significant hostility and resentment. After several years of separation, a young manager felt abandoned by her mentor and decided that the relationship was over. While it is uncertain whether someday the relationship might be renewed, now it has ended with bitterness. The young manager felt that her mentor no longer took an interest in her career, and at a social event, felt he was inappropriately flirtatious toward her.

> Well, there is quite a bit of distance there now, and quite a bit of fear on my part—and things have changed. Since before I always knew I had an ally in my old division—a friend who happened to be in a critical level of power. It was a very secure sort of feeling. . . . After a time, and after the social encounter I became quite fearful—I mean, he might go around all of a sudden and change his mind about my competence, and no longer support me! I feel very uncomfortable now—I could never go back to work in his division. . . .
>
> I don't know how healthy it is careerwise to let a relationship like that become so important. I think I was putting eggs all in one basket, having one sponsor and being very dependent on that one sponsor. . . . I don't want to cultivate that kind of relationship again. . . .

Perhaps the emotional intensity and the hostility allow for psychological separation. As this young manager forms new relationships of a different kind and discovers that she can operate effectively without this relationship, her hostility may subside. It remains to be seen how a hostile termination of a developmental relationship affects both managers in later years.

The redefinition phase is, finally, evidence of changes that occurred in both individuals. For the young manager, the ability to relate in a more peerlike fashion with the senior manager and the ability to function effectively in new settings without the immediate support of the relationship, reflect greater competence, self-confidence, and autonomy. For the senior manager, the ability to relate in a more peerlike fashion with the young manager and the ability to redirect energies toward other young managers reflect competence and creative ability. Both have experienced such a shift in developmental tasks that the previous relationship is no longer needed or desired.

Over time, these developmental relationships may continue as distant friendships or gradually fade into positive memories. As an extension of the senior manager, the young manager is proof of a significant contribution to the next generation of talent for the organization. Because of changes in developmental tasks and organizational circumstances, each individual moves on to new relationships, and eventually the young manager values new relationships with peers and subordinates. The senior manager finds other young managers to pass on wisdom and experience to and finds peers who become equally important as the challenges of mid-career and late-career are faced.

## IMPLICATIONS

This phase model illustrates how mentor relationships evolve over time as they move through the phases of initiation, cultivation, separation, and redefinition. Each phase is characterized by particular experiences, developmental functions, and interaction patterns that are shaped by individuals' needs and surrounding organizational circumstances. This dynamic perspective has implications for individuals who want to manage their developmental relationships effectively, for organizations that want to encourage effective mentoring, and for researchers who want further knowledge of relationships in organizations.

First, the phase model demonstrates how a mentor relationship can enhance both individuals' development. When primary tasks are complementary, a mentor relationship reaches the cultivation phase and provides a range of career and psychosocial functions. These functions enable the young adult to meet the challenges of *initiation* into the world of work and the senior adult to meet the challenges of *reappraisal* at midlife. However, when the young adult begins to feel established and more autonomous, he or she will no longer look toward the senior adult for the same kind of guidance and support. If the senior adult has other avenues for expression of generative needs and can accept continued growth and advancement in the younger adult, then the relationship will continue through separation and redefinition.

Individuals can use this perspective on developmental relationships to understand significant events in their own relationships. If, for example, a junior manager attempts to establish a mentor relationship with a senior colleague and is unable to do so, it is likely that the two do not have complementary needs and that the senior colleague, for whatever reasons, is not available to coach or mentor. This does not reflect on the junior's competence, but rather indicates that their developmental needs are not complementary. Similarly, if a previously enhancing developmental relationship becomes laden with resentment or competition, the separation phase has evolved due to changes in individuals' needs and/or organizational circumstances. Relationship phases are inevitable; to the extent that individuals use this perspective, they will develop more accurate interpretations of the course of events.

Given that these developmental relationships are limited in value and time as a result of changing individual needs and organizational circumstances, an individual will have, over the course of an organizational career, several developmental relationships that provide a range of critical career and psychosocial functions at each stage. The junior manager who wishes to find one senior manager to carry him through his career and to continue to respond to personal and professional concerns is likely to be disappointed and disillusioned.

Individuals should investigate the variety of relationships that are available to them at successive career stages in order to identify other developmental relationships as alternatives to the primary mentor relationship. Not only is the mentor relationship limited in value and duration, but it may not be readily available to all individuals in the early stage of a career because of organizational conditions or limits of individuals to provide mentoring functions. Peer relationships appear to offer a valuable alternative to the mentor relationship; they provide some career and psychosocial functions, they offer greater mutuality and sense of equality, and they are more available in numbers (see Chapter 6).

The delineation of relationship phases highlighted some important limitations found in cross-gender relationships. The lack of an adequate role model in a male mentor caused young female managers to seek support and guidance from other female peers. Collusion in stereotypical behavior encouraged women to maintain feelings of dependency and incompetence when they attempted to become independent contributors and to enter the separation phase of their relationships. Concerns about increasing intimacy and concerns about the public image of the relationship caused both individuals to avoid interaction that had the potential to provide a wide range of career and psychosocial functions; thus the cultivation phase was significantly limited.* Similar patterns are likely to exist in interracial relationships as well.

---

*For further discussion of the dynamics of cross-gender relationships, see Chapter 5.

The phase model illustrates how, under certain conditions, a mentor relationship can become destructive for one or both individuals. For example, a young manager may feel undermined and held back by her mentor, or a senior manager may feel threatened by his protege's continued success and opportunity for advancement. Either occurs when a senior adult enters a difficult midlife transition or a young adult encounters organizational barriers to advancement. Further research in a variety of organizational contexts will illuminate the factors that contribute to these dysfunctional dynamics as well as the range of organizational circumstances that facilitate movement through the phases of a mentor relationship in a manner that maximizes benefits to both individuals.

For now, however, organizations have some options for encouraging mentor relationships. First, through the design of jobs and norms about communication, opportunities for interaction can be created to facilitate the initiation phase by bringing together juniors and seniors who may have complementary needs. Second, job rotation policies and promotion decision practices can take into account the natural evolution of mentor relationships, so that the cultivation phase is not interrupted prematurely by a move that disrupts the relationship, and thus, either individual's development. Finally, organizational response to midcareer individuals can reduce potentially destructive relationship dynamics by insuring continued challenge and recognition for those who have the potential to provide critical mentoring functions to junior colleagues.

Organizations can also provide educational programs that will increase individuals' understanding of mentoring in organizations and their interpersonal skills so that they will be able and willing to build developmental relationships. For example, newcomers and young managers, through experiences with peers, would learn about their own concerns and relationship needs and how they might initiate and cultivate complementary relationships with their senior colleagues. A similar effort for senior managers would enable these individuals to understand particular concerns of midcareer and to explore how providing career and psychosocial functions to younger colleagues might support their own development. In both contexts, information about mentoring functions and relationship phases would prepare individuals to build effective developmental relationships.

Comparative studies of relationships in different settings would show if phases vary significantly in different contexts. Perhaps in organizations where job movement is frequent the cultivation phase of a mentor relationship is much shorter and the range of functions provided more limited. Or, in organizations where promotional opportunities are few and jobs very stable, the separation phase may be elongated and more stressful for both individuals because supportive job changes are not forthcoming. Perhaps these variations have an impact on individual development at each career stage.

The phases of a mentor relationship illuminate predictable patterns in individual development and relationship development. These patterns suggest the need to systematically evaluate the impact of a number of possible educational and structural interventions designed to foster effective mentoring. To the extent that individual and organizational factors support movement through the four phases of initiation, cultivation, separation, and redefinition, mentor relationships will support individual development and career advancement.

# Relationships at Successive Career Stages

Individuals bring current developmental tasks and previous life experiences to their significant relationships at work. Current developmental tasks include those concerns about self, career, and family that become important during different life and career stages (Levinson et al., 1978; Schein, 1978; Hall, 1976). Previous life experiences, including relationships with parents, other authority figures, siblings, and peers, influence how an individual behaves in current relationships (Levinson, 1976; Zalesnik et al., 1970). Understanding these psychological forces helps explain why certain career and psychosocial functions become important in a relationship and why a relationship follows a particular course through its phases.

This chapter illuminates how developmental relationships are shaped by the career stages of the two individuals who create and participate in them. Research in the area of career development has delineated particular vocational or career stages that individuals experience as they move through adult life (Super, 1970; 1957; Hall & Nougaim, 1968;

Miller & Gould, 1951).* These general stages can be called *exploration, establishment, advancement, maintenance* and *withdrawal* (Hall, 1976). However, such models do not fully take into account the effects of outside work involvements and concerns on an individual's experience of these stages. Variations in choices, dilemmas, successes, and difficulties cannot be explained simply by looking at career-related activities (Levinson et al., 1978; Schein, 1978).

In order to understand how individual career stages shape developmental relationships, we must consider how life experiences affect experiences in a work setting. Research in the area of Adult Development highlights how psychosocial development unfolds over the life course. Erikson (1963) defines predictable dilemmas that individuals experience in early, middle and late adulthood. Levinson et al. (1978) define the life structure (the individual's relationship with his or her external world) and how it moves through periods of stability and transition over a lifetime. Gould (1972, 1978) highlights assumptions that must be confronted at each major life stage, and Vaillant (1977) identifies alternative coping strategies and defenses that promote or inhibit movement through successive life stages. While each researcher makes a unique contribution to a complex view of adulthood, all converge on major life stages and their predictable developmental tasks and dilemmas.

The interviews with managers about their career histories suggested that both adult development and career development perspectives should bear on their personal accounts in order to understand how their histories and current concerns affected their relationships. It was not enough to consider only career-related events but rather the interaction of experiences with self, with one's career, and with one's family (or significant outside work relationships) had to be analyzed. By considering all spheres of life, a more complex view of an individual's current developmental tasks was possible.

The patterns of concerns about self, career, and family that characterize managers in several corporate settings were derived from interviews with individuals in three different studies: the study of mentor relationships, the study of peer relationships (see Chapter 6), and an earlier study of individuals anticipating retirement (Kram & Jusela, 1978). When possible the unique examples, such as contrasting the experiences of women and men in managerial roles, are highlighted.†

---

*Career is defined here as a series of job-related activities through all or part of adult life that build on one another and are concerned either with an organization or an occupation.

†It is beyond the scope of my own work to consider with sufficient depth the individual who begins a career at midlife, and how his or her developmental tasks would affect significant relationships at work. I will attempt, however, to speculate about this and other important deviations from the usual paths.

   The delineation of developmental tasks that shape relationships at work are organized into three major eras: *early career, middle career,* and *late career.* When life stage and career stage coincide, as with the individual who begins a career in early or mid-twenties after completing school, and continues in that career until retirement, we can say that each era roughly coincides to the life stages of early adulthood (ages 22-40), middle adulthood (ages 40-60), and late adulthood (60- ) (Levinson et al., 1978). When age and career stage are greatly out of synch, developmental tasks are different from the general patterns.

   As the patterns of developmental tasks are described, several examples highlight how these patterns affect significant relationships at work. Developmental tasks are observed in the tensions and psychological work that an individual experiences in creating or modifying each sphere of life. For example, developing a sense of competence and self-worth is a developmental task that involves an individual's relationship to self. Or, learning to navigate effectively in the organizational world is a developmental task that involves an individual's relationship to his or her career. Finally, managing the tensions between family and work commitments is a developmental task that involves an individual's relationship to career and family spheres. A particular set of developmental tasks can create the need for particular developmental functions in the context of a relationship. In addition, a particular set of developmental tasks can make it likely or difficult for an individual to provide certain functions. A relationship will thrive when developmental tasks and concerns of two individuals are complementary.

   While previous life experiences are not the focus of this chapter, the individuals interviewed frequently likened current developmental relationships to earlier significant relationships. In these instances, it was possible to identify ways in which their earlier experiences may influence a current developmental relationship. For example, in likening a senior manager to his father, a young manager illustrates how the warmth and comfort (or alternatively, hostility and conflict) experienced in a developmental relationship reflect feelings from an earlier relationship. Similarly, in likening a young manager to her children, a manager at midcareer illustrates how the excitement and satisfaction experienced in passing on personal wisdom and knowledge reflect feelings from relationships with offspring. These psychological mechanisms, shaped by earlier life experiences, give a particular importance, character, and potency to a developmental relationship.

## THE EARLY CAREER YEARS _____

An individual in the first stage of both a career and adulthood is concerned with the kind of occupation and lifestyle apart from the family of origin that he or she will pursue (Levinson et al., 1978; Hall, 1976; Schein, 1978). During this period, one explores an initial course and makes provisional decisions to shape a life and career that are both confirming and satisfying. An individual carries some notion of who he or she wants to become; this notion is expressed in goals and aspirations related to an identity as a manager or professional and as a person outside of the work context. It is a period of new beginnings and initiation (see Figure 4-1).

## Concerns About Self

At the outset of an organizational career a young adult has concerns about competence and the ability to function effectively in the corporate world. During the first years of employment, the primary concern is to succeed on the job and to provide for self and/or family members. There is initially less concern about future advancement possibilities and more concern with meeting the immediate challenges of work. During this period, individuals are likely to be either recently married and adapting to the roles of spouse and/or parent, or recently entering the single adult role in the work world. Entering new roles in career and family spheres presents a major developmental task that involves developing a sense of competence and identity in these two spheres of life (Levinson et al., 1978). Erikson (1963, 1968) describes these primary challenges in this era in terms of two polarities that become the focus of attention for the young adult: "Role Identity vs. Role Confusion" and "Intimacy vs. Isolation."

Concerns about competence are most important for individuals in their initial jobs as well as each time they move to a higher organizational level. The unfamiliarity of a new setting and the new responsibilities associated with advancement to a new level create anxiety about their ability to perform effectively (Louis, 1980a,b). In general, however, success at first level management results in greater confidence about one's capacity to thrive in the corporate setting. Often, developmental relationships begin when the young adult is faced with a significantly new kind of job (either a first job or a job at a new organizational level). Emergence of the relationship coincides with concerns about one's competence. This suggests that a young manager's efforts to achieve a sense of competence are the catalyst for a new developmental relationship. Both career and psychosocial functions facilitate the psychological work involved in developing a sense of competence in new surroundings.

I came to work for Michael about a year and a half ago. He is just a super guy. I've never met anybody like him before in the company. He's a guy — I think what he does most for me is — just by his example. He's a model that you watch and see how he works. He is just an interesting guy. I'm learning a higher order of organizational skills that I will take with me wherever I go.

Concerns about identity in a work role are linked to concerns about competence. An appropriate and consistent self-image is a central concern when developing a sense of competence. For example, clarifying what it means to be a manager involves confronting the extent to which one will conform to organizational expectations and norms and the extent to which one will conflict with these expectations and norms (Schein, 1978; Van Maanen, 1976). Choices about behavior and values are critical steps in clarifying one's identity as a manager. These choices are made continuously throughout one's career; however, forming a clear sense of identity in the managerial role is particularly important during this first stage.

Efforts to clarify one's identity as a manager are often facilitated in a developmental relationship. In the senior manager, the young manager finds a model of what one might become or what one might choose not to become.

> Well, we might be getting into things, such as, do you really want to put up with this shit to be a manager? That type of thing. Is it worth it? Look what happens if you continue to be the workaholic type and all this other stuff, what is it going to get you? Is it going to be worth it? Are you going to be satisfied with yourself? Do you see what it has done to some of these other people? Is that really what you want to be? It was that kind of thing. What I respect is that it was the kind of a boss/subordinate, no, I really didn't view it as a boss/subordinate thing, it has got to be hard for a boss to say that to a subordinate, but he did. We would talk about it and I didn't even have to initiate it.

Psychosocial functions confirm and support the manager's evolving sense of self. Seeing alternatives and making choices about how to carry out the managerial role are major developmental tasks of early career years.

Forming a professional identity appears to be more complex for women. Becoming a manager is an acceptable and expected direction for young male managers, but for more than half of the women, identification with the role of manager was both inconsistent with earlier life experiences and socialization, and often disconfirming to self in the current organizational context. A critical developmental task for these women was to find an image of self that was both attractive and viable in the corporate world (Bardwick, 1970; Epstein, 1970; Stewart, 1976). Some women experienced a radical shift in their career experiences when their marriages ended or were in crisis. For them, the upset in their personal lives pushed them to invest a lot more of themselves in their work.

**Figure 4–1.** Characteristic Developmental Tasks at Successive Career Stages.

|  | Early Career | Middle Career | Late Career |
|---|---|---|---|
| Concerns About Self | *Competence:* Can I be effective in the managerial/professional role? Can I be effective in the role of spouse and/or parent?<br><br>*Identity:* Who am I as a manager/professional? What are my skills and aspirations? | *Competence:* How do I compare with my peers, with my subordinates, and with my own standards and expectations?<br><br>*Identity:* Who am I now that I am no longer a novice? What does it mean to be a "senior" adult? | *Competence:* Can I be effective in a more consultative and less central role, still having influence as the time to leave the organization gets closer?<br><br>*Identity:* What will I leave behind of value that will symbolize my contributions during my career? Who am I apart from a manager/professional and how will it feel to be without that role? |
| Concerns About Career | *Commitment:* How involved and committed to the organization do I want to become? Or do I want to seriously explore other options?<br><br>*Advancement:* Do I want to advance? Can I advance without compromising important values? | *Commitment:* Do I still want to invest as heavily in my career as I did in previous years? What can I commit myself to if the goal of advancement no longer exists?<br><br>*Advancement:* Will I have the opportunity to advance? How can I feel productive if I am going to advance no further? | *Commitment:* What can I commit myself to outside of my career that will provide meaning and a sense of involvement? How can I let go of my involvement in my work role after so many years?<br><br>*Advancement:* Given that my next move is likely to be out of the organization, how do I feel about my final level of advancement? Am I satisfied with what I have achieved? |

**Concerns About Family**

|  | | |
|---|---|---|
| *Relationships*: How can I establish effective relationships with peers and supervisors? As I advance, how can I prove my competence and worth to others? | *Relationships*: How can I work effectively with peers with whom I am in direct competition? How can I work effectively with subordinates who may surpass me? | *Relationships*: How can I maintain positive relationships with my boss, peers, and subordinates as I get ready to disengage from this setting? Can I continue to mentor and sponsor as my career comes to an end? What will happen to significant work relationships when I leave? |
| *Family Role Definition*: How can I establish a satisfying personal life? What kind of lifestyle do I want to establish? | *Family Role Definition*: What is my role in the family now that my children are grown? | *Family Role Definition*: What will my role in the family be when I am no longer involved in a career? How will my significant relationships with spouse and/or children change? |
| *Work/Family Conflict*: How can I effectively balance work and family commitments? How can I spend time with my family without jeopardizing my career advancement? | *Work/Family Conflict*: How can I make up for the time away from my family when I was launching my career as a novice? | *Work/Family Conflict*: Will family and leisure activities suffice, or will I want to begin a new career? |

Way deep down in back of my mind, I never admitted it though, my idea was always that I would get married and that I would not have to work. I can't verify that fact but I am pretty sure it was. I think getting married showed me that that was not the case. I was making more money than my husband, and in many ways, supporting him, and it was my money that allowed us to do what we needed to do. When I got divorced, I lost a lot of money on the divorce and realized that it was me against the world and that was when I truly began thinking career. Up until that time, a friend of mine and I could walk around and say—this is a tough job and it's a good job, but we're in better shape than the boss. Our boss was single. If we wanted to quit, we could quit. She can still quit—I can't anymore.

For the other women, frequent promotions and recognition provided a source of confirmation that enabled them to feel more comfortable in the managerial role.

Young female managers also described a sense of loneliness as they moved beyond entry-level positions. As the only woman in a particular department, forming an identity as a manager was difficult because there were no female models and because often they were either not taken seriously or resented by male peers. In searching for effective ways to navigate in the organization, they either felt pressure to behave in ways that were inconsistent with their self-images, or they felt disconfirmed and rebuffed in their attempts to assume more traditionally male styles. In either case, internal conflict was significant during the search to find an identity that would be acceptable to others and to themselves. This struggle was addressed through counseling and modeling functions in their developmental relationships, and frequently their relationships with female peers were particularly helpful.

## Concerns About Career

Closely linked with competence and professional identity is the concern about how committed to one's career an individual will become. As years pass and the decision to stay with an organization continues, an individual is likely to feel committed to staying rather than consider alternative careers (Schein, 1978; Hall, 1976). With movement to higher levels in the organization, more emotional energy is invested, and it becomes difficult to see the decision to stay as a provisional one. A common concern after reaching second or third level management is reflected in ambivalence about progressing any further. Managers become more aware of the extent to which their lives have been shaped by continued experience in the organization, and the personal costs involved in continuing down that path. Questions about one's commitment, advancement possibilities, and relationships at work encompass a range of career-related concerns.

**Commitment.** There are two aspects to the ambivalence that raise concerns about commitment to an organizational career. One has to do with how much conformity is required in order to advance further — that is, to what extent one can maintain one's individuality and identity and not be coerced into adopting certain values and behaviors in order to continue to be successful. The other has to do with the amount of time and energy that may be taken from one's personal life in order to be successful. Young adults feel their efforts to advance conflict with other parts of life. Relationships to the organization and to one's family are examined.

> I don't mind doing anything like that on a temporary basis, until I get proficient enough so I can cut corners and cut that out, but if it's going to be the kind of job where it's a steady diet and it's expected of me, then I don't want it. I'm really very firm on my personal life. It's just that life's too short and I really enjoy my home and my husband and my family. Even that type of job now, I won't take it because of that. A lot of the managers feel that that's a stepping stone that I should take in manufacturing to get to a higher level. I don't know, if I have to do it, maybe I'll look at it differently.

Whether to stay, and how much to invest, are larger questions for some than for others. Some maintain the possibility that they may leave the organization — they may begin a second career, become a fulltime mother, or consider the possibility that one's professional aspirations might be met better in another setting. For these individuals, the option to leave seems very important on an emotional level; it provides a sense of freedom to counteract the fears of conformity that are associated with continued advancement. For the others, staying in the organization is almost certain. None, however, appear to be completely without conflict. If they are not considering leaving the organization, their ambivalence lies in whether they want to assume positions that demand greater responsibility, authority, and investment of self.

Commitment and ambivalence reflect a developmental task involving the nature of one's attachment to the organization. This task can be addressed explicitly within the context of a developmental relationship. Often, the senior manager's behavior provides a model of one way to resolve the ambivalence and tension that this particular task creates. For some this model is appealing; for others it is discomforting and keeps the tension alive.

**Advancement.** Uncertainty characterizes predictions of the future. This uncertainty is due, in part, to the young adult's ambivalence about continued commitment to the organization and to continued advancement in the corporate world. As one experiences pressures to conform or experiences personal sacrifices in family life in order to advance, the young adult experiences internal conflict regardless of the opportunities that may exist.

> I would really hate to find myself in a position where there is no time to spend with people who are important to me. And I can see certain levels of responsibility where that could easily happen. And, as a matter of fact, at _____ I found myself in a number of very serious discussions with some of the men who were discussing the stress and the strain their careers were having on their relationships with their wives and their children. I don't have those responsibilities, yet my father just passed away and I have a mother who right now needs a lot more of my time, and so it's something I must consider. So I'm sure that it's going to temper any career decisions I'm going to make.

Individuals may feel the desire to stay put for a while even though advancement is likely; the pressure to advance further combined with the opportunity to do so is counteracted by an internal sense that moving ahead would create more personal costs. Others expect to advance but express a similar concern about how to maintain one's own values and stance toward the world at higher organizational levels. A smaller number question whether advancement opportunity will present itself.

The organizational pyramid begins to narrow as the young adult achieves management status. In the earliest career years, opportunity was vast, particularly with the formation of a positive developmental relationship. Now, with a narrowing pyramid, an individual is more conscious of both competition with peers for fewer positions and the impact of political processes on winning the race to the top. Concerns about the future stem from this uncertainty about options as well as from the ambivalence about whether such options are desirable. In contrast to many midcareer managers, however, the young manager anticipates a change in status and a continued struggle with whether to continue the upward climb.

**Relationships at Work.** In addition to concerns about commitment and advancement, the young adult must establish and manage relationships with peers, superiors, and subordinates within the organization. These relationships are important because they provide psychosocial and career functions that can enhance one's development. In addition, they frequently supplement the functions provided by a primary developmental relationship. Ineffective relationships can interfere with work and can lead to a sense of frustration and incompetence. These relationships are always important since the particular constellation of relationships continues to change while moving through the organizational hierarchy. In launching a career, one continually establishes new relationships. Relationships with superiors begin with the first boss. In personal accounts, most young managers recall this relationship as a critical one.

> Alan was very influential. I respected him as being pretty sharp and pretty astute. He had a lot of guts to tackle the problems that existed in the area and that was the union-management business. I was really identifying with him.

> In terms of what and how you run something, how you manage something. You would sit down and talk about or debate how you do certain things, what should we do in this kind of situation. We would be right in line. I think it was the way I came at a problem — it might be similar to the way he would come at a problem.

> I also respected him as an individual that I saw as very articulate, smart, sharp, and the kind of boss that you would respect at least from where I was. Maybe a good way to say it would be that he was a good role model for me. I think it also helped because we are not that different in age. I think that made a difference too.

Either this relationship provides critical career and psychosocial functions that aid socialization into the organization or it blatantly lacks such functions, resulting in frustration and the desire to leave the organization. The experience with the first boss inevitably leaves a strong impression with someone in early career; one knows afterwards more about what is needed from a boss and more about how to effectively work with superiors (Hall & Berlew, 1966). Most often, the first boss is close enough in age and experience to the young adult that he is engaged in similar developmental tasks. While he could provide a model (and other functions) for the young manager, most of his energy is directed toward personal career concerns and less is directed toward subordinates (Baird & Kram, 1983).

Because of frequent job movement in early career years, the first boss relationship generally lasts about one year. Then the young adult must establish new relationships with direct superiors and more distant superiors. Managers feel ambivalent in most of these relationships — on one hand wanting to please and gain acceptance, and on the other hand resenting the authority and control that people at higher levels have over their careers. Characteristic postures toward authority emerge that are undoubtedly influenced by earlier life relationships (Levinson, 1976; Zalesnik, 1970). Some described these relationships as full of conflict; they resisted and fought the significant authority figures in their work context. Others describe these relationships with apprehension; they reported fear and anxiety when encountering a senior manager. The remaining describe these relationships as amiable but distant; there is a certain mystery about these figures that made engaging them both attractive and difficult.

Young managers usually learn in the early years of their organizational experiences that relationships with more senior managers are important. These senior managers can provide sponsorship, coaching, and visibility to the young manager; their approval, support and interest are critical for career advancement. A developmental relationship often helps the young manager learn to establish other relationships with more senior colleagues.

> Once there was a bond of trust, I think formed between us, where I felt I could be completely open with him and I presume he felt the same — at least he said so — we were talking about that a number of times. I felt very comfortable, and I could talk openly about what was on my mind — insecurities as well as other things and vice versa — and I think that we were able to operate very effectively together.

> He as a subordinate, I think, I hope, could talk about his insecurities and problems with me without feeling that it might affect him in performance evaluation. I think, at least I hope, it would develop confidence that I would evaluate his performance and potential objectively, irrespectively of the most intimate sharing that we had.

> There are a lot of things that cause you to chew your fingernails, and it is nice to be able to emote and talk about them and get them off your chest.

Often the senior manager coaches the young manager on how to establish rapport and credibility with other senior managers. Experience in this relationship provides a useful model for coaching; the key senior manager paves the way for other relationships through exposure and visibility to significant others.

Relationships with peers become increasingly important over time. These relationships provide an alternative and supplement to a mentor relationship.

> Arlene had just arrived from Seattle, which is different — different mores there. I had just arrived from Ohio. Which . . . a different way of interacting with people. So we had to adjust to the New England style, and very specifically, to the _____ business' style which is (of its own set). So we . . . there were a lot of dilemmas. The business facts, initially, weren't as critical as the personalities and how people treated each other and interfaced (you). We talked about these things a lot. . . .

Peers provide psychological support as well as a point of comparison for how one is progressing; thus, there is often ambivalence in these relationships because of the potential competitive feelings. When developmental relationships are lacking in some way, one can turn to peers for critical psychosocial functions. Alternatively, the developmental relationship provides support and counsel in the face of problematic relationships with peers. Relationships with peers not only have the potential to provide support, but they are often critical sources of information and assistance in getting work accomplished.

Relationships with subordinates become more important with advancement in the organizational hierarchy. Both increasing age and organizational rank contribute to greater concern for subordinate relationships. As second and third level management levels are achieved, the young adults become interested in contributing to subordinates' development. This responsibility provides a new kind of relationship in which they find themselves the experts and the ones who can influence the development of others in ways that their senior managers have done. The tension between looking out for one's own career and looking out for one's subordinates' careers surfaces with this new responsibility (Baird & Kram, 1983). Often, feelings of inadequacy emerge when a young manager must provide career and psychosocial functions to subordinates. It is also a time of discovery; the young managers find new ways to expand their own identities to include the roles of teacher, coach, counselor, model, and sponsor.

## Concerns About Family

During the early career years, a young adult also faces the developmental task of developing a family structure apart from the family of origin. This task concerns one's relationships with a partner and/or children. Concerns about competence and identity extend to new roles in the family. Concerns about family include how one creates satisfying personal relationships as well as how one manages conflicts created by these new commitments.

An individual's relationship with a spouse affects the ability to address concerns about self and career. Some spouses provide a source of support. In doing so, the relationship serves many of the psychosocial functions characterizing a developmental relationship. Concerns about competence, advancement potential, one's identity in a professional role, or one's career commitment, are openly discussed with the spouse. These relationships are significant during stressful periods at work. Much of the psychological work created by other developmental tasks is eased by relating to a partner who provides acceptance-and-confirmation, counseling, and friendship.

But the spouse relationship can create tension that shows up as guilt or anger (Bartolome & Evans, 1979). An individual may feel guilty for spending so much time and energy at work when his partner feels deprived or rejected. This person may also feel angry at his partner for imposing what seem to be unrealistic demands at a time when high energy is needed to address concerns about identity in a new managerial role.

> I was very much into my work, she'd call me a workaholic, so, conse-quently, I didn't give her the support that I should have given. That's one side. In fairness to myself, I was being asked to do an awful lot, and I was never in a position where I was able to do what I had to do, but maybe I overdid it.

A discontented spouse presents a threat to one's new and evolving iden-tity. Problems in a spouse relationship inevitably result in greater tur-moil about one's relationship to the organization and to one's career.

These work/family stresses can have greater consequences. Separa-tion or divorce can result; relationships end after considerable struggle, leaving one with unresolved guilt and anger about the impact of work on the breakup of a marriage. The trauma of separation or divorce is a significant disruption to one's sense of identity as well as to one's sense of competence in both spheres of life.

In a tense spouse relationship, the emotional struggle associated with balancing commitments to work and to family is often brought to a developmental relationship.

> I emulate the way he is able to keep that high energy level—and still—the guy still invests a lot of time, it seems to me, with his family. He manages his time well with his family and that's one fear I always had. The higher you go, the lesser importance your family takes on. Your job gets to be domi-nant and I think that's not true with Michael. The quality of time he gives his family is exceptional. We talked about that. I told him that one of my fears was that I'd become Mr. Company and the worst or whatever might happen—I don't devote enough time to my family. He said, there is a way around that—manage your time at home so you make sure that doesn't hap-pen. But he said, "you will, if you go up a level or two, you will devote more time to the job. There's no question about it." So he is very honest with me—he didn't try to say that doesn't happen.

Some young managers discuss the conflict with their senior managers, or look to senior managers for a model of how to manage the tensions. Thus, through counseling and/or role-modeling functions, the relation-ship responds to this developmental task. A young adult's concerns about family also stem from the parenting role. Becoming a parent initially creates concerns about building a career, rather than merely succeeding at a job, because of the additional responsibilities that parenting entails. Parenting becomes another source of tension for the person in early career who fears missing the growth of children because of the potential for total immersion at work.

Parenting presents a particular concern for many women. Becoming a parent is frequently experienced as being in conflict with pursuing one's career.

> I do try to consider whether we'll have children. How that's going to affect careers. Whether I'll take a leave of absence or whether I'll stay and try to get day care. It's really complex. Right now I'm twenty-eight. I'm watching the biological time clock.

Some decide definitely not to have children; others, whether married or single, are uncertain as to how they would combine the desire to have children with the desire to continue working. The degree of optimism concerning how it is possible to integrate the roles of mother and manager varies (Stewart, 1976; Hennig & Jardim, 1977). The women who are most pessimistic about integrating these roles yearn for female role models who have effectively achieved such an integration.

The developmental tasks facing the young manager are reflected in concerns about self, career, and family. The particular set of concerns is shaped by previous life experiences, incoming expectations, and current organizational and life experiences. How the young adult works on these concerns influences his or her developmental relationships. The particular career and psychosocial functions important in a developmental relationship are those that enable such work to proceed. To some extent, however, the senior manager's developmental tasks also influence what finally evolves.

## THE MIDDLE CAREER YEARS

The individual at midcareer is confronted with a unique set of developmental tasks. In contrast to the individual in early career he or she has a substantial career and life history that influences current concerns about self, career, and family (Levinson et al., 1978). While the young adult is launching a career and creating an identity, the individual at midcareer is reappraising the past and modifying the present in order to reconcile past aspirations with current circumstances (Osherson, 1980; Jacques, 1965; Dalton, 1959). Thus, the concerns he or she brings to a developmental relationship result from a different orientation, a different time perspective, and a primary task of reappraisal rather than initiation (see Figure 4–1).

### Concerns About Self

People generally experience a shift in identity as they approach midcareer. For some the shift is an exciting process, and for others it presents emotional turmoil as they reluctantly give up the familiar identity established in earlier career years (Levinson et al., 1978; Hall, 1980; Hall & Kram, 1981). In either instance, new roles in work and family give rise to a view of self that is quite different from that of the past. Acceptance of an evolving and changing identity frees energy for developmental relationships, while resistance or confusion prevents the individual at midcareer from effectively providing career and psychosocial functions. Erikson (1963, 1968) suggests that the polarity of "generativity vs. stagnation" becomes important as the individual must modify his basic stance toward relationships and toward himself.

One moves from being a novice to being an expert. With experience, organizational tenure, and organizational rank, others look to him for advice and support. Structurally, the individual at midcareer probably has greater responsibility than he did in early career years. Emotionally, he finds that more novices depend on him. Both of these changes are alternately experienced as enriching or frightening. Those individuals who have been in middle management for about ten years probably accepted a shift in their professional identities; providing consultation, leadership, and support to novices is viewed as an integral part of their managerial identities.

Part of the shift in identity is stimulated by the new status of "senior adult." This shift reinforces the notion that one is no longer a newcomer but rather someone assumed to be more knowledgeable than younger colleagues. With this status also comes the awareness of one's age.

> I think I'm becoming more aware of the eventuality of death and I'm just beginning to think. Is the continued sacrifice worth the potential reward, and the potential is diminishing. Meanwhile, you're doing everything in reverse and trying to motivate your people, even though they may be older, and all that kind of stuff. My friend Dick keeps sending me those obits from the Times, and he keeps sending me material on how to plan for the future, and I always thought I could adjust very well to age, and uncertainties of middle age, the rising doubts in your mind, and death and other things. Last summer he convinced me that I should write my goals down, and I did. As I wrote them, I was surprised at what I was writing. They were more in line with what my friend's objectives were than what I am working for—higher level in the company—and so perhaps, I am at a crossroads. . . .

Many individuals at midcareer make note of their age and the implications of being "older" for further advancement. Awareness of aging is managed in different ways; some yearn to be young again in order to redo past choices, and others welcome the status and the opportunity to provide for and support others. Most often, individuals respond ambivalently. Acceptance of oneself as a senior adult is a primary task for the individual at midcareer. Effectiveness and satisfaction in a developmental relationship provide confirmation and support for this aspect of a person's evolving identity.

In contrast to early career, the person at midcareer has demonstrated competence and has achieved repeated recognition with each successive movement in the organization. However, concerns about competence reemerge with critical events that challenge one's positive views of self.

> I think that everybody is always concerned, and I guess I'm at that middle aged period where suddenly you begin to question how good you are, are you really effective. You see a lot of young people coming in with new skills, new drives, more daring and more risk-taking than you are and I know I've begun to sometimes question my own level of energy and enthusiasm on the job — my own stomach for some of the politics, the lobbying, and some of the things that have to get done for the right thing to happen. You begin to look around to see who your competitors are and who is with you, or supportive of you — so I've had some concerns and anxieties. . . . Top openings are so few that competition is always significant, age becomes a factor, your own ability to continue to achieve, and how long are you going to stay in the race. Very significant!

A transition to a new management level, the experience of being passed over for a promotion, the experience of stagnation in one job after a history of rapid movement, or the awareness of young professionals who are entering the system with greater technical expertise and greater opportunity for rapid advancement, can heighten such concerns.

In the eighteen mentor relationships studied, three of the senior managers had recently moved from middle management into one of the top seventy-five positions in the organization. They describe this transition with excitement and anxiety. For all of them the move was a desirable one, and for all of them there was anxiety about whether they would perform effectively at a new hierarchical level. The promotion involved developing new networks of relationships with peers and superiors, as well as expanded responsibilities in the new position. Two of those senior managers experienced difficulty in their developmental relationships; anxiety in the new role probably interfered with providing career and psychosocial functions. The third found confirmation and support from a subordinate who conveyed respect and loyalty during a tumultuous period. The process of moving to the new level is similar to that experienced by the younger manager at the outset of a career. The senior manager's anxiety about competence, however, is in conflict with the expert role that he or she is expected to fulfill. The private fears expressed during the interviews affected the course of the developmental relationship even though they were rarely articulated.

In the same study, six of the senior managers described the experience of being "passed over" for a promotion as one that threatened their sense of competence.

> I'm not so sure that you always come to terms with it. I think you come to terms with it given several factors, or several dimensions which then come to mind. . . . You come to terms with it depending upon how many times you're passed over. . . . Another factor entering into it is that I don't think there is a guy around who doesn't know that profits are involved. We all get put into categories and I may be in the one that says "not promotable." You come to terms with it, if you're in a higher category and all of a sudden, you're 55 or 56 years old, the young jets are coming up, they're more versatile — you may have been locked into a job for so long, not that you're obsolete — you're really good at it, and what have you, but the versatility is extremely important. And at a certain age, you lose that!

For half of these managers, realizing that further advancement was unlikely started a significant period of reassessment, self-reflection, and resolution of anger and frustration. At the time of the interviews, these individuals had "come to terms" with the fact that they were not going to advance further. They had found ways to regain a sense of self-worth and competence by either externalizing the reasons for blocked opportunity to organizational politics or by developing a view of self that was valued because of contributions not necessarily rewarded by advancement. These three managers report more energy directed toward subordinates and less energy directed upward when accepting final hierarchical status. The acceptance and resolution of being "passed over" enables the senior manager to engage more fully in a developmental relationship.

However, the lack of acceptance of being "passed over" created resentment toward young managers who still had opportunity to advance. The remaining three managers who experienced being "passed over" had not accepted it; at the time of the interviews they were quite frustrated, angry and unsettled.

> There's a few ways to look at this. Either I wasn't as good as I thought I was, and nobody ever told me, or I was and I'm just not politically popular. But nobody ever told me anything. The company has this thing where everybody is supposed to have a periodic interview and be told — in the first place you shouldn't have to wait for any particular time — it should be timed on what seems to be the proper time to tell somebody, about where they stand and what their chances are. I not only haven't had any of those impromptu ones, but I've never had a formalized interview with any boss

since I got to this level, and that's as I say, 18 years. . . . People haven't leveled with me. People haven't leveled. I wouldn't expect much coaching at this level, but I would expect some leveling. . . .

These feelings were brought to the developmental relationships in two ways: either the senior manager found support and relief in sharing concerns with the young manager, or the young manager became a target of envy, resentment, and anger. Thus a developmental relationship either confirmed worth and competence, or posed an additional threat.

Concerns about competence become important when the individual at midcareer reflects on the experience of being in the same job for six years after moving every two or three years in previous periods. Frequently senior managers privately compare themselves with younger subordinates. Even those managers who anticipated further advancement are concerned about whether a younger, more competent manager would be chosen instead. Concerns about competence are intertwined with concerns about aging; regardless of prior success, most individuals at midcareer are concerned about whether they will continue to be a valuable resource to the organization. A developmental relationship at midcareer reinforces their sense of competence; they see the positive results of their efforts to support younger colleagues.

Reassessment during midcareer is caused by both internal and external forces. The passing of time and the aging process cause one to look backward and to assess where he or she is today in comparison with earlier expectations and aspirations. For those who perceive blocked opportunity or being "passed over" for a promotion, the disappointment and anger stimulated by an organizational event set the reassessment process in motion. The majority describe a period of rather intense self-reflection during which time new concerns about competence, values, and accomplishments surface.

## Concerns About Career

Like the individual in early career, the person at midcareer has concerns about commitment, advancement opportunities, and relationships at work. The content of these concerns differs; long term commitments have already been made, advancement opportunities are more certain, and relationships with peers, subordinates, and superiors have a long history. Previous experiences both inside and outside of the organization shape these concerns as one reflects on the consequences of long-standing commitments, comes to terms with limited advancement opportunity, and adjusts to changes in significant relationships.

**Commitment.** The individual at midcareer has had to choose whether to stay, when to conform, and how much time and energy to invest in the organizational career. These choices and prior commitments are reflected upon at midcareer. A person no longer sees these commitments as provisional, but rather as ones that have significantly shaped his or her identity in work and family roles (Levinson et al., 1978; Osherson, 1980). There is a range of feelings about past choices. For those who are optimistic about the future and enthusiastic about the present, past choices are valued. For those who are frustrated and pessimistic, past choices are reported with regret.

In either instance, the senior manager wants to share the benefits of experience in a developmental relationship. The opportunity to pass on personal wisdom and experience to a younger colleague provides a new direction for energy and commitment.

> It is hard to describe . . . I light up. I do. I have done that with other people. I have been fortunate I think for many years to have reasonably intelligent people and younger than I am and hard-working people working for me, and I guess my wife would say that I am a frustrated teacher, that I love to see people grow and expand in their ability to think and approach problems and life in general. I am sure that Tom and I get off on some other subjects that have nothing to do with the business at times. To pass on something that I had found out in living, that might be useful to him, is very important to me. . . .

The developmental relationship is increasingly important when the senior manager enables a young manager to emulate (or avoid) his or her past choices. The opportunity to provide critical career and psychosocial functions enables the midcareer adult to rework past experiences and to commit himself to developing young managerial talent.

Coming to terms with the personal costs of previous commitments presents major psychological work during midcareer. Not having to achieve a niche in the corporate world through rapid movement and demonstration of competence allows for time and energy to reflect on the intense years of rapid change in one's career. Most managers find themselves reflecting on how their previous commitments to work have affected their personal lives and their families.

> I look back now and I don't know how I did it. I don't think I ever questioned it. It just had to be done. It was very stressful. That's my one regret looking back at that period. I took everything so seriously that I wish I had more fun with the kids than I had. We're doing some of that now but it would have been nice to have some of it when they were growing up. They are also getting over what I am getting over now, feeling that life is supposed to be constant work and working toward things and that you can't take time

out just to have a lot of fun. I can do that now but it's been a long time getting there.

While a young adult is beginning to confront work/family tensions, the midcareer adult is assessing the ways in which these conflicts have been managed up to this time. Counseling and coaching functions are stimulated by these parallel concerns.

At midcareer there is little question about leaving the organization; the commitment is usually considered irreversible. However, other commitments will be modified or created during the second half of one's career. For many, relationships with younger colleagues involve a new major commitment. In earlier years, demonstrating competence for career advancement was most important; at midcareer, a shift toward developing other managers and attending to personal and family life occurs. For some, failure to make meaningful commitments may lead to depression, withdrawal, anger, or low self-esteem (Levinson et al., 1978; Osherson, 1980; Hall, 1980).

**Advancement.** Those who still have advancement opportunities express ambivalence similar to that experienced by individuals in early career years. As the pyramid narrows, midcareer individuals are aware of the political processes involved in reaching the top of the corporate structure. They question whether or not to participate in these processes in order to obtain the (possibly) last promotion, since greater personal costs are likely. This concern appears in the developmental relationship as senior managers observe parts of themselves in younger colleagues' similar struggles.

Managers experience varying degrees of self-acceptance during midcareer. Some have succeeded beyond their initial aspirations, and others are discontented with their accomplishments. Blocked opportunity often causes feelings of inadequacy. These feelings are brought to a developmental relationship in subtle ways. Envy, resentment, competitiveness, or hostility may underlie the positive bond to the extent that a senior manager remains at odds with self. Those who are more self-accepting and less concerned about advancement seem to be less ambivalent about their younger colleagues' successes and advancement.

Concerns about the future emerge when the end of one's career is in sight. Both those who perceive further advancement opportunity and those who will move no further confront the reality of a more limited future. Whereas the person in early career starts with a wide range of options, the person at midcareer feels the constraints of time and opportunity.

The midcareer manager needs to be challenged for the remaining fifteen to twenty years of his or her career. The opporunity to contribute to younger colleagues' development can provide an important alternative to advancement.

**Relationships at Work.** The individual at midcareer has had considerable experience in building, maintaining, and ending relationships with peers, superiors, and subordinates. At first, relationships with superiors were most important, but at midcareer the players are not new, and one's concerns about position in relation to significant others are different. What distinguishes those at midcareer is a perspective shaped by a history of relationships (both helpful and unhelpful) and a future limited by time and opportunity.

Managers come to rely on subordinates to provide loyalty and accomplish the work in their areas of responsibility.

> The more I think about that—that's important to me. It is hard to know when people are talking straight to you—especially when you're looking for feedback and observations that might help you personally—especially from subordinates. In many ways, your subordinates know you better than anyone else, so if you can somehow develop a relationship and get their own feelings—how do you really see me and the department—what bugs you—what pleases you—and feel that you are getting it straight. It means a lot.

Most managers at midcareer begin to develop subordinates when they achieve second and third level management positions. This development becomes more important as the senior manager gets farther away from actual work.

Many managers are concerned about adapting to technological and social changes. Younger colleagues provide an opportunity as well as a requirement for the senior manager to stay in touch with new values brought into the organization. There is a mixture of delight in and resistance to the younger generation's perspectives. Working with a young manager with greater technical expertise, or working with a young manager who challenges the authority structure, or working with a young manager of the opposite sex all present the opportunity to learn, as well as to falter in responding to the younger colleague's concerns and interests.

> Quite frankly, I am trying to hold on to what I've got without goofing and having the energy to do it and also to have the intelligence to respond to the changing world that's around me, and it's changing very rapidly. Our whole business world now is becoming computerized. I have forced myself to do that, and I think I'm one of the few of my peers who is able to use the computer as much as I do. I'm not bragging with that. It took discipline to do it. So I keep saying to myself, if the change is there, respond to it, work with it, and I have found by working with it, hey, it's a help. Your first reaction is,

oh, that garbage, you don't want it, but after you deal with it and see what it can do for you, then that stimulates you, but you have to discipline yourself to do it. I think the whole environment keeps changing like that, and I think, you have to respond with it. I think most of us at my age level and my peers somewhat feel the same way—that we're here and hopefully we can hang on. . . . I've seen a pattern over a period of years and the pattern runs, at first they will take younger people and jump them into management. They want the young blood. . . .

Interest in subordinate development is stimulated by both instrumental and psychological needs. Successful subordinates reflect well on the midcareer manager; a subordinate's promotion symbolizes the manager's effectiveness in providing developmental functions that enhance the young manager's growth and advancement. Midcareer managers who provide mentoring functions identify between three and eight junior managers who benefit from their attention, guidance and support. They describe the success of these individuals with pride and note that the young managers' successes reflect on their judgment and ability to develop young managerial talent. In contrast, the young manager who fails to perform excellently reflects poorly on them. There is both risk and necessity in taking special interest in particular young managers.

Psychological needs also stimulate interest in subordinate development. Guiding and counseling a young manager in learning the ropes of organizational life help the individual at midcareer pass on his own experience and compensate for his own wrong career decisions (Levinson et al., 1978; Dalton et al., 1977). He wants the young manager to benefit from his experience. A young manager derives a greater sense of self-worth by avoiding similar mistakes and learning to navigate the system more rapidly. The young manager becomes a symbol of the midcareer manager's wisdom and insight.

Most senior managers liken their interest in young managers to parental concern. They feel that they helped the young manager, and they feel pride, satisfaction, and responsibility. Just as a parent marvels at what a child has become, the senior manager marvels at the success of a young manager who has become more than a novice in the corporation.

Maybe if I could say this without sounding corny. . . . I kind of look at it as if Anne—and she could be, she is just a little bit older than my daughter—could be my child and that as a parent, I would want my children to be able to stand up on their own two feet. I would like to think as a father that I had made some contribution to what they stood for and what they believed in and what they wanted to aspire to, so that as they succeeded as I would hope they would on their own, without me bringing them along like I owned the business, but once they got to a point even . . . if I thought at some point, I could measure what a child of mine was doing was the best thing in the world that they could possibly do, no matter what level it was or anything else, then I would feel if I had made some contribution to that, that would be a sense of tremendous satisfaction. I think I feel kind of that way about Anne, although I don't think of her as a child. I think of Anne as almost a peer. . . .

The senior manager often sees parts of himself or herself in the young manager. The subordinates who become important to the senior manager are those with similar values, ambitions, or perspectives on the world. The young manager thus becomes an extension of the senior manager, a legacy, carrying on the attributes that the senior manager values.

The quality of developmental relationships is influenced by relationships experienced earlier in one's career. Most midcareer managers recall two or three senior managers who were particularly helpful when they were novices. These previous developmental relationships left impressions and feelings about what kind of relationship aided growth and development. Thus, in current relationships with selected subordinates the midcareer manager emulates those who contributed to his or her career or, alternately, acts in contrast to those who interfered with growth and development. Current career and psychosocial functions are shaped by the senior manager's experience of past relationships.

Current superiors may have less organizational experience or may be younger than the midcareer manager and yet have greater organizational authority. This situation is uncomfortable. Current superiors may have been former peers or subordinates, and the transition to a subordinate-superior relationship requires a major adjustment. Early in one's career it is generally easier to accept the authority of more experienced superiors. At midcareer there is more ambivalence because difference in status is the only attribute that justifies such an accommodation. The current superior, in most cases, is viewed more like a peer who happens to occupy a more senior position.

This ambivalence involves intense positive and negative feelings. Strong positive feelings result from a superior's help in early career years. At the same time, the superior's impending retirement might create an opportunity for further advancement. There exist both gratitude toward the superior as well as a wish for his retirement. These conflicting feelings contribute to an uneasy stance toward one's superior. It is like the ambivalent stance of the individual in early career, but it tends to be more intense for the individual at midcareer because of the long relationship history and the limited future.

Most individuals at midcareer feel superior relationships are less important than relationships with peers and subordinates. Psychosocial functions are generally found more in the latter two kinds of relationships. There is a sense of aloneness since there are fewer superiors to look to for support; also, one is expected to be an expert at the senior management level. Senior managers often contrast their current situations with earlier years by noting that there is no longer someone looking out for their careers. When they become senior managers, they realize that they are totally in charge of their own careers.

The extent to which an individual desires further advancement affects his or her attitude toward superiors. If advancement is still important, the superior may be viewed as an obstacle or someone to make further promotion possible. Again, these feelings are likely to be intensified with a time limit. If the individual is content to stay at the current position, the superior relationship is less cumbersome. In this instance, the relationship is less ambivalent and more cooperative and the individuals can enhance each other through mutual respect and support.

Senior managers describe peer relationships as becoming increasingly important in recent years.

> At the earliest stages from where I was, I don't think I needed peer relationships. For one thing, I don't think I had time for it. I was too busy trying to get ahead, and I don't really honestly think that they were that important. I do feel, as you go up into management, I think that's where you really need it. You need support, somebody, and it's got to be somebody that understands where you're coming from. So it should be really a peer who has lived a similar experience. I think it's really helpful, I really do. Sometimes I think it keeps you from losing all your marbles.

Often the new senior manager receives coaching and counseling in new peer relationships. More experienced peers share insight into the network of relationships at the top of the organization, which helps the new senior manager navigate at a new hierarchical level. Peer relationships become an important source of information as well as a source for valuable subordinates. Each senior manager identified up to five peers who they relied on as confidantes, providers of information, and providers of valuable younger managers on a rotational exchange (see Chapter 6).

Current peers also represent serious competition for the few positions at the top of the organization. Mutual respect is colored with competitive feelings, particularly for those who aspire to higher levels. There is underlying fear and anticipation that someday one may work for, or be the boss of, a current peer. These feelings interfere, at times, with the interdependency that characterizes peer relationships at this level. So while peers can potentially empathize with current developmental tasks, they are, at the same time, contenders for promotion. Peer relationships have been through many changes over the years; now they pose both an opportunity and a threat.

## Concerns About Family _____

The senior manager's reassessment process is influenced by changes in the family sphere as well. Children have grown and for many they have begun to leave home to enter the adult world. In contrast to the person in early career, the midcareer individual is not entering the parental role but rather seeing the results of parenting efforts. There is concern about how well one's children are prepared to stand on their own. With pride or disappointment, managers reflect on their effectiveness as parents. For those who feel pride, efforts with children can be transferred to efforts with subordinates. For those who feel disappointment, efforts with subordinates can compensate for a sense of failure with one's family.

The anticipation or reality of children leaving home provides a stimulus for reassessing one's relationship to work. For some the change in family structure presents a new freedom to explore other parts of self; for others it presents a loss that leaves a painful void. The new freedom or the new loss requires adjustment. The satisfaction and importance of contributing to a younger colleague's development is, in part, explained by the loss that the midcareer manager experiences as children leave home.

Many senior managers who made sacrifices in order to achieve in their careers now feel some degree of guilt.

> It took me years to be able to walk out of this place and leave it. I didn't do that for years. As a matter of fact, I'll always remember a comment my wife made. My kids were pretty small, the oldest one was about six, I guess — I have four of them. I was working every single night, Saturday and Sunday, and I was getting tired, no question about it. I was pushing way too hard. I really didn't have to push that hard, as I reflected back on that, there was no need for that. There were other ways to do it, but I came home one night and I had supper, and I had to go right back. I was going out the door and my wife looked at me and said, 'Oh, by the way if you get the time, why don't you let me know, and I'll introduce you to your children.' And she meant that — she was very serious about it.

The senior manager questions the value of such sacrifices and whether continued intensive involvement at work is worthwhile. The confusion about past choices parallels young managers' concerns about how much time and energy to invest in their careers. This common concern can become a subject for mutual exploration in a developmental relationship.

Spouses are generally viewed as key supporters. A marital relationship can develop in which one's spouse provides critical psychosocial functions that support the senior manager's development. The senior manager learns to count on this relationship for support and acceptance. Changes in the spouse relationship are frequently stimulated by children leaving home. This often disrupts an important source of support that was taken for granted as one pursued a career. For senior managers whose marital separation occurs during the formation of current developmental relationships, young managers can become an important alternative source of support.

The person in midcareer is confronted with a variety of concerns stimulated by aging, changes in organizational circumstances, and changes in the family structure. The particular set of concerns depends, to a great extent, on one's personal appraisal of past accomplishments and future opportunities. Common to all in this era is the primary task of reassessment, the experience which affects what one brings to a developmental relationship.

## THE LATE CAREER YEARS

The individual in late career is confronted with a unique set of developmental tasks. As the midcareer manager is in a process of reappraisal and reassessment, so the individual in late career faces the fact that his or her career will soon end. This era marks the beginning of the end of a work life that has met central needs during adult life. Whereas the midcareer individual acknowledges that his career is half over, the individual in late career faces impending retirement and must consider what life will be like without a work identity (see Fig. 4–1).

### Concerns About Self

A shift in work identity occurs during the late career era. Often organizational processes require a shift from an authoritative role to a more consultative role. Only a minority of late career individuals maintain powerful positions as they age; more often, as individuals approach sixty, they are replaced with younger colleagues who are viewed as having greater potential to perform the most central work tasks because of their current technical knowledge and the continuity they provide for the future.

The individual at this stage struggles to maintain a sense of usefulness and centrality while becoming aware of the age gap between himself and the majority of those who are now most responsible for the organization's operations. He must find ways to make the later career years productive even though he is no longer central to organizational functioning.

I'm a firm believer, Kathy, that life doesn't really begin at 55, no matter what the wonders of the world are today — but I don't think anything has really basically changed when you are in a company as to what your chances are when you've reached a certain age. I'm not feeling sorry for myself, I'm trying to be practical.

If they are going to broaden somebody's background, say on a lateral move — why do they want to broaden mine? What good is it going to do them? You see, they only put me in this job as an expedience, not because they were trying to broaden me for anything. If they were thinking — "okay, he's a contender for something better, then let's have him have this and that other thing to broaden him so that when he goes up to that new level, he'll have the kind of background we want." That's not happening given this move. I'm out of the running now.

Years of experience in the organization make the late career manager particularly valuable as a consultant for younger colleagues (Dalton et al., 1977). The late career manager is not likely to have unique technical expertise; however, he is likely to have a special wisdom of experience that can shape future policy for the organization.

The extent to which a person can embrace a more consultative work identity depends on both psychological and organizational factors. If organization members provide rewards and positive recognition to the late career individual who becomes a consultant, mentor, or coach, he will probably welcome the new role (Hall, 1980; Hall & Kram, 1981). However, if organization members convey the message that he is no longer needed or valued, then the new work identity will be resisted. If the shift in identity coincides with significant decreases in recognition and influence, the individual feels lost, depressed, and angry. The loss of a work identity that comes with retirement may be encountered during the late career years.

The experience of late career is also influenced by one's anticipations of retirement. For those who hold a positive fantasy of what life without one's career will be like, the last years are not dreaded and perhaps even welcomed. Some consider second careers to do a kind of work that was never previously an option. Others look forward to increased leisure time to pursue hobbies and visit family members and friends. However, for those who have no positive image of life after their careers have ended, the late career years can be painful and frightening. Those who are immersed in their work lives and only minimally involved in other spheres find approaching retirement threatening; these individuals met most of their central needs at work.

I don't really like to think about retirement. I am constantly hoping to forget that I have to retire. I am jittery about leaving the company — and sad. It has been like my family. . . . Everyone keeps saying that I'm going to feel good to have all that time to myself. . . . I'm not so sure.

Finally, the individual in late career must accept whatever course his life has taken and confront the reality of his one and only life cycle. A primary developmental task of this era is to consolidate a lifetime of experience and to achieve some sense of having had an effect through work and family spheres during adulthood.

> It came about maybe five years ago. And I determined that this was probably the level at which I was going to go and I stopped and said maybe consciously or maybe unconsciously, "Is that good or is that bad? And it's not all that bad. It's okay. It's a good job. Most of the time it's a challenging job. The salary is good, and I've done good work over the years. Can I live with that? Yeah." And I guess you might call it coming to terms with yourself, or with oneself.

Anticipations of the future do not fully account for the experience of late career years. An individual's sense of what legacy he will leave behind is equally important. If he feels as though he has made an important contribution, it will be easier to leave than if he does not have that sense. For the individual who is still striving to feel good about his career accomplishments, impending retirement may seem premature and disruptive. For the individual who feels she leaves behind a positive legacy, however, it may be difficult to leave the organization if alternative opportunities for being productive and creative are not yet envisioned. Coming to terms with what one will leave behind is an important developmental task that allows the individual to direct energies toward retirement years. Erikson (1963, 1968) defined this task as one of establishing a sense of "ego integrity" in which the individual feels satisfied with her life choices and actions so that she sees it as meaningful and is willing to leave it as it is. The failure to achieve such integrity can result in a fear of death—the one and only life cycle is not accepted as the ultimate. The alternative to ego integrity is *despair*, a feeling that there is not enough time to start over again in order to find a path to integrity.

## Concerns About Career

For late career managers, the end is in sight. In contrast to early and middle career individuals, there is no longer the opportunity to revise their course or to change their accomplishments and aspirations. Instead of strengthening their commitment to the organization, they look for other commitments as retirement approaches. Similarly, their concern is not whether they will advance further, but rather can they accept what has been achieved. Finally, late career managers are uncertain about what will happen to significant relationships at work as they begin to disengage from the organization.

**Commitment.** One's work role serves some essential functions. It provides economic resources that are a means to other ends. It allows individuals to view themselves as contributors to society and gives them self-respect. It helps them define personal identity. It provides opportunities for interactions with others, and it allows them to structure time and to ward off discomforting feelings (Sofer, 1970).

> A lot of people say retirement is very nice. I don't think it will be that nice — my gut feeling is that it won't be. If you have a goal, that would be good. I don't want total freedom to go and do without a schedule. I need to commit myself to doing things. I couldn't be happy without goals. . . . Anyone who has worked for 38 or 40 years knows — work is a big part of life!

Given the range of functions that a work role offers, it is not surprising that most individuals build a strong commitment to work by late career. A developmental task at late career is to discover what can replace one's work identity so that one can commit to other worthwhile endeavors.

The search for alternatives is both exciting and frightening. The prospect of beginning a new career or new community activities or spending more time on leisure pursuits is exciting; the routine of a familiar work role and setting will be replaced with something new to tap one's personal resources and creative energies. On the other hand, one's commitment to work may never be replaced with something as involving and one may move into a great emptiness upon retirement.

For those who carried commitments to family, leisure, and community pursuits along with work commitments, the future may be predictable, and the potential loss is not as threatening. Even for those who have been workaholics, the opportunity to reorient themselves toward other endeavors can be intriguing.

> It won't be a scheduled life. It will be great! Relaxing and peaceful. I'll have more time to be active with friends and the condominium association. Life will be less regimented — doing only the things you want to do. I hope I can stay healthy and do the things I like to do for enjoyment. I want time for reading, travel, people, perhaps part-time work, and cultivating new friends.

The transition into retirement begins, at least emotionally, during late career years. Leaving one's organizational commitments creates ambivalence. Both potential loss and excitement characterize the impending separation from one's work role.

Some begin the search for alternative commitments several years before retirement, and others refuse to give it attention until they are faced with reality. The latter stay involved with work activities, work relationships, and the events inside the organization; for them it is important not to lose a sense of belonging any sooner than necessary. The former, in contrast, begin to invest their energies elsewhere and maintain only peripheral involvement in the work sphere.

**Advancement.** The next move for a person in late career is either to a less central position at the same organizational level or out to retirement. At this career stage, the concern is not whether one will advance further, but rather whether one is satisfied with what has been achieved. At midcareer further advancement may not be likely, but it is still possible, at least to build a respectable role during the second half of one's career. In late career, however, time is running out, and the primary task is to accept what has occurred.

Achieving a sense of integrity is an ongoing process at this career stage, and the individual in late career years reviews his career history thoroughly, reworking previous decisions, successes, and failures. At the same time he views younger colleagues with delight and possibly with envy; they are learning from those in late career, and they have opportunities that are no longer available to those for whom retirement is near. The individual in late career may see parts of self in both the novice and the midcareer employees; this identification enables him to develop a sense of continuity, knowing that parts of self will live on through others.

For those who achieved what they set out to do, or more, late career is a time when they feel some sense of closure in their careers.

> I thoroughly believe that your life doesn't begin at this age. As a consequence, I think more about the experiences that I have had and what I can call upon from what I learned, and I never really stopped to think about them so much before. Things get sucked up by osmosis, by experience in learning, and you don't stop to think, "where did I learn that?" Now at this particular age, you begin to realize how much you can call upon that 32 years you gave. And how much you have to teach others because of your experience.

They have energy for coaching and advising peers and junior colleagues; they enjoy the consultative role precisely because advancement concerns no longer exist. For those who are dissatisfied with their accomplishments, the late career years become a period of depression and psychological withdrawal as they come to terms with what has been achieved. In the latter instances, managers feel the consultative role is either belittling or a burden; they have difficulty maintaining a positive attitude with a work role or with others in the work setting.

**Relationships at Work.** By the time an individual reaches late career, he has many long-standing relationships with peers, superiors, and subordinates. At this stage, he is less concerned with building relationships and more concerned with maintaining or withdrawing from them. Relationships during this career stage allow him to pass on wisdom and experience and leave a legacy behind. They also support him as he confronts the transition into retirement. Finally, they are the most obvious and durable link that an individual has with the organization he will soon leave.

Relationships with peers are particularly important during late career years. The individual in late career reflects on the past and shares concerns about the future with those of the same age and similar organizational histories.

I'm more open with my peers now than I was in my younger years. I guess back then I was aggressive, I wanted to do things, and I suppose in some instances I might have even stepped on toes to get things done, without regard for what I was doing to people around me. As you grow older, I think you get a little better perspective of how important these relationships are to you. . . .

Peers empathize with the fears and anxieties about retirement. They also remember all of the events and changes over the years that had an impact on their careers. Talking about how it was different in earlier years with someone who was also a part of that history is important; it unites the past with present.

Peers provide psychological support for reviewing and integrating one's entire career. They also provide information about retirement. Those in late career watch their peers who leave the organization before them to see what the transition is like. When others have positive experiences in their new leisure time, concerns are somewhat alleviated and replaced with positive anticipations of the end of a career. Discussing changes with peers who left the organization helps late career individuals manage the transition.

Competition in peer relationships is not as great during this career stage as in earlier years. Individuals no longer aim for the next promotion; they direct their energies toward coaching younger organizational members and advising on strategic or policy issues. Those who find the movement into a less central (or more consultative) role difficult might resent peers who remain more integrally involved in the operation of the organization. The individual in late career who is unhappy with his or her accomplishments may feel competitive with peers. The inability to develop a sense of integrity, with the confidence that one leaves behind a positive legacy, interferes with the potential benefits of relationships with peers in the final years of one's career.

Relationships with subordinates during the late career years allow the manager to pass on wisdom and experience. Through mentoring and coaching roles, an individual still feels valuable to the organization and develops confidence that he or she will leave a legacy behind.

> I think the business needs it, and I'm astute enough to know that there are many younger people in the business today who have inherently more capability than I have. If the business is going to grow, and they're going to grow, and we're going to continue to meet the challenges of providing our basic services, you've got to raise people along as younger managers. You can't sit back and say you're the only people who can manage because we're really not. I think probably that's one of the biggest parts of my job now — not written or documented anywhere — is watching out for young people like this and offering challenges that they can take and grow with.

Relationships with subordinates also allow the late career manager to get reacquainted with youthful parts of himself. He identifies with those junior colleagues for whom he provides mentoring functions. This identification is, in part, an attempt to relive some of the earlier experiences of his career as the process of moving into retirement begins. One's ability to let go of an organizational career may be facilitated by periods of reflection within the context of a developmental relationship.

If the individual in late career fails to develop a sense of "ego integrity" as the end of her career nears, she probably will not be able to engage in supportive relationships with subordinates. She may resent that younger colleagues have their youth and their opportunities to advance.

> It begins to raise doubts in your mind when you see very competent younger people doing those things that you used to do, or had greater opportunity to do because of the pyramid, and so those concerns, I think everybody, if they're realistic or honest, experience.

In addition, negative self-esteem and anger or depression interfere with providing mentoring functions to others. Paradoxically, close relationships with subordinates are an important source of support during late career years; at the same time, those who need support are often unavailable to participate in these alliances.

In late career, superiors play a unique role. They are not there to promote or develop the individual, and possibly they are younger than the individual. The formal role relationship necessitates interaction, and this relationship can contribute to or interfere with the transition into retirement. The impending retirement and the reversal in age difference make this relationship complex.

A superior can help the individual in late career feel valued even with a shift into a more consultative role. He can provide task assignments that tap the late career person's experience and historical perspective.

Or, a superior can make the late career manager feel obsolete and worthless by providing only trivial work assignments and by disregarding the individual's suggestions because he will be leaving the organization. The nature of this relationship depends, in part, on the current developmental tasks of the boss (Baird & Kram, 1983).

In contrast to early or middle career years, relationships with superiors may be less important than relationships with peers or subordinates. A superior can be a good sounding board and confidante for some of the concerns of the individual in late career. More often than not, however, peers are sought out for this purpose.

> I have other people to talk to—other than my boss. It would create preconceived ideas about my readiness to retire—to talk with him about some of my concerns.

In late career, as one anticipates leaving the organization, a range of feelings about current relationships may surface. An individual may fear the loss of significant relationships and either withdraw prematurely from them or attempt to solidify them. Withdrawal dulls the pain of separation, while attempts to solidify relationships minimize the fear of losing them completely. Since relationships contribute to one's sense of identity at every career stage, the prospect of losing them in late career can be awesome, particularly as one faces loss of a work role as well. Significant others may have similar reactions as the individual in late career moves closer to retirement; they, too, will experience loss when the career has ended, and they too, are unclear about continuing the relationship after the individual's departure.

## Concerns About Family

The individual in late career either anticipates major changes in the family sphere or chooses not to acknowledge that they will occur. After having a career for so many years, the prospect of leaving a work identity behind has significant implications for nonwork life. Relationships with family members are likely to change, leisure time becomes more abundant, and the anticipated loss of a work identity becomes reality.

Some late career individuals do not think much about these impending changes and how they may be affected by them. They are immersed in their work and discomforted by thoughts of retirement so that they avoid considering what lies ahead. Frequently, a spouse will be concerned about what their lives will be like after retirement.

> She is not very happy about my talking about retiring. In fact, it upsets her. Maybe it is because she feels that I'll be hanging around the house when I retire. We haven't planned together about it too much.

The late career individual's impending retirement affects family relationships. Spouses react to the impending change, possibly with both enthusiasm and trepidation. How their new life structure will evolve is uncertain.

The individual in late career who does think about impending retirement has other concerns as well. He wonders what his relationships with spouse and children will be. He may fear becoming financially or emotionally dependent as he envisions life without a fulltime career.

Some individuals, however, have positive fantasies of increased time to spend with family members after so many years devoted to their careers. They may even begin to plan their second careers at this time.

Perhaps the most fundamental concern in later career is the fear of losing a sense of purpose in life after retirement. For those who have been extremely involved in their work, the threat of boredom and atrophy is very real and frightening. Late career managers afraid of life without their current work role are likely to avoid thoughts of the future.

## IMPLICATIONS

This chapter examined how individuals' needs and concerns change over the course of a career and how these changes affect significant relationships at work (see Figure 4-1). What individuals seek in relationships and what they offer others shift with movement to a new career stage. When a relationship responds to concerns of both individuals, it is a *complementary* relationship. In contrast, when a relationship interferes with either person's concerns, it is a *noncomplementary* relationship.

*Complementarity suggests the opportunity to complete oneself.* For example, a manager in the later career years may see aspects of his younger self that are brought to life in relating to a manager in the early career period. Participating in the young manager's development enables the senior manager to rework the past and to become reacquainted with aspects of himself that have been dormant in previous years. Similarly, a young manager may discover valuable parts of himself in the senior manager who becomes a role model and an object of identification. He develops previously unknown parts of himself by relating to the senior manager. Both individuals are enhanced by the relationship.

*Noncomplementarity suggests a potential threat to self.* For example, a senior manager may feel that a young manager's growing strength and autonomy threaten his influence, self-esteem, and opportunity. As the young manager develops a separate identity, the senior manager may feel rivalrous and competitive and may no longer be willing to provide career and psychosocial functions. Similarly, a young manager may see the senior manager as an obstacle to continued growth and development; he may feel smothered or undermined by someone who previously enabled him to develop competence and effectiveness in the managerial role. Each individual experiences a loss of esteem and feels uncomfortable relating to the other.

*All developmental relationships begin as complementary ones.* For example, if a young manager is concerned about competence and about learning how to be effective in the managerial role, and if a midcareer manager wants to pass on her wisdom and experience by developing young talent in the organization, a complementary relationship will probably emerge between these two individuals if they have opportunities to interact. The relationship becomes mutually important because it allows both individuals to address important developmental tasks. This mutuality is the basis for the initiation phase of a relationship and what causes the emergence of a range of career and psychosocial functions.

*Relationship complementarity exists for a limited period of time.* Because of changes in individual needs or organizational circumstances, relationships are not likely to continue as complementary. For example, a young manager with a few years of organizational experience may no longer need coaching and guidance from a mentor. Or, a midcareer individual may enter a period of reassessment and redirection and no longer be interested in counseling, guiding, or sponsoring younger colleagues. Similarly, the individual in late career may find, as retirement nears, that he prefers to establish and maintain relationships with individuals outside the organization rather than with colleagues at work. Organizational changes, including transfers, promotions, and policy changes, frequently shift a manager's concerns, and this shift can cause him to move away from a relationship that no longer responds to his developmental tasks.

*Individuals can experience complementarity in several relationships simultaneously.* It is a fallacy to assume that only one relationship which provides a range of developmental functions can respond to an individual's needs and concerns at any one time. Relationships with individuals of another generation can be complementary because younger colleagues get the guidance they need and older colleagues meet generative needs. At the same time, relationships with individuals of the same generation can be complementary because peers find empathy as well as reflections of their own experiences in each other. Similarly, individuals in midcareer or late career find that only with peers can they share their most central concerns about aging, the threat of obsolescence, or impending retirement. At every career stage, then, a number of relationships have the potential for complementarity.

Individuals at every career stage can identify the possibilities for complementary relationships. Too often, however, young managers wait for good relationships to "happen to them." They fail to recognize what they have to offer to others as well as how to initiate a relationship with a potential mentor. Alternately, those who have outgrown relationships with mentors overlook opportunities for enhancing relationships with peers who can provide important developmental functions (see Chapter 6). At every career stage, in many organizations, individuals feel alone in their experiences of personal and professional dilemmas; they assume that others would not understand or recognize the significance of their concerns.

Scanning the organizational environment for opportunities to build complementary relationships is self-enhancing. It is of equal value to acknowledge and accept those instances in which noncomplementarity is inevitable. For example, if boss and subordinate are of similar age and career stage, the boss probably will not provide many critical mentoring functions to the subordinate (Baird & Kram, 1983). In addition, competitiveness will result if both aspire for similar advancement opportunities. The young manager who persists at building a developmental relationship with a boss in this situation is likely to be disappointed and frustrated.

The individual, then, can become a diagnostician. He can identify primary concerns about himself, his career, and his family and the kinds of relationships that support them. He can also assess which individuals are likely to have concerns that are complementary. Finally, the manager can anticipate which individuals may be unavailable to provide certain career or psychosocial functions because of his or her career stage and associated dilemmas. In undertaking these diagnostic efforts, the individual becomes an active agent in developing relationships that support career development.

For individuals whose life stage and career stage are out of synch, it is challenging to build complementary relationships. The manager who is launching a career at midlife, for example, may find that potential mentors are the same age or younger. This can create discomfort and awkwardness for both individuals. The newcomer may feel reticent to ask for coaching or may resent having to report to and take advice from a superior who does not have more experience. And the senior colleague may feel uneasy about coaching or counseling someone who is older than most other junior colleagues, or she may feel threatened by a subordinate who has experience outside of this career or organization. In these instances, relationship dynamics add complexities; potential resentment, competition, or fear will have to be managed effectively.

Organizations can support the development of complementary relationships by creating conditions that help individuals assess their needs and build valuable relationships. Through educational efforts, individuals can understand how needs change over the course of careers, as well as know the diagnostic and behavioral skills needed to build complementary relationships. Educational programs that bring individuals of similar career stages together allow individuals to discover the value of peer relationships. Educational programs that bring individuals of different career stages together allow for learning about those of other generations, thus enhancing the likelihood that relationships with those at other career stages will evolve outside of the educational context.

Outside of the educational context, organizations create conditions through the nature of work design, the reward system, the norms, and the general culture. To what extent does the organization encourage individuals to pay attention to their relationships? Do jobs provide opportunities for interaction with those of similar and different career stages? Are jobs and people matched so that, for example, midcareer individuals can provide mentoring functions as part of their primary responsibilities? Does the reward system reinforce efforts to provide mentoring functions as well as efforts to pay attention to the quality of peer, subordinate, and superior relationships? These are diagnostic questions for the organization that recognizes the important role of developmental relationships in individuals' careers and that is committed to insuring that conditions encourage complementary relationships.

In periods of retrenchment conditions often emerge that do not support relationship-building efforts. Educational programs may be cut in order to reduce expenses, and managers are likely to feel the pressure to be results-oriented and less attentive to the socio-emotional features of their departments. The paradox, however, is that during such a time, individual stress and anxiety increase in response to the uncertainties about job security or the future of one's career. During retrenchment, personal and professional concerns will heighten. Relationships are a critical source of support in finding ways to manage uncertainty, stress, and anxiety so that effective work can continue.

More research is needed on both the individual and organizational forces that support the formation of complementary relationships at each career stage. It is still not entirely understood why some individuals manage to build a number of complementary relationships while others fail to do so. There is also much to learn about the forces that contribute to noncomplementary relationships and how these can be managed effectively by individuals and organizations. Finally, the study of relationships at different career stages in a variety of organizations would help us understand how features of organizational life shape relationships that have the potential to respond to individuals' developmental tasks.

5

# Complexities of Cross-Gender Relationships

During the last decade the number of women in professional and managerial positions has increased dramatically. One important consequence of this trend is that relationships between junior and senior colleagues, and between peers, will more often involve members of both sexes than in previous years (Kanter, 1977). This chapter explores the complexities of developmental relationships at work that involve both sexes.

Both men and women are searching for ways to build and maintain effective working relationships with members of the opposite sex. Young female managers frequently report how difficult it is to develop a sense of autonomy and independence in their interactions with their male mentors. Male managers describe their discomfort when they find themselves behaving in overprotective ways toward their female subordinates. Both men and women allude to the sexual tensions and fears of increasing intimacy that cause anxiety, ambivalence, and confusion in their relationships with colleagues of the other sex.

These dynamics are not surprising. Earlier socialization experiences have not prepared men or women for the challenges created by these new forms of work relationships (Sargent, 1977). Men, for example, worked effectively in teams with other boys and young men in sporting events. In their adolescent and early adult years, they learned to relate to women as girlfriends, lovers, or secretaries who occupied lesser status positions. None of these experiences prepare them to work with women as peers or supervisors (Kanter, 1977; Epstein, 1970; Hennig & Jardim, 1977).

Similarly, women historically have had little training in team sports and more experience in solo sports if at all involved in athletics as a child (Hennig & Jardim, 1977). In terms of relationships with potential mentors, women have had socialization experiences that leave them inclined to behave in dependent and nonassertive ways with male colleagues (Baker-Miller, 1976; Josefowitz, 1980). In addition, they are unlikely to have had any experiences that would prepare them to assume positions of authority and to provide mentoring functions to others, particularly to men. They are, like men, not sufficiently prepared for collaborative and effective working relationships with individuals of the other sex.

Individuals must now figure out how to manage work relationships with those of the other sex. They must meet this challenge by managing the internal relationship as well as the external relationship. The internal relationship is what transpires between two individuals whether they are peers or in a hierarchical role relationship. The external relationship is the boundary between the two individuals and the rest of the organization (Clawson & Kram, 1984). Both of these are important since either can present dilemmas for those who work together. The external relationship in cross-gender relationships is particularly critical, since it is frequently scrutinized.

In these studies of mentoring and peer relationships, five major categories of cross-gender relationship complexities can be identified. The first three are part of the internal relationship, and the last two are part of the external relationship. Each of these complexities is shaped by individual and organizational factors, and each has the potential to be destructive by limiting the competence and effectiveness of both men and women.

First, men and women are inclined to assume stereotypical roles in relating to each other in work settings (Bunker & Seashore, 1977; Kanter, 1977). These roles are defined by assumptions and expectations about appropriate behavior for each sex. In order to reduce the uncertainty, ambiguity, and anxiety created by the emergence of cross-gender work relationships, individuals rely on what is familiar. Thus, sometimes unknowingly, men and women assume traditional roles that they learned from past situations. These roles tend to constrain behavior and to reduce individual competence and effectiveness. People perpetuate stereotypical roles because it is what they know. In developmental relationships, the challenge is to figure out how men and women can be freer to behave in a variety of ways that are most appropriate for a given work context.

Second, in cross-gender developmental relationships, the role modeling function is frequently unsatisfactory to the younger individual and sometimes to the mentor as well. While women in the early career years face developmental dilemmas similar to those of male counterparts, women face some that are unique to being female in male-dominated organizational contexts (Kanter, 1977; Missirian, 1982; Baker-Miller, 1976). Concerns about the appropriateness of a particular behavior may appear unwarranted to the male mentor who does not understand that what works for a man may not work for a woman. Concerns about balancing work and family commitments are exacerbated for women in their thirties who are simultaneously advancing their careers and assuming the roles of wife and/or mother. These unique gender-related concerns make it difficult for male mentors to empathize, to provide role modeling, and to identify with their female proteges.

Third, in cross-gender developmental relationships, the mutual liking and admiration characteristic of all significant work relationships may lead to increasing intimacy and sexual tensions. This growing intimacy and sexuality is a source of anxiety that can be both threatening as well as exciting to men and women who work together. Such mutual attraction can lead to testing the boundaries of the relationship, to withdrawing from the relationship because of the anxiety and fear that is evoked by continual involvement, or to assuming stereotypical roles of a father/daughter connection in order to eliminate the possibility of sexual involvement. Concerns about intimacy and sexuality add stress to a developmental relationship; the manner of dealing with them determines whether the relationship is strengthened or weakened by this complexity.

The last two categories of complexity have to do with the external relationship; they pertain to how the two individuals relate to the organization as a whole. Cross-gender developmental relationships are particularly vulnerable to these complexities because they are still a relatively rare occurrence in most organizations. This, combined with heightened awareness due to Affirmative Action efforts, makes the relationships more visible.

Cross-gender developmental relationships are subject to public scrutiny; others study the relationship with interest and, more likely, with some suspicion. If the external relationship is not carefully managed, rumors develop that can be destructive to one or both individuals' careers as was evidenced in Mary Cunningham's career at Bendix (*The*

*Boston Globe*, October 2, 1980). The possibilities of sexual involvement and favoritism rather than competence as the criterion for sponsorship can threaten the reputations of both individuals. This puts considerable stress on the relationship as the public image becomes the priority, increasing the likelihood that certain developmental functions are forfeited.

Finally, cross-gender relationships are subject to peer resentment. This complexity occurs for women with male mentors who are working in a predominantly male peer group. Because of the competitive dynamics that occur among peers aspiring to advance, the solo woman stands out as one who receives special attention if she is regularly coached by a male superior. Although this relationship may be important for her, she may be reluctant to maintain it for fear of becoming isolated from or ridiculed by her male peers. As a result, the solo woman in this situation can experience considerable stress as she confronts having to choose between relationships with peers and a valuable relationship with a male superior. With this complexity, it is likely that the senior colleague is unaware of the stress created by peer resentment since the resentment is directed at the junior colleague.

With an understanding of the factors that contribute to relationship dynamics, it is possible to manage them so that individual competence and effectiveness is not diminished or threatened. It is also fruitful to consider the hidden advantages of each of these complexities for men and women who are in cross-gender mentoring and peer relationships. By focusing on these advantages, there is the prospect of directing the uncertainty and ambiguity into productive action. If managed effectively, these relationships can serve both individuals well.

## COLLUSION IN STEREOTYPICAL ROLES

One way that both men and women deal with the uncertainty and ambiguity of working with members of the other sex is to rely on traditional (and familiar) roles learned in other settings. While these roles may not maximize work effectiveness, they do reduce anxiety and the internal conflict that may emerge in cross-gender relationships. It is not inevitable that individuals fall into stereotypical roles; however, they are likely to when organizational members bring traditional socialization experiences to a changing social context at work.

Stereotypical role relationships are powerful because two individuals may collude to maintain familiar ways of relating to one another, even though these ways may not be in either individual's best interests. For example, a young female manager looks to her male mentor for direction and advice excessively, enacting the role of the dependent one who cannot act autonomously. At the same time, the male mentor embraces the role of helper and protector because it makes him feel powerful and dominant. Both individuals participate in the collusion; they try to fulfill what they think are others' expectations of them, and to fulfill what they internalized as appropriate sex-role behavior (Bunker & Seashore, 1977; Epstein, 1970; Kanter, 1977).

Stereotypical roles constrain behavior and therefore reduce competence and effectiveness at work. The woman who colludes in playing a helpless and dependent role forfeits the opportunity to demonstrate her skills and competence. The male manager who maintains the role of tough, invulnerable expert forfeits the opportunity to ask for help when it would be useful for needed support or information. Both men and women contribute to the collusive behavior that limits the range of available behavioral options. While in same-gender relationships these dynamics might occur because of status differences and personality traits, they are more likely to occur in cross-gender relationships where stereotypical assumptions and expectations are easily triggered (Kanter, 1977; Bunker & Seashore, 1977).

There are many forms that the collusion can take. Four reciprocal role relationships have been identified (Bradford et al., 1975; Kanter, 1977; Kram, 1980). These relationships are observed most frequently because they involve the most commonly held traditional assumptions about appropriate behavior. Most men and women initially report that they behave no differently in same-gender and cross-gender relationships. However, when probed further about their actual experiences in relationships, the tendency to fall into traditional patterns that have women feeling incompetent or men feeling overly responsible are shared. The following examples illustrate the effects of collusion in stereotypical roles and how they diminish individual effectiveness.

The most commonly experienced stereotypical role in mentoring relationships was that of the "father" and the "pet" as defined by Bradford et al. (1975) and Kanter (1977). In this situation, usually involving an older male manager and a young female manager, the former takes on a protective role, providing coaching and advice and shielding her from the risks and struggles of organizational life. At the same time, the younger female manager feels most accepted and most comfortable when she is behaving as one who needs support and who is less competent. Her role in a work group evolves into that of the "cheerleader" for others, rather than one who makes substantive contributions. It is, in the end, a protective father-daughter relationship.

One young woman described being in this role with her mentor as well as with her male peers.

> I couldn't control the fact that I was a woman. All I could do was try to fit in without compromising myself personally. . . . I became someone who was a nice little girl on a pedestal. . . . They wanted me to be either their

daughter, their girlfriend, or their wife. . . . At meetings, I noticed it was
hard for me to be heard. . . . They listened to each other, but not to my
ideas. . . .

This woman behaved in ways she thought would be acceptable and
then found she was making few substantive contributions at meetings.
Her male mentor also noted that he felt protective of her because he
knew it was difficult for women in male-dominated organizations. Both
individuals had good intentions, and both caused the female manager
to reduce her competence and the male manager to be protective in a
way which did not allow for greater equality and collaboration.

A closely related situation is that of the "chivalrous knight" and
"helpless maiden" (Bradford et al., 1975; Kanter, 1977). Here the male
sees himself as stronger and more competent than his female peer or
subordinate. He does not perceive the woman as having many task-
related skills. Thus, he is unlikely to challenge or make the same
demands on her that he would on males. The woman who plays the
complementary role manipulates the man by feigning ineptness (sometimes unconsciously) and getting the man to serve her. Men in this
situation frequently resent having been "enslaved" in such a protective
stance, and women suffer from overlearning. They are trapped in a
helpless role and lose the opportunity to take care of and assert
themselves. This pattern is less likely to occur in developmental relationships since, by definition, the woman is believed to be competent.
However, in times of stress, both men and women report falling back
on these stances.

In both mentoring and peer relationships, men and women tend to
put the female colleague into the role of "nurturant mother" (Kram,
1980). She finds herself serving primarily as a confidante to whom
others can bring their problems and look for support. She nurtures and
supports when she might otherwise accomplish work and face work-
related conflicts or disagreements. As the following male manager
illustrates, her behavior is reinforced by the male manager who finds a
comfortable sounding board in his young female subordinate.

> I personally feel more comfortable talking to a woman about feelings than I
> do to a guy. . . . I guess I can talk more at the level of feeling with her, per-
> sonal things, than I can normally feel comfortable with talking to a male col-
> league. . . .

For many men it is important to maintain an image of being tough
and independent, suppressing all emotions, particularly with their male
colleagues. The role of "tough warrior" (Bradford et al., 1975) prohibits
men from expressing emotions and from being other than rational and
logical—thus the need for a confidante who can provide a listening ear
as well as a psychological support.

In the fourth set of stereotypical roles, that of "macho" and "seductress" (Bradford et al., 1975; Kanter, 1977), the mode of relating is sexual, with elements of game-playing and flirtation. While this can be fun for both individuals, and self-affirming of one's attractiveness as well, this mode also ignores the woman's competence and intellectual contributions and leaves the man distracted from work and focused on winning her approval. While the expression of sexuality can be energizing, these roles become entrapping when they do not allow for intellectual exchange and collaboration. For example, in one mentor relationship the young female manager wondered whether her senior manager viewed her as a serious, competent professional.

> I think he has difficulty accepting a woman as his mental equal . . . some of the uncomfortableness that I still feel with him, is that he fancies himself as quite a ladies' man. He even makes allusions to wearing my skirts too long because I have nice looking legs, and that kind of stuff. . . . I don't feel comfortable when I pick up on stuff like that . . . suggesting that if we were ever at a party together, or out for a drink, he would put the make on me. I've got to really watch what I say and how I conduct myself . . . so that I'm taken seriously for my work contributions.

While the male mentor in this situation acknowledges his sexual attraction, he is not aware of how his comments affect his female protege. And while she feels his behavior indicates that he does not respect her as an intellectual equal, he maintains that she is one of the most competent subordinates that he has. Both are relatively unaware of how the sexual banter affects the other. This creates misunderstanding in an otherwise productive and enhancing developmental relationship.

These stereotypical roles are more significant in relationships that are not particularly enhancing to individual development. However, even in the most valued developmental relationships, men and women note instances where cross-gender relationship dynamics interfered with their competence and effectiveness. And even with the good intentions of wanting to foster development and effective collaboration on work tasks, they find themselves falling into stereotypical roles. Collusion, then, is often unconscious; individuals assume traditional roles that reduce their competence or that of a colleague without awareness of doing so. Individuals working in cross-gender relationships need to become aware of when traditional expectations and assumptions are driving their behavior in dysfunctional ways. When these roles become "entrapping" (Kanter, 1977), individual effectiveness is reduced, and the relationship is no longer an enhancing one.

Effects of the lack of experience with cross-gender relationships are most evident in the situation of a token woman in an all male department (Kanter, 1977). Introducing a woman into an all male department is disruptive and anxiety-provoking. In order to reduce these effects, stereotypes are employed so that the token woman is rapidly placed in one or several stereotypical roles. Sexual tensions, resentment, competitive feelings, and the possibility of her disrupting the formerly all male group are managed by putting these stereotypes in place. The tendency to entrap the token reduces her competence, since her behavior is constrained by the traditional expectations for her. Everyone colludes in this situation, albeit unknowingly, to make her feel helpless, incompetent, like the "nurturing mother" or like a sex object, but not as a competent, contributing member of the team.

In developmental relationships, the powerful effect of tokenism that entraps women in dysfunctional roles can be counteracted by trust and an interpersonal bond. The more two individuals have the opportunity to work together, the less likely they are to need stereotypical behavior and expectations. Thus, the best way to reduce the collusion is to increase interaction. When men and women working closely together is no longer a rarity, there will be less need to reduce uncertainty and anxiety.

Individuals are likely to assume some, but not necessarily all, of these stereotypical roles. Because of earlier socialization, some roles will come very naturally, and they may be difficult to resist even with a genuine commitment to breaking dysfunctional collusions. The senior manager who naturally assumes a "protective father" role finds it difficult to refrain from overprotective behavior with a junior female manager. Similarly, the woman who finds it easier to play "helpless" than to assume an equal, and sometimes dissenting, stance with a male authority figure also has a difficult time resisting the familiar stereotypical role relationship. As individuals become aware of their inclinations in cross-gender working situations, they will probably choose alternative behaviors that are more effective.

The individual who violates stereotypical assumptions in relationships where the other party is living by them is likely to encounter disappointment or anger. For example, the woman who is assertive and competent with a man who enjoys being the "chivalrous knight" has a discontented colleague; she breaks a collusion that he wants to maintain. Similarly, a man who refuses to assume the role of "protective father," insisting that the female subordinate behave autonomously and stand up for her own ideas, evokes anger and abandonment from the woman who wants to be protected like the "pet" or "daughter."

There are some hidden advantages to maintaining collusions in sex-role stereotypes. The stereotypes seem to reduce anxiety and ambiguity; to give them up involves risks that might be intolerable for some individuals. The option to continue with familiar patterns rather than search for alternative behavior (which may be more effective) is attractive. In addition, traditional roles reduce the guilt or conflict that a man or a woman might feel about deviating from a sex-role stereotype. Thus, a woman feels more comfortable continuing in a "helpless" role; becoming more assertive might create guilt and internal conflict. Similarly, a man feels more comfortable continuing in a "father" role than risking loss of power to, or becoming sexually aroused by, a woman who no longer appears to be a "good girl."

There are times when collusion can be self-serving even if it reduces the competence of the other person involved in a cross-gender relationship. The traditional roles support the power discrepancy and empower the more senior male in the relationship. Stereotypical role relationships reinforce the power dynamics inherent in a hierarchical relationship. However, when a woman occupies the more senior position, the stereotypes are not likely to prevail; in fact, these situations can be particularly difficult at first, since there are no stereotypical assumptions and behaviors to rely on. These instances force both men and women to discover a wider range of alternatives for interacting in cross-gender relationships.

## THE LIMITATIONS OF ROLE MODELING

One of the primary functions of a developmental relationship is to provide role modeling. For the individual in early career years, role modeling is critical for learning the ropes of an organization. When one attempts to master the technical, political, and managerial tasks of a new professional role, the opportunity to watch someone who is successful and who embodies what one wants to become is invaluable (see Chapter 2).

Role modeling is limited in cross-gender relationships. Some of the personal and professional dilemmas that young women bring to a work context are very different from those of their male senior colleagues; thus, whatever strategies and solutions the latter have developed for coping with career concerns may not be useful to their female proteges. In addition, even when concerns are identical, strategies for managing them may diverge because what works for a man in a particular work setting won't necessarily work for a woman (Kanter, 1977; Gordon & Stroeber, 1975; Missirian, 1982). While the intention to provide a model may be genuine, in the most critical domains of personal or professional development many efforts are inadequate.

In some instances the desire to provide a role model weakens (albeit unconsciously) in cross-gender relationships. In same-gender relationships, a junior colleague discovers a model of whom he might become, and the more senior colleague finds a younger version of himself in the one for whom he is a model. This mutual identification strengthens the role modeling function. In cross-gender relationships, however, identification is more difficult to achieve because the gender difference makes finding fundamental similarities more remote. Without identification, neither individual sees parts of self embodied in the other, and the senior person becomes less of a model for the junior colleague.

Role modeling involves both interaction and identification (Spiegler, 1981). When professional and personal dilemmas are quite different, interaction concerning how to manage these is of limited value because empathy and joint problem-solving are difficult to achieve. When neither individual sees central parts of self embodied in the other, the identification process is lacking. Both interaction and identification are unlikely in cross-gender relationships.

Discussion of the limitations of the role modeling function in cross-gender relationships is based on the study of relationships involving junior women and senior men. Situations in which the female is senior and the male is junior are not irrelevant, but these are still relatively rare in most managerial contexts. One can speculate that the same kinds of limitations will exist; personal and professional concerns will differ, making empathy and mutual problem-solving difficult, and the lack of identification will weaken the role-modeling function.

The personal and professional dilemmas women face that are foreign to their male colleagues can be summarized into three general categories. The first has to do with the individual's professional role and the personal conflicts that arise when carrying out the role effectively. The second has to do with the stresses and conflicts that arise when managing multiple roles in career and family and the dilemmas of successive life stages. The third encompasses the uncertainties and challenges that arise for the female professional as she builds and manages her relationship with the organization and the unique dilemmas created by being a minority in a professional setting. The role modeling function has limitations when responding to these concerns.

Women entering professional roles in this era face considerable internal conflict concerning how to effectively carry out their new positions. Earlier socialization encouraged behavior which is inconsistent with what is now demanded (Hennig & Jardim, 1977; Bardwick, 1971). Thus, the female manager experiences internal conflict which is quite different from that of her male counterparts. For example, she may find it difficult to be assertive, particularly in male-dominated settings (Baker-Miller, 1976). Or she may find it frightening to consider that she may succeed and surpass her male colleagues (Horner, 1969). The discrepancy between what is expected in the professional setting and the traditional roles learned earlier creates stress, guilt, and anxiety (Bardwick, 1971; Epstein, 1970).

Such reactions interfere with learning about an organization and a particular role. While both men and women are anxious and concerned about competence in early career years (Schein, 1978; Hall, 1976), women must contend with the internal conflict created by the discrepancy between what is required in the new setting and what was learned earlier. While everyone has to learn the technical, managerial, and political requirements of a new role, these may present greater challenge for those who must adopt foreign behaviors in order to survive.

An example of how this internal conflict affects learning the ropes and how it affects the nature of cross-gender developmental relationships is reflected in a young female manager's account of her first years on the job. Five years later, and with much difficulty, she became a successful second level manager. She maintains that the struggle was one that she could never share with her male mentor.

> At first I used to cry at home at night. I knew I wasn't being effective, and yet I couldn't do what I had to do. I would have anxiety attacks every time I went to a department meeting. I wanted to speak up more and show them I knew something, but I always ended up retreating into my shell, and then I would blame myself afterward for being so passive and unassertive.
>
> Gradually I learned how to deal better — but it wasn't from talking with Bob [her mentor] about it. The few times I attempted to discuss it with him I felt that he didn't understand the problem, and I got embarrassed. So I stopped bringing the concern to him.
>
> Somehow, after 2 years of hell, I found myself being more assertive, speaking my mind, and being more of a leader. And I even grew to like myself in this new way. I had to change my whole conception of myself. . . .

While she gained other kinds of support and guidance from her mentor this young woman found little empathy or guidance on how to manage internal conflicts that interfered with her effectiveness. The anxiety, guilt, and fear associated with behaving in new ways presented a difficult challenge in the early career years.

She faced dilemmas unique to being a woman, and her mentor was only able to empathize, understandably, with experience and struggles that were similar to those he faced earlier in his career history. The role-modeling function is limited because the central concerns of the younger person are foreign to the senior colleague. This is most likely to happen in cross-gender developmental relationships.

While the first category of personal and professional dilemmas involves the intra-role conflict that women experience carrying out new work roles, the second category involves the conflicts created by multiple roles or the prospect of assuming multiple roles. Both men and women face the choices as to whether to marry or stay single, whether to have a family, and how to manage both spheres of commitments effectively. However, the psychological work surrounding these challenges may differ for the two sexes (Bardwick, 1971; Gilligan, 1982). These differences affect the role-modeling function by making empathy and identification less likely.

The decisions to marry and have children are not seen as in conflict for men who are launching new careers. The two often go hand-in-hand as evidence of one's ability to establish a satisfactory life structure (Levinson et al., 1978). Frequently, a man wants to become established at work before assuming responsibility for a family; however, these are seldom viewed as mutually exclusive commitments. While women are beginning to combine work and family roles, they experience significant conflict in doing so. First, the role of mother is viewed as potentially interfering with one's career (Hennig & Jardim, 1977). Second, the decision not to have a family or not to marry may threaten one's sense of femininity (Bardwick, 1971). Third, even when roles are combined, women may experience considerable conflict and confusion concerning what is expected in each role (Epstein, 1970). Thus, the challenges associated with building career and family commitments are enlarged for women for biological, psychological, and cultural reasons.

One third level female manager in her early thirties identified several inter-role conflicts that were clearly related to her sex. Prior to assuming her last promotion, she became concerned about what implications this new position had for her self-image, as well as for how others viewed her. She experienced a direct conflict between career advancement and motherhood.

> I almost didn't take the promotion. I had a lot of questions about how feminine it was—you know, did I really want to take this new position—after all, wasn't I going to have babies and all that good stuff? I knew I was getting older, and I felt like I wanted to consider—so how could I take this promotion. . . .

At the time of the interview, she had yet to decide to have a child, but she was beginning to accept herself in a position of considerable responsibility. She overcame emotional barriers to assuming the middle-management role, but still felt incomplete about the prospect of becoming a mother. Consumed by the demands of her new position, she was distracted from this concern. Instead, she was now grappling with the tensions created by her role as wife.

My husband has been very supportive of me and he takes pride in the successes that I have — kind of brags about me.

But we have some problems — I have always made more money than he has — and that makes both of us uncomfortable. Also, even though he respects my career and likes the fact that I work, he wants me to walk out at 5:00 to be home on time. . . . He didn't want me to care so much about my work. Maybe it was a threat. . . .

The demands at home were in conflict with the demands at work. This alone, however, is not unique to women. What is unique is the discomfort both husband and wife experience in their relationship when a female professional assumes any number of several nontraditional stances (Epstein, 1970). The fact that she earned more money than he, and her unavailability to assume traditional responsibilities at home, created considerable guilt, confusion about priorities, and anxiety. The stress associated with inter-role conflict is of a different sort for women since what is expected at home is at odds with what is expected at work. Given earlier socialization, failure to meet traditional expectations in the wife role can be devastating (Epstein, 1970; Bardwick, 1971). Here again, the role-modeling function would be limited in a cross-gender relationship where a male senior colleague is unlikely to have solutions based on experience.

The final category of personal and professional dilemmas that limit the role modeling function contains many concerns that the individual has about his or her relationship with the organization. This individual-organization interface is most important when a person is launching a new career (Schein, 1978; Hall, 1976). Much of what a developmental relationship provides is the opportunity to learn how to manage this interface effectively. While all are concerned with establishing competence, developing a professional identity, and learning the ropes, particular challenges arise for women in male-dominated settings (Kanter, 1977; Bunker & Seashore, 1975). The challenge presented by being a token are sometimes difficult for those in the majority to understand. Thus, when a female manager feels isolated, lonely, or entrapped by sex-role stereotypes, it may be difficult for her male senior colleague to empathize with her.

One young female manager explains how much her male mentor has provided sponsorship, opportunities for exposure, and challenging work. Yet in talking further about his role in her development, she is disappointed.

I have yet to meet someone that I work for directly that I really want to emulate. That bothers me a lot. Jerry is close to it, but he does a lot of things that just aren't right for me. He will get on my case, because we are women, he will say that we are pussycats. . . . But he just doesn't fully understand that women, just by being women, can't do exactly the same thing that a man will do.

It is almost like I need another woman to be in that job, where you can see her style and really try it her way. There are a few women in similar jobs but none that I have been close enough to say, let's see how you operate. . . .

She had found that Jerry's assertive and aggressive style was not only uncomfortable for her to adopt, but frequently offensive to her male clients and peers. She experienced Jerry as being overly critical of her "different style," and she found if difficult to emulate his. The yearning for a female manager to observe in this organizational setting indicates her need for a role model of the same gender. She cannot identify with her male mentor, which limits the extent to which he can provide this critical developmental function.

There are a number of individual and organizational factors that limit the role-modeling function in cross-gender developmental relationships. First, both men and women make assumptions that create a self-fulfilling prophecy. Women assume that their male senior colleagues cannot understand or provide a model for how to manage their particular dilemmas, and men assume that they have little in common with their female colleagues, preferring to establish supportive relationships with other men. Thus, women will consciously or unconsciously seek out women role models to help them manage their conflicts and dilemmas. At the same time, male senior colleagues will gravitate toward younger male colleagues (rather than toward younger female colleagues) for those who can become objects of identification. The women's skepticism about their male colleagues' capacities to provide relevant modeling and the men's inclination to identify with and seek out other male colleagues combine to reduce the role modeling function in cross-gender relationships to a minimum.

One consequence of the limits on identification and role modeling in cross-gender relationships is that women are turning to female peers for this developmental function. Thus, the limitation has provided an impetus to seek out and to develop connections with same-gender peers that can be mutually enhancing.

We all had a common bond. It became a very good opportunity to share problems, successes, for helping one another. It was great to find out that others had the same kinds of problems that I did or that I could be of assistance to someone else. Workwise it was helpful in that it was more possible to find out what was going on in other parts of the company—there was now somebody to call if you wanted to find out about possible jobs or if you were looking to transfer a person somewhere. It became a power base and a support.

The opportunity to discuss concerns about work/family role conflicts, concerns about managing oneself in a professional role, or challenges in operating in a male-dominated organization is highly valued by those who discover their same sex peers. Modeling then occurs in other relationships and isolation and loneliness are reduced.

It is possible, too, that members of cross-gender relationships will discover a unique value in the role-modeling function. While identification and empathy may be far less than in same sex relationships, there may be opportunities to enhance one's skills and perceptions of the organization through observing how someone of the other gender manages particular situations. For example, while the male mentor may not have much to offer on the internal conflicts concerning career and motherhood, he may, through his actions, provide a valuable model of how to manage organizational politics effectively. Similarly, the female colleague may offer a perspective on how to manage work/family conflicts as well as other organizationally related experiences that a male colleague, as a member of the majority group, may not have thought of or understood. Clearly, there are options for increasing the value of cross-gender role modeling once the limitations are clarified.

## INTIMACY AND SEXUALITY CONCERNS

Since mutual liking, respect, and attraction are part of the interpersonal foundation of developmental relationships, it is not surprising that intimacy and sexuality concerns surface in cross-gender relationships (Bowen, 1983). As men and women work together and experience the mutual benefits of career and psychosocial functions, intimacy increases, and sexual attraction often develops. This erotic component can provoke anxiety. While mutual sharing and closeness may be satisfying and enjoyable, they can also be frightening since the boundaries of the relationship are called into question.

Increasing intimacy and sexual attraction are more likely to provoke anxiety or seem threatening than to be viewed as a positive source of synergy and creativity in a relationship, even though the latter is a unique benefit of cross-gender interactions. Both men and women are fearful and ambivalent about extending the boundaries of their relationships. To do so might destroy the positive attributes of a strong developmental relationship or pose threats to personal relationships with spouses and friends outside of work. It may also affect the career advancement or cause personal hurt since increasing involvement in any relationship increases one's vulnerability.

These issues cannot be avoided since whenever a man and a woman work closely together and find value in relating to each other, feelings of intimacy and/or sexuality are inevitable. These feelings lead to ambivalence and add considerable stress to the relationship. There are negotiations at each phase of the relationship regarding which developmental functions will be provided and how each individual's needs will be met. Personal boundaries around closeness, intimacy, and sexuality must also be clarified.

There are several ways that individuals manage the ambivalence and stress created by these particular cross-gender relationship dynamics; each has impact on the overall nature of the relationship as well as on the development of each individual. For example, individuals may attempt to test and expand the boundaries of the relationship to include greater intimacy and a sexual liaison. Alternately, individuals may withdraw somewhat from the relationship in order to reduce increasing intimacy. The managers may avoid any one-on-one meetings at work or outside of work or simply reduce the frequency of contact and range of issues discussed. Finally, individuals may deny feelings of attraction and intimacy by accentuating qualities that resemble a father-daughter connection; this makes any thoughts of a sexual liaison taboo. Interestingly, most individuals that report increasing intimacy and sexuality tension also indicate that they never talked with their significant others about the strategies both had adopted.

Testing and expanding the boundaries of a relationship to respond to growing mutual attraction can enhance or destroy the relationship. In one instance, a male mentor noted that his female protege had become his closest confidante in his work setting. With her he could discuss many personal concerns about work and family life that he could not do with other colleagues or even with his wife. Similarly, his female protege noted that they had a strong and "unusual" friendship. Both valued the shared intimacy, and both desired to continue to share. When asked about the sexual dimension of their relationship, both knew the boundaries; the fact that both were married made any sexual liaison out of the question. In fact, this made it possible for them to become closer over several years since there appeared to be no threat of a sexual liaison.

When managers agree on the nature of intimacy to be shared in a relationship, the mutual liking and attraction can be motivating, enjoyable, and synergistic (Bowen, 1983). Problems arise, however, when one individual wants to expand the boundary to include a sexual liaison while the other does not. This is particularly stressful in a hierarchical relationship between mentor and protege when the consequences (for further career advancement opportunities) of not accommodating the other's desires are great. Sexual dynamics are so closely linked with power dynamics that this can become a struggle for those involved.

One young female manager described, with considerable anger, the demise of her relationship with a male mentor. In five years he had provided a range of developmental functions including sponsorship, coaching, exposure, challenging work, and friendship. Then, at a social gathering, he made a sexual advance. She was very upset by it and immediately refused, expressing considerable anger and a sense of betrayal as well. A year and a half later, their relationship is still tense, and she is now concerned that he may no longer be a strong supporter as future promotional opportunities arise. She felt hurt, violated, and very concerned about the impact of this event on her future career. While for him the event may have been much less significant, her reaction had longstanding effects on her as well as on their relationship.

> I couldn't believe it—after so many years of working so well together. I don't know if I will ever be able to trust him again. I know for certain that I will never allow myself to get so close to another man that I work with. It's dangerous to put all your eggs in one basket. . . .

> Unfortunately, he still has a lot to do with my advancement. If there is an opening in his organization—because people have known for such a long time that he has been my main suppport—if he does not seek me, that would be very detrimental to me. At the same time, if he did seek me out again I wouldn't want to work for him. So I am also fearful that he might seek me out—it won't look good if I refuse the offer in others' eyes.

> I don't know if I could have prevented it. I am now doubting my own style here—should I dress differently? Should I behave differently? It's hard to sort the whole thing out. For now I'm still hung up with lots of anger and hurt. . . .

She began to have self-doubts about her managerial style, wondering if she had in some way encouraged the encounter. In addition, she hesitated to get close to other male managers that she would work with in the future. This boundary testing not only destroyed a previously enhancing developmental relationship, but it probably made forming new relationships with potential male mentors and colleagues very difficult.

When the desire for greater intimacy is not mutual, the risks of testing the boundaries are great. The prospect of creating a situation like the one just described causes some individuals to maintain considerable distance in their developmental relationships. Other fears also cause managers to withdraw to insure that the opportunity for a sexual liaison will never present itself. Men and women fear the consequences for other relationships (i.e., a spouse or partner) of increasing their intimacy and involvement in a developmental relationship. They also fear for their careers; the learning component of the relationship may be altered, public scrutiny may result in rumors that can destroy advancement opportunities, or increased personal investment may detract from one's managerial effectiveness.

The most apparent form of maintaining distance in a relationship is exemplified by the manager who consciously chooses not to have one-on-one meetings with a female subordinate. He is concerned both with rumors created if he is seen at dinner with his protege and his own feelings of attraction for her. By eliminating private encounters in the office or outside of work, he controls his own temptations.

> I would never do those things with her that I did with the men—go out to lunch, one on one, stop for a drink, or many other things of that nature that you would do with people of your own sex. I just completely avoid one-on-one situations, other than those that are completely work related.

> The reactions others might have if you're seen with a younger subordinate of the opposite sex—what they might think if you happened to be going out for lunch other than in the cafeteria, or seen after hours . . . what are they thinking? So I prefer to avoid those situations that make other people suspect, and me more vulnerable. . . .

These efforts have consequences for the developmental relationship. The actions reduce opportunities for the coaching and counseling functions that frequently occur in informal one-on-one interactions. Thus, this kind of avoidance behavior narrows the range of developmental opportunities available to a female protege. The attempt to effectively manage sexual tensions limits the overall value of the relationship in providing critical developmental functions.

Attempts to avoid frequent and intimate contact may also be observed among women who share similar concerns about their attractions for their male colleagues. Without being fully aware of their behavior, they contribute to their own isolation by cutting off contact that may provide critical information, coaching, and career opportunities. Thus, men and women collude in distancing their relationships in order to eliminate sexual tensions; these same efforts, however, also eliminate critical developmental functions.

Managing increasing intimacy or the fear of a sexual liaison is also accomplished through accentuating qualities of the relationship that resemble a "father-daughter" connection. By doing so, individuals suppress any sexual desires that might otherwise be aroused with their opposite sex colleagues. Since incest is such a taboo in this culture, it is easy to have no sexual feelings or fantasies for a mentor or protege when that person represents a parent or a child. Thus, the stereotypical roles described earlier are assumed as a defense against anxiety and sexual tensions.

> I like Gene a great deal, but there was never any attraction between us. I mean, he's objectively good looking, but to me he's more like a father than a potential lover—and I'm sure I remind him of his daughter . . . I'm about her age, and he seems to be concerned about me like I was family.

While this practice reduces the threat of sexual tension, it also tends to reduce the competence and effectiveness of the junior female colleague. In assuming the role of daughter, she is put in a less powerful position as someone who needs guidance and support. Sometimes this stance is entirely appropriate, but it can become problematic when a female colleague would benefit from acting in an assertive or autonomous manner. If she is trapped in a stereotypical role, she will have difficulty behaving assertively when required to do so.

Occasionally men and women choose to increase their involvement and introduce a sexual component to their relationship. Little is known about how such a decision affects both individuals' work effectiveness or career development. Most managers in developmental relationships feel the risks of a potential liaison are greater than the anticipated benefits (Missirian, 1982). The dynamics of mentoring suggest that a sexual liaison could increase the dependency of a female protege so that it interferes with her developing sense of competence and autonomy (Sheehy, 1976). Thus, concerns revolve around how to manage increasing intimacy and sexual feelings so that they do not interfere with an already valued relationship. Most of the strategies reduce the value of the relationship because they limit the range of critical developmental functions provided.

## PUBLIC SCRUTINY

All developmental relationships are, to some extent, subject to public scrutiny. Organizational members are aware of the relationship and have opinions about its role in each individual's development. Managing the external relationships involves both individuals' awareness of how others perceive their alliance and conscious attention to how their behavior affects the public image of their relationship. In cross-gender  relationships, public scrutiny frequently leads to views which can be damaging to either individual's reputation or career advancement.

Cross-gender developmental relationships are more vulnerable to public scrutiny because they are fewer, they are still relatively rare in managerial settings, and they often evoke jealousy and resentment from colleagues. Organizational members are surprised at these relationships and wonder why a male senior manager is interested in a female junior manager. In addition, the credibility or competence of either individual may be questioned if there are rumors about the nature of the alliance.

All of these possibilities create stress and ambiguity for the individuals involved. When career functions like sponsorship and coaching are provided in a developmental relationship, the relationship becomes visible to colleagues whether it involves individuals of the same sex or opposite sex. As a senior manager speaks in favor of a promotion for a protege, his or her peers conclude that a supportive alliance exists and that the junior individual is being coached and supported by the senior colleague (Kanter, 1977). This alliance links the two individuals together; if either fails, or develops a poor reputation, it will reflect poorly on the other.

> I think that, if you ask, many people would know that she worked for me, that I sponsored her. It's no secret. If word got out tomorrow that I was demoted, she would feel like, and in fact, be in trouble. Because I supported her, she would be off the potential list or moved down unless there were others who supported her. It's really important to have other supporters.

> It's okay as long as she's respected and I'm respected for what we have done. But the day that I'm not respected or she gets the tag of not being capable she will be through, and I won't look so good for having sponsored her.

In cross-gender relationships there is the tendency to question why the supportive alliance exists. In same-gender relationships, it is assumed that the senior perceives the junior as very competent; in cross-gender relationships, this is not so readily assumed. Rumors about sexual involvement and favoritism spread in reaction to frequent statements of support for the junior's advancement. This public scrutiny, characterized by skepticism and accusations creates stress for both individuals. In addition, the impact of sponsorship is diminished as the credibility of the senior and the competence of the junior are questioned.

This kind of public scrutiny can create self-doubts in both the junior and the senior manager. The former questions her competence and whether she is indeed being sponsored because she is a valued organizational member. The latter questions whether it is wise for him to publicly support a younger female colleague because of the possible negative consequences for his own career. Affirmative Action pressures counteract these self-doubts, pushing individuals to provide career functions in the face of public scrutiny.

A male mentor describes the concerns and self-doubts he had as he sponsored a female protege for a promotion to third level management.

> It's like crying wolf. If you recommend good people, people will respect your judgment... It's very important that you save your praise and your recommendations for those who are deserving—otherwise your reputation goes downhill. And I knew that she was competent, but it wasn't clear to me that others saw it as clearly as I did.

> She was attractive, young, and very friendly... and I was afraid that they would think that that was why I wanted her promoted, not because she was competent. I was afraid that rumors would spread, and that I would lose credibility with my peers. It took me a while to go forward with the recommendation—it worked out ok, finally, but it could have backfired.

Public scrutiny caused this manager to doubt his own inclinations to sponsor his female protege. It is possible that he was projecting his own ambivalences toward her, but clearly there were enough reactions from colleagues to cause him to act cautiously. This created stress in the relationship as well. Not only did he withdraw his efforts to sponsor his junior colleague to some extent, but she, too, reacted with doubts about her competence.

> The first thing I asked John when I was promoted—I said, if this is Equal Employment Opportunity I want you to tell me, because I don't want to be just a year-end quota. He assured me that it wasn't to fill quotas, and I wanted to make sure it was me that they wanted.

Public scrutiny affects both individuals' perceptions and behaviors. The senior may be reluctant to actively sponsor his female protege, and the junior may begin to question her mentor's support as he becomes reluctant to take action, or as rumors spread. The mutual trust which previously characterized the relationship is threatened by external challenges and skepticism. In addition, both individuals may respond to the scrutiny by withdrawing somewhat from the relationship. As this occurs, the range of career and psychosocial functions that can be provided is diminished, and the quality of the relationship suffers.

Such avoidance behavior is understandable. In an effort to reduce the potential negative consequences of public scrutiny, individuals minimize the opportunities for other organizational members to see them together. This results in fewer informal meetings after work over a drink and fewer one-on-one meetings behind closed office doors. Unfortunately, these are precisely the contexts in which valuable coaching and counseling occur. Thus, in attempts to eliminate public scrutiny of the relationship, both individuals lose valuable interaction with their significant others.

In some instances individuals discuss their concerns about the public image of their relationship with each other. This allows them to reduce these concerns and to make conscious decisions about how they will manage the external relationship. One senior manager had privately decided never to be seen in public alone with his female protege again, for fear of what others might say and of how this might affect both of their careers. After sharing this concern with his junior manager, she convinced him that it was okay for them to continue to get together since their meetings were valuable to both of them.

> I asked her once, do you mind being seen with me alone in a restaurant? She said, "Are you crazy?" You know, she was self-sufficient and she didn't give a damn, although possibly at some point, she might want to think about it a little bit. I know what we're doing and she knows what we are doing, so what difference does it make? I guess I was afraid of what people would say. We agreed to be somewhat sensitive to what we heard, but that we would continue to meet periodically over a drink to discuss office politics.

Often the pressures created by public scrutiny of the relationship lead to avoidance behavior. Individuals shy away from public interaction that would create rumors, rather than continue to meet, discussing concerns about the public image of the relationship as they arise. Those who choose to interact freely in settings which could result in doubts about reasons for the alliance risk being pushed out of the organization by the growth of damaging rumors. Individual careers are threatened by public scrutiny as exemplified in the Bendix case (*Time*, October 6, 1980).

Other individuals do not feel as vulnerable to public scrutiny and do not alter their behavior in order to reduce rumors or challenges to their credibility or competence. This may be a risky strategy if public scrutiny should undermine the credibility of either individual. Finally, there are individuals who choose a strategy somewhere between these extremes; they do not eliminate interaction that is valuable, and they are conscious of the potential impact of certain actions. This proactive management of the public image of the relationship increases the likelihood that public scrutiny will not have negative consequences.

The potential negative consequences of public scrutiny are great. The hidden advantage is that public scrutiny forces individuals to manage their relationship with each other and with the organization as a whole. This challenge can bring individuals closer together, serving as a catalyst for frequent dialogue about organizational politics and interpersonal relations. If men and women explore how to manage the external relationship effectively, they can avoid the negative consequences of this complexity.

## PEER RESENTMENT

Closely related to public scrutiny of a relationship is the resentment of one's peers created by the perceived special relationship between mentor and protege. Competitive feelings and limited opportunities for advancement can cause the junior manager's peers to react negatively to a supportive relationship with a senior colleague. This rivalry is exacerbated in a cross-gender relationship where the solo female protege is viewed as getting special attention from the male boss because she is female.

Peer resentment causes problems for the individuals and for the relationship. Junior female managers are more likely targets for resentment than male senior colleagues, and they feel internal conflict and guilt about the supportive relationship. In addition, they feel increasingly isolated from their peers. Thus, the more important and valued the mentor relationship becomes for the female protege, the more likely she is to feel internal conflict and guilt and to become isolated from her male peers.

> It was terrible as far as peer relationships go. That is the biggest problem that I have had. While my boss took me seriously, and we were developing a very good relationship, my peers didn't take me seriously. They began to refer to me as "the pet" of my boss, and they began to get hostile the more successes I had. . . .

The young female manager feels that she must choose between a valued relationship with a senior colleague and effective relationships with her peers. This creates considerable stress, and relationships suffer as well. She must either withdraw somewhat from the mentor relationship or tolerate the resentment from her peers.

The organizational context affects the extent to which peers become resentful of a developmental relationship between a female peer and male senior colleague. When competition for promotion is severe, and Affirmative Action is strong, resentment is more apparent. The result of such resentment is increased distance and diminished support between male and female peers. Male peers are threatened by the competence of their female colleagues and find it difficult to support them, given their own career advancement obstacles.

> With objectives and consent decrees I have to realize that it's a fact of life that a capable woman should compete and be eligible for higher positions . . . they will get some of the jobs and it's that simple. I'm damned if I'm going to sit there and say it shouldn't happen. I can certainly see why it should and I can see that it's happening. So there is more competition, and I just want to make sure I get my fair chance . . . sometimes it seems like

there is more incentive to coach and sponsor the women in this department. . . .

This complexity creates ambivalence in the cross-gender relationship; increasing involvement results in increasing alienation from one's peers. There are no apparent strategies for managing this dilemma, but the external relationship must be consciously managed so that a developmental relationship does not negatively affect relationships with peers or vice versa. Finding an appropriate balance of involvement with peers, bosses, and mentors is the basic challenge.

## IMPLICATIONS

The complexities of cross-gender relationships have a range of effects on individual development and on the quality of development relationships. The potential negative consequences command attention. Strategies for managing the negative consequences must be identified so that the hidden advantages can be maximized and the potential destructiveness minimized.

Each complexity illustrates how the value of a developmental relationship is limited by particular cross-gender dynamics. Collusions in a variety of stereotypical role relationships reduce the competence and effectiveness of the female junior colleague, entrap the male senior colleague in overprotective stances, and diminish the value of the working alliance to both individuals and to the organization. The limitations of the role-modeling function can leave female proteges at a disadvantage and without the support needed to resolve personal and professional dilemmas. Intimacy and sexuality concerns can cause individuals to withdraw from an otherwise valuable developmental connection. Finally, the public scrutiny or peer resentment of a cross-gender relationship can create rumors and personal stress which interfere with career advancement and the continuation of a valued alliance.

The less obvious advantages of these complexities are also significant. The potential complementarity in cross-gender developmental relationships is great; both men and women can increase their skills and modes of expression through relationships with the opposite-gender colleagues. In addition, the synergy, enjoyment, and excitement possible in a male-female work alliance is a positive side of increasing intimacy. Finally, in order to have equal opportunity for advancement, both men and women must have access to relationships with senior managers that can provide critical mentoring functions; cross-gender relationships offer these to young female professionals.

There are several ways to manage these complexities effectively. However, it should be noted that it is important to supplement these ways with organizational efforts designed to eliminate the potential negative consequences. Individual efforts are limited by the work setting in which they are attempted. A combination of individual and organizational efforts is the most promising.

Individual self-awareness is a critical first step. If men and women understand how they create and perpetuate collusions in stereotypical roles that reduce competence and effectiveness, they will be able to choose not to do so. Entrapment in stereotypical roles continues because individuals are not aware of their contributions to these dynamics. Similarly, managers can change their reactions to public scrutiny and peer resentment by being aware of these consequences; they must manage the external relationship in a way that preserves the integrity of the internal relationship while supporting career advancement of both individuals. Finally, awareness of intimacy needs and sexuality in the workplace helps individuals become more at ease with increasing intimacy in a cross-gender relationship. With increasing comfort and self-understanding, withdrawal from a relationship that provides critical developmental functions will be unnecessary.

Self-reflection and discussion with others may identify alternatives to one's current practices. For example, in a discussion with colleagues, a female manager may discover how her interpersonal style contributes to an overprotective response from a male manager, thus perpetuating a stereotype. She could then modify her style to increase respect and equality in her relationship. More assertiveness, less automatic deference to authority, and obvious self-confidence would break the stereotypical response. Peer relationships often involve mutual coaching and strategy planning about how to manage relationships with senior colleagues effectively.

Self-awareness can be increased in an educational context. Courses offered within an organization, as well as public seminars or workshops, increase awareness of how one contributes to dysfunctional dynamics. In educational settings, participants are acquainted with new perspectives on career development and the role of relationships in supporting career advancement. They may also discuss cases that reflect many of their own experiences (Spelman & Crary, 1983). Through lecture, discussion, case study, and simulation formats, the complexities of cross-gender dynamics can be highlighted and explored until participants learn how to manage them. An important outcome of such education is a new sense of options and a personal sense of one's capacity to change one's immediate environment.

Educational contexts are particularly helpful when they bring together individuals who face similar challenges in the workplace. Thus, women professionals at similar career stages can discuss the dilemmas that they encounter in their relationships with significant others (George

& Kummerow, 1981). Or male managers can learn about their contributions to difficulties in mentoring young women in discussions with their peers. When such forums are offered within an organization, an added benefit is the networking that occurs as a result of the educational experience. While public seminars offer the greatest amount of anonymity and confidentiality, in-house seminars offer greater opportunity for follow-up support back on the job.

Individuals can further enhance their capacities to manage the complexities of cross-gender relationships in the context of their other relationships. In same-gender relationships, they examine the dilemmas encountered in cross-gender relationships and jointly develop strategies for managing them. For example, two managerial women might help each other develop ways to eliminate dysfunctional stereotyping in their relationships with male colleagues; or two male managers might help each other provide mentoring to female proteges while maintaining appropriate levels of intimacy and distance. Same-gender colleagues can provide counseling and role modeling concerning issues that cannot be adequately addressed in a cross-gender relationship.

The positive effects of other relationships on a particular cross-gender relationship should not be underestimated. Through discussion with others, predictable dilemmas become less awesome and individuals develop strategies for managing them. And when a complexity detracts from the value of a given relationship, other relationships can compensate. For instance, a female manager can turn to her female peers for a role model of how to manage work and family conflicts or how to be assertive without alienating her colleagues. The stresses, ambiguities, and disappointments that characterize cross-gender relationships can be reduced through positive interactions in other relationships.

Individuals can improve the quality of their cross-gender relationships in several ways. However, none of these will have lasting impact unless certain conditions exist in the organizational context. Until there are more women in managerial ranks, the tokens will have difficulty eliminating dysfunctional collusions in stereotypical roles (Kanter, 1977). And until the culture of the organization genuinely supports equality and collaboration between the sexes, individual efforts will be undermined, since attempts to eliminate stereotypes and public scrutiny will be viewed as deviant behavior. Finally, organizations must encourage the development of cross-gender relationships by providing the educational opportunities for individuals to develop relationship skills and by rewarding individuals who pay attention to people and relationship development.

Increasing the numbers of women in managerial positions at all levels has the greatest potential to reduce negative consequences of cross-gender relationships. As more women are promoted to senior positions, both men and women will have more experience working with members of the opposite sex. Not only will this help individuals develop skills, but the unfamiliarity of working in cross-gender alliances will be reduced. As a consequence, fewer organizational members will be as anxious about cross-gender relationships, and the extreme public scrutiny will diminish. When it is no longer rare for men and women to work closely together, the negative consequences of public scrutiny, peer resentment, and concerns about intimacy and sexuality will lessen.

As the numbers of women in male-dominated settings grow, it will be more difficult to perpetuate dysfunctional stereotypes. Individual women who break the collusions that reduce their competence will be supported by their peers; both men and women who maintain stereotypes will be challenged by the more frequently observed alternatives. With more women present, a wider range of styles, assumptions, and interactive patterns will be exhibited. This diversity violates traditional stereotypes, offers new alternatives, and empowers those implementing new strategies. Perhaps most importantly, with more numbers of women the pressures of tokenism are reduced, and each woman is free from the stress of being the only one (Kanter, 1977).

If an organization succeeds in increasing the numbers of women in managerial positions, several unplanned consequences may occur. The number of cross-gender relationships with the female in the more senior position will increase, and these relationships will have unique complexities created by the power relationship being directly opposite of traditional sex-role relationships. In addition, as the number of cross-gender relationships increases, organizational values, norms, and practices may be questioned as more and more women assume positions of authority. Finally, there will be more female mentors to provide the role-modeling function; however, unless tokenism is eliminated, the stresses associated with being a woman in a position of authority may make it difficult to assume the role of mentor.

It cannot be assumed that an organization will agree to implement these strategies. In fact, the culture of an organization may be the greatest barrier to implementation (Deal & Kennedy, 1982; Beer, 1980). While affirmative action programs and equal employment opportunity legislation have created movement toward this end during the last decade, the increasing numbers of women in middle and upper management probably will be met with ambivalence among certain groups. There is still much to learn about how to effectively address this resistance to change (Beer, 1980; Beckhard, 1969; Kanter, 1977).

Until such obstacles are surmounted, organizational members can make some things happen which do not require such dramatic changes in the overall culture. In addition to the individual efforts described earlier, those with authority can develop reward systems and educational programs that encourage individuals to improve the quality of their cross-gender relationships. Such organizationally sponsored education demonstrates the value attached to managing relationships for the purposes of increasing individual and organizational effectiveness. If these are supplemented with rewards for people development, relationship development, and affirmative action efforts, individuals will be encouraged to consciously manage their relationships and to minimize potentially dysfunctional dynamics.

Cross-gender relationships offer benefits to both men and women. Both individuals learn new ways of relating to the world from their opposite-gender colleagues. Junior women have greater access to power, information, and desirable positions through their alliances with male senior colleagues, and the potential for synergistic and creative work is enhanced by the mutual attraction and intimacy that may develop. The complexities of these relationships are not trivial, and they may discourage individuals with opposite-gender colleagues. These complexities must be managed effectively if individuals and organizations are to reap the benefits that positive cross-gender alliances have to offer.

6

# Mentoring
# Alternatives

Mentor relationships have both great potential and significant limitations. Relationships must end, and they can become destructive to one or both individuals as needs and organizational circumstances change. In addition, mentor relationships are relatively unavailable to most individuals in organizations; individuals' capacities to mentor and organizations' lack of encouragement for the activity prevent this kind of developmental relationship from being widely accessible. It is essential, therefore, to consider alternatives to this kind of relationship.

The importance of relationships in the world of work and career development has not been studied sufficiently. The premise that many relationships are important to development has a long history (Sullivan, 1953; Storrs, 1961; Neugarten, 1964). Social psychologists created the idea that one's personality develops within a social nexus of relation-

The research for this chapter was conducted in collaboration with Ms. Lynn
Isabella of Boston University and Mr. Manny Berger of Beth-Israel Hospital in
Boston. Both actively shaped the research design, data collection, and analysis.
In addition, Ms. Isabella co-authored an article, which will appear in the
*Academy of Management Journal* in March, 1985, on which this chapter is
based. I gratefully acknowledge their contributions and their colleagueship.

ships (a core group) from which one learns new behaviors and gains a positive sense of self (Ziller, 1963). Sullivan (1954) defined personality as a relatively enduring pattern of recurrent interpersonal situations. Storrs (1961) postulated that each individual develops directly through his or her relationships with others. Most recently, Levinson et al. (1978) developed the concept of the life structure which effectively describes an individual's relationship with different parts of the external world; they further articulate that an individual selectively uses and is used by his or her worlds through evolving relationships. Each perspective maintained the importance of relationships in enabling individual development and growth at successive stages.

In work settings, there are many relationships that could provide developmental functions. One alternative to the mentor relationship is the peer relationship. Peer relationships provide some critical mentoring functions, and, at the same time are relatively available to individuals. One likely has more peers than bosses or mentors in a hierarchical organization and the lack of hierarchical dimension in a peer relationship facilitates communication, mutual support, and collaboration.

Many individuals refer to the importance of peer relationships when they lack a mentor relationship, when a mentor relationship is in the process of changing or ending, or when a particular relationship fails to provide critical developmental functions. For example, individuals approaching midcareer and beyond feel peer relationships are essential because they offer empathy and support for the dilemmas encountered at this career stage. In addition, female managers at every career stage refer to female peers as providing role modeling or counseling functions that were absent from a mentor relationship with a male senior colleague. Peers offer important alternatives at every career stage.

When "level peers" are also of the same age, relationships are most likely to become quite intimate and enduring. When level peers are of significantly different ages, relationships can take on qualities of a mentor relationship. One person has more experience because of his longer tenure or greater age and thus can coach his peer in some domains. Similarly, "age" peers (those of the same age but different organizational level) also take on some qualities of a mentor relationship, but are peerlike in the sharing of common experiences and career dilemmas.

Peers offer important alternatives to the mentor relationship, and critical career and psychosocial functions can be provided in several kinds of peer relationships. Examining the types, functions, and characteristics of these developmental relationships suggests that they are more readily available and more enduring than the mentor relationship. Peer relationships in successive stages of adult and career development expand the range of options for individuals and organizations. (See pp. 5–8 for a description of the research sample.)

## CHARACTERISTICS OF
## PEER RELATIONSHIPS _____

Peer relationships provide a range of functions. Many of these functions are similar to the developmental functions observed in mentor
relationships (see Figure 6-1). In providing career functions, a peer
relationship aids organizational advancement; in providing psychosocial
functions, a peer relationship supports an individual's sense of competence in a professional role. The functions that characterize a particular relationship vary, and peer relationships can be significantly
different from each other. Such variations can be explained by considering the individual and organizational factors that shape these relationships.

Peer relationships can provide several career functions.

Basically, it was the type of relationship, I think. I was always ahead of her
one assignment. I would feed back to her about the other assignments that
I've heard of and how the assignments were. Mainly, what I was trying to do
was have her benefit from my experience and recommend jobs that I thought
were better or worse for her to go after. I think we developed a career
counseling relationship.

**Figure 6-1.**   Developmental Functions: Comparison of Mentor and
                 Peer Relationships.

| Mentor Relationships | Peer Relationships |
|---|---|
| **Career Functions** | **Career Functions** |
| Sponsorship | Information sharing |
| Coaching | Career strategizing |
| Exposure-and-visibility | Job-related feedback |
| Protection | |
| Challenging work assignments | |
| **Psychosocial Functions** | **Psychosocial Functions** |
| Acceptance-and-confirmation | Confirmation |
| Counseling | Emotional support |
| Role modeling | Personal feedback |
| Friendship | Friendship |
| **Special Attribute** | **Special Attribute** |
| Complementarity | Mutuality |

Within the context of a relationship of this kind, *information sharing* gives both individuals technical knowledge and perspective on the organization that help them get their work done. In addition, through *career strategizing*, individuals discuss their career options and dilemmas, using a peer to explore one's own career. Finally, peers give and receive *feedback* concerning work-related matters to evaluate their own experiences and clarify their own strengths and weaknesses.

Psychosocial functions are more frequently observed in peer relationships that are more intimate, of longer duration, and characterized by higher self-disclosure and trust.

> He is one of my closer friends right now. . . . I'll walk into his office and bounce off gripes that I have or things that I am doing or ask advice that I need, and he'll do the same thing — I think a lot of sounding-board stuff.

> Our careers are kind of parallel in that we're about the same age, we're both single, we both like to go out and party a lot and are a little less serious about work than some other people. And we're doing similar types of jobs at work.

Within the contexts of these relationships, peers provide *confirmation* to each other through sharing their perceptions, values, and beliefs related to their lives at work, and through discovering views they have in common. Secondly, peers provide *emotional support* by listening and counseling each other during periods of transition and stress. Third, by providing feedback in areas that extend beyond the job-related concerns in career functions, peers offer each other a personal level of *feedback* that can be invaluable in learning about one's leadership style, the impact one has on others in the organization, and how one is managing work and family commitments. Finally, peer relationships provide *friendship*, encompassing concern about each other that extends beyond the work. This function reduces the sense of alienation or stress individuals experience at every career stage.

While many of these functions are similar to those in mentor relationships, several attributes of peer relationships make them unique. First, peer relationships offer *mutuality*; both individuals are the helper as well as the recipient of help. In a mentor relationship, one individual specializes in the role of guide or sponsor, and in a peer relationship, each assumes both roles. This mutuality allows individuals whose career is advancing to develop a sense of competence, responsibility, and identity as an expert. As individuals provide information, career advice, and feedback to colleagues, they feel like an equal with expertise and knowledge to share.

Second, peer relationships are more available at every career stage than mentor relationships are. Everyone has, in his or her immediate work context, more potential peers than potential mentors because of the organizational pyramid and the ease in contacting those at the same age or hierarchical level. In addition, individuals can provide the developmental functions outlined previously to a number of peers, and then receive a range of these functions from several peers. In general, these relationships are less exclusive than mentor relationships.

Third, peer relationships endure far longer than mentor relationships; whereas the latter generally last between three and eight years, some peer relationships begin in early career and last through late career, and can last as long as twenty to thirty years. Such long-term relationships provide continuity over the course of a career, a variety of functions through periods of change and transition, and a unique perspective on where one has been.

Peer relationships have some negative attributes as well. Most important is the potential for competition that interferes with providing career and psychosocial functions and that can even lead to destructive interactions. Attitudes toward self and characteristics of the organizational context can fuel competitive dynamics. For example, if an individual feels uncertain about her competence, she is less inclined to form a trusting and supportive relationship with a peer with whom performance may be compared in the future. If the organization rewards individual effort and discourages collaboration, it is difficult for peers in the same setting to support one another. It is not surprising that the closest relationships frequently occur outside the immediate work context where competition is minimized.

Even if competitive dynamics are absent, peer relationships can undermine individuals' development if certain views of self or the organizational world are reinforced. In providing confirmation, feedback, career strategizing and friendship, a peer often influences how one perceives one's advancement possibilities, one's competence, one's relationships, etc. Peers often get together in the first place because they hold a set of common beliefs, values, and attitudes about how things get done and what the organization values. A problem arises, however, when certain points of view are not in the individuals' best interest. For example, several entry level professional women may increase their sense of powerlessness by reinforcing each other's views of futility and inability to develop positive connections with senior colleagues. While the barriers are real, the increasing pessimism and a growing inability to see alternative strategies for establishing themselves in the system result in the belief that they can do nothing to improve their position in the organization.

Relationships with peers can provide a variety of developmental functions, can endure significantly longer than mentor relationships, can be more readily accessible, and can develop a sense of mutuality, expertise, and connectedness. Each of these characteristics varies in quality and limitations of individuals' attitudes and skills as well as the organization's attributes.

## A CONTINUUM OF PEER RELATIONSHIPS

There can be considerable variation in the combinations of developmental functions provided. Several types of peer relationships can be identified, and each type has a particular set of career and/or psychosocial functions, a unique level of trust and self-disclosure, and a particular context in which the relationship has evolved (see Figure 6–2).

We describe the primary functions, tone, and context of three distinct points on a continuum, since these exemplify three major types of relationships. A continuum suggests that these are points of reference, rather than the only variations. Criteria used for placement along the continuum are listed in Figure 6–3.

### Information Peer

Individuals in the *information peer* relationship benefit most from exchanging information about their work and about the organization. This peer relationship is characterized by low levels of personal self-disclosure and trust. As a result of the focus on information exchange and the low frequency of contact, individuals receive little confirmation or emotional support from an information peer. While they may receive a small amount of job-related feedback, there is insufficient trust for personal feedback.

> I think it's just a friendly exchange, very little giving back and forth. It's primarily informational. . . . That's probably what he gives to me and

**Figure 6–2.** A Continuum of Peer Relationships.

| Informational Peer | Collegial Peer | Special Peer |
|---|---|---|
| **Primary Function** | **Primary Functions** | **Primary Functions** |
| Information Sharing | Career Strategizing<br>Job-related Feedback<br>Friendship | Confirmation<br>Emotional Support<br>Personal Feedback<br>Friendship |

**Figure 6–3.**  A Continuum of Peer Relationships: Criteria for Placement Along Continuum.

| Criteria | Information Peer | Collegial Peer | Special Peer |
|---|---|---|---|
| Level of commitment | Demands little, but offers many benefits. | Information sharing joined by increasing levels of self-disclosure and trust. | Equivalent of best friend. |
| Intensity of relationship | Social but limited in sharing of personal experience. | Allows for greater self-expression. | Strong sense of bonding. |
| Issues worked on | Increases individual's eyes and ears to organization (work only). | Limited support for exploration of family and work issues. | Wide range of support for family and work issues. |
| Needs satisfied | Source of information regarding career opportunities. | Provides direct and honest feedback. | Offers chance to express one's personal and professional dilemmas, vulnerabilities, and individuality. |

I think that's what he would say I give to him. I don't think he would look at me as giving him any insight into how he's running his business — we don't get into shop in that regard.

If you look at it and sum it up, Ron and I have a friendly relationship, feel comfortable in talking with each other, have a lot of outside things we can talk about comfortably. He's a bright enough guy, sincere enough, and so forth, so that you value his input, and that's about career and how to handle politics and so forth.

The information peer relationship is common in organizations. Individuals maintain large numbers of such relationships; it is not uncommon for individuals to identify five or more such relationships as part of their "network." Such relationships demand little and offer a number of benefits. In addition to general information sharing, information about career opportunities is often exchanged as well. While this kind of peer relationship provides some familiarity or friendship, it offers little of the ongoing psychosocial support characteristic of the other two types.

## Collegial Peer

The *collegial peer* relationship is typified by a moderate level of trust and self-disclosure and is distinguished from the information peer by increasingly complex and widening boundaries of interaction. In this kind of relationship, the information sharing function joins with emotional support, feedback, and confirmation. Individuals participate in more intimate discussions about work and family. With this greater self-expression in the context of the relationship, there is increased confirmation of self-worth.

Nathan and I, oh, he's ten feet away. I see him many times. When one of us has a tough thing we'll wander over to the other's office and bitch a little bit and commiserate. . . . He goes to the Y and I go there. We've been running on a track indoors so we talk while we're running as well.

There's a lot of give and take — on a professional basis and on a social basis. Professionally, we're both learning at the same time. He's a manager a little less than a year more than me, so he had a bit of an advantage, but I think we're growing and experiencing things simultaneously. There's a lot of sharing about experiences with people and about different situations arising. So we reinforce one another in that respect.

Individuals usually have a limited number (2–4) of such relationships, and they tend to have them with people who work in the same department where work contact encouraged the relationship. The primary functions provided in the collegial peer relationship are career strategizing, job-related feedback, and friendship, as well as some information sharing, confirmation, and emotional support. These distinctions are best highlighted when set against the unique offerings of the *special peer*.

## Special Peer

The farthest point right on this continuum represents *special peer*, the most intimate form of peer relationship. Becoming a special peer involves revealing ambivalences and dilemmas in both work and family realms. Pretense and formal roles are replaced by greater self-disclosure and self-expression. Through the widest range of career and psychosocial functions, individuals find support, confirmation, and an essential emotional connection that enables more profound work on developmental tasks.

> I can say anything to Art and he will be understanding. I am able to get frustration and anger out in a more constructive fashion talking to him. We do that for each other, often at lunch.

> It's relatively intangible. . . . I think we enjoy one another's company when we're doing things, skiiing, tennis, or whatever. It is nice to have somebody to talk to about certain things that you might not be able to talk about, perhaps, with the person next to you.

> We are genuinely happy for each other's successes, and we try to help each other with major decisions. . . . The thought that would be depressing if either of us leaves, is the fact that friends of different levels come and go, but we've had much more of a sustained relationship. I generally always have one close friend, and this has been the longest.

The special peer relationship is rare. Individuals typically have a small number of these (1–3), or none at all. They take several years to develop, and they tend to endure through periods of change and transition. Thus they offer not only intimacy and confirmation but continuity and stability as well. In addition to the benefits from information peer and collegial peer relationships, special peers often have a sense of bonding with one another. This can provide security, comfort, and belongingness on the job. This type of peer relationship provides reliable and candid personal feedback, emotional support, career strategizing, and ongoing validation of individuals' competence and potential.

It is interesting to note that relationships can begin as information peers and evolve into collegial or special peers. Over time, interaction and individual needs and skills become more intimate and take on more of the qualities of a "best friend." This occurs when both individuals seek closer connection with individuals in their work setting and initiate discussion of personal and professional problems with another who has similar concerns, experiences, and values.

Most mentor relationships evolve into peer relationships during the redefinition phase (see Chapter 3). After a period of separation, both junior and senior colleagues must discover a new form for their relationship since earlier career and psychosocial functions are no longer possible or desired. For example, a junior manager, having advanced to middle management, may no longer need coaching and sponsorship. The senior manager, though perhaps older, now travels in similar circles in the organization, and is unable to sponsor or provide protection. But if the interpersonal bond was strong, as is frequently the case, both individuals will search for opportunities to relate on a new and more appropriate basis.

As the junior advances and no longer needs an active coach, and as the senior comes to recognize his or her former protege as a contributing colleague, the two individuals will perceive each other as peers. Whether they will evolve a special peer or information peer connection depends on current organizational and personal circumstances. If both need to discuss personal and professional problems, and the opportunity for frequent interaction presents itself, the relationship will probably move toward greater intimacy and self-disclosure. This can be particularly rewarding for both individuals; the new peer relationship symbolizes growth for the younger individual and satisfaction in developing the junior colleague for the older.

## Factors Causing Movement on the Continuum

Many factors may cause a relationship to move along the continuum from an information peer to a collegial peer or even to a special peer. These can be categorized into individual needs and attitudes, interpersonal skills, and organizational characteristics.

At different career stages, individuals have more or fewer needs for intimate connections in the workplace, and current developmental tasks shape a particular peer relationship. For example, in early career years, individuals seek guidance and coaching more from mentors than from peers because they do not yet feel prepared to participate in an equal connection. But in middle and later career years, peers are a natural connection as one becomes a mentor for younger colleagues. In addition to career stage needs, the other relationships in one's life affect whether a particular relationship will become more intimate. Not only do individuals vary in the range of relationships they desire in the workplace, but the current constellation of relationships affects the course of a particular peer relationship.

Individuals vary in the range of interpersonal skills that they bring to potential relationships. They may form close relationships with peers, but unless they know how to initiate and build relationships, and are skilled in listening, communication, self-disclosure, and conflict management, it will be difficult to move relationships along the continuum toward greater intimacy and trust. Even information peer relationships require certain relationship management skills, although not the capacity for intimacy and increasing commitment or involvement. Understanding of how relationships begin and develop over time, practice in communication skills, and appreciation for the organizational context and how it shapes opportunities for interaction are essential for building relationships with peers.

Finally, an organization can encourage or discourage the formation of peer relationships (and different types of peer relationships) through the nature of task design, reward systems, promotional practices, and the overall culture of the system. For example, if competition and individualized effort are encouraged, it will be more difficult for individuals to form collegial and special peer relationships within a work unit. Or, if individuals move around frequently and interdepartmental interaction is discouraged, then it will be more difficult for individuals to form any lasting relationships with peers. Similarly, if the reward system encourages only results and does not require relationship-building activities, individuals will not be inclined to give energy to mentor and peer alliances. Thus, the peer relationships that organizational members experience will differ across work settings, depending on the organizational characteristics that shape relationships.

## RELATIONSHIPS AT DIFFERENT CAREER STAGES

The three types of peer relationships on the continuum are perceived differently by individuals at different career stages. These variations are related to the particular developmental tasks that each person brings to the relationships. Since developmental tasks are concerns about self, career, and family that characterize each career stage, it is not surprising that these shape what is brought to a peer relationship (Dalton et al., 1977; Schein, 1978; Levinson et al., 1978). Thus, while the primary functions of each type of relationship do not change, the content of what is discussed and how that content is shared differs at successive career stages.

These differences in the content of peer relationships are captured in dominant themes of each type of relationship at each major career stage (see Figure 6–4). Differences that appear to be related to individuals' developmental tasks clustered roughly around the *establishment, advancement, middle,* and *late career* stages. The establishment stage was comprised of people in their twenties, the advancement stage with people in their thirties, middle career with people in their forties to early fifties, and late career with people in their mid-fifties and beyond.

**Figure 6–4.**  Peer Relationships at Successive Career Stages: Dominant Themes.

|  | Information Peer | Collegial Peer | Special Peer |
|---|---|---|---|
| **Late Career Stage** | Maintaining knowledge. | Assuming consultative role. Seeing others as experts. | Preparing for retirement. Reviewing the past. Assessing one's career and life. |
| **Middle Career Stage** | Networking. Maintaining visibility. | Developing subordinates. Passing on wisdom. | Threats of obsolescence. Reassessment & redirection. Work/family dilemmas. |
| **Advancement Stage** | Preparing for advancement. Gaining visibility. | Gaining recognition. Identifying advancement opportunities. | Sense of competence & potential. Commitment. Conformity vs. individuality. Work/family dilemmas. |
| **Establishment Stage** | Learning the ropes. Getting the job done. | Demonstrating performance. Defining a professional role. | Sense of competence. Commitment. Work/family dilemmas. |

## Dominant Themes in the
## Establishment Stage _____

Concerns about competence and a sense of professional identity generally characterize the developmental needs of a person in the *establishment* phase of *early career* (Hall, 1976; Schein, 1978; Levinson et al.,
1978; Super, 1957). People in their twenties are concerned for their professional identity—who they are as managers and professionals—and
desire to feel self-confident and competent as they learn the ropes of
organizational life.

Peer relationships in the establishment stage are similar to some
aspects of a mentor relationship in that the other has more wisdom or
experience and is a model and career guide, even though he or she is a
peer.

> Terry struck me to be very intelligent, career-oriented, knowing where she
> wanted to go. Those were all the kinds of things that I need to look up to.

> Terry was really leading me around. It was virgin territory we were getting
> into. Terry was really a good one to get in there and plow and pioneer it.

> I think Terry has a better way of dealing with some situations than I do. She
> says she is going to do something and she does it, whereas I tend to procras-
> tinate a little more, not so willing to take a risk that she will take. She has
> guided me in that sense.

Thus, this special peer relationship in the establishment stage, through
providing confirmation, emotional support, personal feedback, and
friendship, helps the individual define a professional role and acquire
competence and confidence. These relationships, especially the collegial
peer and the special peer, involve a sense of "looking up to" one's peer
for guidance, offering a mentoring alternative.

## Dominant Themes in the
## Advancement Stage _____

As the individual becomes established in his or her chosen profession
and has a sense of competence and mastery, needs and concerns
associated with advancement in the organization and the profession
take on new importance (Hall, 1976; Schein, 1978; Super, 1957). No
longer the burgeoning novice, individuals in the advancement stage
want to burrow in and get ahead. They work through the problems
which arise between work and family commitments, and, most of all,
they "settle down" (Levinson et al., 1978) into their lives and build a
career niche.

Dominant themes for peer relationships in this career stage are
shaped by these developmental tasks (see Figure 6–4). The information

peer relationship provides information that enables an individual to advance through increased knowledge of the organization as well as increased visibility among those who make promotion decisions. Similarly, the collegial peer relationship, in providing career strategizing or feedback, gives the individual recognition and identifies advancement options. Finally, through sharing with a special peer, an individual grapples with work/family dilemmas and with concerns about one's potential and the extent to which one is willing to make a commitment and to conform to the demands of the organization.

Relationships at this time are no longer characterized by the elevation of one member to a higher level. People in their thirties tend to perceive themselves as equal to the others, even if the others are older or at a different career stage or organizational level. There seems to be a real *need* among these people to perceive and experience this sense of equality.

> I don't consider him like a boss. It's more like a peer relationship. I don't feel equal in responsibility, but I feel equal in ability to influence his thought. I mean, I will go and deal with him more on an equal basis than I did with other supervisors. In fact, it's the first time that I've felt this way. I've always felt really subservient to the people that I worked for, whether it was true or not. . . . Maybe it's just getting older and maturing that has done that.

Some individuals speak of this equality as the ability to influence the other person in work-related or technical matters (no longer being the learning novice taking advice). Others describe a flexibility of roles, at one time giving advice and at others receiving. Peer relationships at this stage are especially malleable and receptive to differences in day-to-day needs.

## Dominant Themes in Middle Career

During the forties and early fifties, people are generally concerned with reworking old issues or learning new ways to approach situations in life and career (Levinson et al., 1978; Hall, 1976; Hall & Kram, 1981). Individuals in middle career have a history created by the choices made and passed up, situations dealt with effectively or ineffectively. Midcareer is a time for re-evaluation and rethinking of those choices and events. Midcareer is also a time to depend on others to accomplish the tasks of the organization. No longer an individual contributor, the manager at midcareer is responsible for developing and supervising others, or for coordinating and incorporating the work of others.

The dominant themes for peer relationships in this career stage are shaped by these developmental tasks (see Figure 6-4). Thus, a collegial peer relationship, by providing career strategizing and job-related feedback teaches how to develop subordinates and how to depend on, as well as coach, junior colleagues. Similarly, a special peer relationship provides several psychosocial functions which help manage fears of obsolescence and the reassessment and redirection that might occur.

The relationships in middle career years, particularly in collegial peer and special peer relationships, are similar to the mentor's view of mentoring relationships. Peer relationships for individuals in this career stage are generally with younger people. People in their forties and early fifties see in younger peers the issues experienced earlier and live out alternative ways of confronting those issues vicariously.

> I think I envy a lot of . . . some of her characteristics. She, I think, is more dedicated to her job, and to things than I am — the job, people, and principles. I could fluctuate. My interests can change. I would tend to do the thing that appeals to me more, and let something else slide. She's more organized, more on top of things. . . . I think maybe too that she probably felt that she had seen my growth as a manager, and maybe she liked that and tried to follow through in those footsteps.

For the individual in midcareer, peer relationships offer a strong sense of security, comfort, and camaraderie, as well as a chance to celebrate oneself through another.

> I think that probably a little bit of our friendship is the fact that he feels that I'm a minority too. And we both worked hard to get where we are, and it's been "in spite of," you know, instead of "because of." We started back early in the days before there was any emphasis on minorities and women. And I think that both of us feel to some extent that we have blazed the trails with no help. . . . This is a sort of little bond between us.

## Dominant Themes in Late Career

As individuals enter late adulthood and career, peer relationships can aid the gradual movement into retirement. Individuals in late career begin to understand and appreciate having accomplished so much in life and in one's career (Levinson et al., 1978). In terms of career development especially, most individuals face moving out of the work force and into new endeavors through retirement (Hall, 1976; Schein, 1978). One's own fallibility and vulnerability take on greater significance.

Dominant themes for peer relationships at this stage reflect one's impending move out of the organization (see Figure 6-4). Thus, information peers provide information to help an individual stay connected with the organization enough to continue to work effectively. The collegial peer relationship and the special peer relationship help the late career manager assume a consultative role, pass on responsibilities to younger colleagues, and psychologically prepare for retirement.

The special peer relationship in late career is both rare and essential. Few individuals can provide emotional support and confirmation to an individual in late career without having had a similarly long career history. Thus, peers of the same age with a similar organizational history offer a unique opportunity for intimate sharing about immediate developmental tasks.

> During the conversation, a lot of times it will come up, where do you think we can go from here, at our age . . . ? I think probably I could feel more comfortable with Ted talking about things that have happened, and making an analysis of it and being able to both understand what's happened. I think that's pretty important because we can relate to each other much better than I could relate to Sara [who is a much younger peer]. First of all, she wouldn't know what the hell I'm talking about because unless you've experienced it, you really can't talk about it.

While differences are relished and appreciated as sources of learning at this career stage, similarities appear to be great sources of security as one experiences the loneliness of anticipating movement out of the organization and one's career. Collegial peer and special peer relationships in late career become, in some instances, like a home away from home — a chance to be understood and liked by someone who has been through it all, too.

## THE RELATIONSHIP CONSTELLATION

Some of the developmental functions of peer relationships are similar to those found in mentor relationships. Peer relationships are more readily available to individuals in organizations, they tend to endure longer than most mentoring relationships, and they offer opportunities to engage in two-way relationships that enable the individuals to both receive and give support to one another. Thus, in peer relationships, an individual can share wisdom and feel like an expert and also learn and derive support from a colleague. It is precisely this condition that enables one to move from the apprentice stage to the independent contributor stage of a career (Dalton et al., 1977).

Relationships with bosses, subordinates, and friends and family members can also provide a range of developmental functions. A preliminary study of engineers and scientists indicates that learning from one's subordinates helps an individual learn the ropes and prepare for advancement (Thompson, 1982). In addition, an exploratory study of managers in their thirties indicates that peers and spouses provide career and psychosocial functions typically provided by mentors (Isabella, 1982).

Career and psychosocial functions that support development at every career stage, then, can be provided by a range of relationships. This range of relationships is the *constellation of relationships* that support an individual's development at any given time (see Figure 6–5). The relationship constellation may not be adequate, in which case an individual feels unsupported, under stress, and in need of several developmental functions. In addition, the relationship constellation will change with time. An individual may choose to develop new relationships that provide critical developmental functions. Significant others may leave the organization, or major organizational changes such as promotions, transfers, or reorganizations may disrupt previously enhancing relationships.

Several case examples illustrate what relationship constellations look like, how they may change over time, and how they may be satisfactory or inadequate. In the first example, a young female manager has a relationship constellation that appears adequate. She has a mentor, two levels above her, who provides critical developmental functions; he has provided exposure, sponsorship, and coaching during the past five years and acceptance-and-confirmation, some role modeling, and some friendship as well. Her boss provides *challenging work* and some

**Figure 6–5.** The Relationship Constellation.

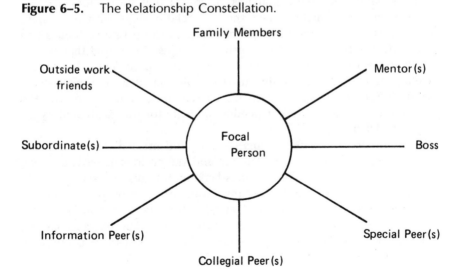

coaching on how to prepare for advancement. She has several collegial peers, several information peers, and a very supportive spouse who provides emotional support, friendship, and occasional coaching or counseling functions. Nonetheless, this individual feels considerable stress in coping with her token status in her department and in managing conflicting demands at work and in her personal life. These are significant developmental tasks that she has not been able to address effectively within the current relationship constellation.

This young manager eventually expands her constellation to include several more information peers and two special peers. The latter are other women facing similar developmental tasks, one working in the same organization in a different department, and another working in a different industry. This change in the constellation did not occur overnight. It required involvement in a professional network for women in her field for several months. In this context, she met women with similar developmental concerns, expanded her network of information peers and, over time, developed two intimate connections with professional women with whom she shares a great deal.

In another instance, a young male manager has a relationship constellation that meets all his developmental needs when his mentor decides to leave the organization for a better opportunity elsewhere. After a period of distress over the loss, the young manager looks for alternative sources of support. He finds some developmental functions in collegial peers, and he considers how other senior colleagues might provide critical mentoring functions like sponsorship, exposure, and role modeling.

Eventually, the young manager discovers that he no longer needs some mentoring functions and that his relationships with peers have become extremely important. He has learned to operate without a primary mentor figure and, in the process, he has discovered that he can provide developmental functions to others, his peers. Thus, the abrupt leaving of his mentor resulted in the evolution of a new relationship constellation that responded to his current developmental needs. His transition from novice to independent contributor was facilitated by his mentor's leaving.

In another case, a female manager in midcareer discovers that her relationships with peers are adequate and she no longer needs a strong mentor figure, but that something is lacking in terms of a sense of well-being and affirmation in the organization. Information peers, collegial peers, and special peers provide friendship, feedback, information sharing, emotional support, and some confirmation. The manager cannot identify what is missing from her constellation until there is an unrelated organizational change.

The department is redesigned, and this manager now supervises a number of young professionals. Within six months, she has assumed a mentoring role for some of these subordinates, and feels confirmed in this new role. The opportunity to guide, counsel, and provide a range of mentoring functions to younger colleagues responded to her current developmental tasks; relationships with subordinates enabled her to assume a generative role and to develop a new creative pursuit. This change provides internal satisfaction and confirmation, and she is seen as an excellent developer of talent for the organization.

Finally, a male manager in late career, facing impending retirement, finds satisfaction in a relationship constellation that has both peers and subordinates in it. While a boss may provide some developmental functions by assigning interesting work and perhaps supplying friendship and emotional support during the transition into retirement, peers and subordinates offer other developmental functions that facilitate leaving the organization with a sense of integrity and accomplishment.

In this instance, peers of the same age offer a sounding board for discussing and grappling with the dilemmas of aging and impending retirement. Younger peers offer colleagueship and continued connectedness with the organization. Subordinates allow him to pass on his wisdom and experience, to leave something of value behind, and to stay in touch with the youthful parts of himself.

## Individual Differences

These case examples illustrate how an individual's developmental tasks shape his or her relationship constellation; the young female manager sought out female peers with whom she could discuss developmental problems, while the young male manager discovered through his mentor's leaving that peers were an important source of support and provided opportunities to experience the mutuality of such relationships. In addition, the manager at midcareer modified her constellation by including subordinates, which allowed her to provide mentoring functions to younger colleagues. Finally, the late career manager found that both subordinates and peers were critical to dealing with his impending retirement. An individual's fundamental attitudes and postures toward relationships also shape which relationships become important. While further research is needed to delineate how particular attitudes shape the relationship constellation, we can speculate about several.

An individual's attitudes toward authority are likely to affect whether he seeks out mentor relationships with senior colleagues or peers and affect the extent to which mutuality in relationships is possible. The individual with a generally rebellious stance toward authority is less likely to seek out supportive relationships that involve coaching and guidance from senior colleagues. In contrast, the individual who seeks and desires approval from those in authority is more likely to gravitate toward senior colleagues for guidance and support and probably form significant mentor relationships. The former may seek developmental functions from peers, while the latter may focus on senior colleagues and overlook the potential value of peer relationships.

An individual's attitude toward intimacy is likely to influence the extent to which she develops open and sharing relationships with mentors, peers, and subordinates. If sharing personal and professional problems with individuals in the workplace is legitimate and she has the relationship skills of self-disclosure, listening, and building trust, then she will build mentor relationships and special peer relationships. An individual who has a radically different view of what is appropriate may have few or no intimate connections at work. In this instance, a relationship constellation might consist of a boss, some senior colleagues, primarily information peers, and perhaps some collegial peers.

An individual's view of his or her competence affects the extent to which it will be possible to develop peer relationships characterized by mutuality and two-way helping. In addition, one's self-concept affects the extent to which, in midcareer, one is available and willing to become a mentor for younger colleagues. For example, in early career years, an individual forms peer relationships of all types if he feels that he has expertise to offer. And in later career years, an individual embraces the mentoring role if he has accepted his accomplishments and can enjoy helping younger colleagues succeed and perhaps go beyond current accomplishments.

An individual's attitudes toward competition and conflict may also affect relationships with peers, mentors, and subordinates. While competition and conflict are inevitable, how one manages them determines whether supportive relationships can evolve. For example, the individual who has strong competitive feelings may not be willing to collaborate with peers; a two-way helping relationship cannot emerge. But the individual who can put aside the competitive dimensions of organizational life when support and collaboration are beneficial will build mutually enhancing relationships with peers. Similarly, if conflict is managed effectively, it will not interfere with relationships at work. If one avoids conflict at all cost, intimate relationships with potential mentors and peers will probably be curtailed.

An individual's feelings toward the importance of work and personal domains is likely to shape the evolution of significant relationships at work. When work is relatively unimportant, developmental functions are provided primarily by relationships outside of work. In contrast, when work is a primary commitment of time and personal involvement, the relationship constellation will contain relationships with peers, bosses, subordinates, and mentors.

Finally, one's attitudes toward learning affects the extent to which an individual looks to relationships for developmental functions. If an individual assumes that learning must be accomplished alone, she probably won't seek out coaching, counseling, or other developmental functions. But if an individual perceives learning as an ongoing collaborative process, she will initiate relationships and build a relationship constellation that provides a wide range of developmental functions.

These fundamental attitudes and postures may change during life, and they certainly interact with each other to shape a relationship constellation. The individual who is dissatisfied with his or her relationship constellation might examine how particular attitudes may be interfering with establishing the kind of relationships that are needed.

However, interpersonal skills are also necessary to initiate and build enhancing relationships at work. Even with the desire to form intimate connections and learn from colleagues, the lack of effective skills in listening, self-disclosure, conflict management, trust-building, and giving and receiving feedback, will thwart the best intentions.

## Organizational Differences

In studies of mentor and peer relationships, organizational features influenced both the characteristics of these relationships and how they unfolded over time. Features of the surrounding organizational context also influence relationship constellations. While further research is needed to delineate how organizational features shape relationship constellations, we can speculate about several.

First, the culture of the organization influences how individuals relate to others at all organizational levels (Deal & Kennedy, 1982). In shaping the fundamental values of an organization, the culture encourages individuals to be more or less self-disclosing at work about personal and professional dilemmas, it encourages or discourages interaction across hierarchical and departmental boundaries, it reinforces or discounts the importance of relationships in both getting the job done and in providing well-being for organizational members, and it supports or undermines relationship-building activities through the systems that it perpetuates. Thus, in some organizations individuals find it easy and are encouraged to initiate supportive relationships with peers and potential mentors; the culture conveys values which support the formation of all kinds of mentor and peer relationships. In other organizations, in contrast, this is more difficult to do; self-disclosure is viewed as deviant or inappropriate, and frequent interaction with individuals at a higher organizational level or in another department violates central rules of conduct. Relationship constellations will look very different in these two contexts; in the former there will be more special peer and mentor relationships and in the latter, fewer of these and more distanced relationships with bosses and information peers.

The reward system of an organization shapes relationship constellations by formally encouraging or discouraging relationship-building activities. Mentor relationships appear when individuals are promoted not only for bottom line results, but also for how well they develop talent. Similarly, peer relationships are more prevalent in organizations that reward collaboration; where individuals are recognized for supporting their peers, it is easier to build information peer, collegial peer, and special peer relationships. The reward system in an organization can facilitate relationship constellations that provide a wide range of developmental functions, or it can, alternately, prohibit their formation.

Task design can similarly allow individuals to connect with others who might become part of the relationship constellation. Such relationships are facilitated when work encourages frequent interaction with peers and potential mentors. In contrast, in organizations where work is highly individualized and solitary in nature, it is more difficult to form alliances that can provide critical developmental functions.

Finally, personnel practices can facilitate or interfere with the formation of relationship constellations. If frequent job rotation is a requirement for advancement, relationships may be disrupted by transfers that are good for one's career, but not necessarily good for one's developmental relationships. Job rotation that is not mandatory allows greater flexibility. Individuals can choose not to move at a given point if staying in a mentor's department is more developmentally desirable.

Educational programs that bring peers together provide a forum for individuals to develop peer relationships of all types. Special peer relationships often begin where common personal and professional concerns are discovered and addressed. Because these individuals have met in a supportive educational setting and because they do not work together every day, it is easier to build a relationship of trust, self-disclosure, and mutuality. Special peer relationships are sometimes difficult to build in an immediate work group where impression management and competition for advancement are both important. Thus, personnel systems that encourage meeting peers from other parts of the organization facilitate relationship constellations that contain special peers.

Personnel practices that encompass formal systems for developing people (e.g., performance appraisals, career planning processes and workshops, etc.), assist individuals in providing critical career and psychosocial functions. Thus, relationships with bosses, mentors, and subordinates are indirectly supported in providing developmental functions when formal systems and procedures require them to do so. Coaching and counseling occur because these systems instruct managers in how to fulfill these functions. In organizations that have such personnel systems, relationship constellations include relationships that provide critical developmental functions, particularly if the systems are followed, and individuals have the skills to carry them out effectively.

Describing what a relationship constellation should look like for a particular individual at a particular career stage is difficult. Much depends on individual attributes, as well as on the nature of the organizational setting. Research to date suggests that predictable developmental tasks become important at each career stage and that relationships help address these tasks (Levinson et al., 1978; Hall, 1976; Schein, 1978; Dalton et al., 1977; Clawson, 1979). Diagnosing individuals' needs, attitudes, skills and organizational circumstances will point to the relationships that can provide critical developmental functions. The relationship constellation offers an important alternative to the search for a mentor; it highlights the range of significant others who might support development.

## IMPLICATIONS

Discussion of the continuum of peer relationships and the relationship constellation highlight how a variety of relationships can provide essential developmental functions at each career stage. The mentor relationship, in providing career and psychosocial functions, is beneficial to both parties. However, it is not the only work relationship that supports career advancement and psychosocial development.

Individuals benefit from a diagnostic approach to managing relationships at work. A systematic assessment of one's developmental needs, one's current relationship constellation, the opportunities for new relationships, and the opportunities for building interpersonal skills, is the first step in managing one's relationships. Such an approach insures that one does not feel trapped in a situation without mentor and peer relationships that support one's development and advancement.

First, a systematic assessment of one's developmental needs requires active introspection and self-awareness. Thus, rather than wait for a mentor to provide developmental opportunities, for example, an individual identifies what she needs in terms of guidance, coaching, exposure, and other developmental experiences. Some of these may be forthcoming; others may be lacking. Most important is recognizing which needs are most important and how they might be met in relationships with peers, subordinates and senior colleagues.

Second, a systematic assessment of one's current relationship constellation indicates what relationships are providing which developmental functions, as well as where gaps exist. For example, an individual in early career may have a constellation which consists of a mentor relationship that provides many career functions but few psychosocial functions and only a small number of information peer relationships. If the individual needs more friendship, counseling and coaching, he might decide that the relationship constellation would be better if several collegial and special peer relationships were added, if the mentor relationship were enriched, or if relationships outside of work were used as sounding boards for professional dilemmas. Alternately, an individual might discover that the relationship constellation is providing just what he needs at that point.

When a gap does exist, the next step in a systematic diagnosis entails identifying the opportunities for new relationships or for enriching existing relationships. Keeping in mind the conceptual schemes that outline the range of possible mentor, peer, and subordinate relationships, an individual can identify who might be available to provide developmental functions, and how to go about building such alliances. It is essential to anticipate what the other's developmental needs might be in order to build a mutually enhancing relationship (Baird & Kram, 1983). For example, a junior manager considers which senior colleagues might be interested in providing mentoring functions and how to approach these individuals in a way that invites further interaction and coaching.

Systematic diagnosis of one's developmental needs, one's current relationship constellation, and opportunities for building new relationships or enhancing old relationships might lead to the conclusion that there are few possibilities to enhance the relationship constellation. An individual may be unaware of others who might have complementary needs, or perhaps such possibilities don't exist. Participation in many departmental and organizational events can expand one's visibility and surface potential new contacts.

Joining networks of various kinds can expand one's options, particularly for information peers and special peers. Networks vary in purpose and structure and in whether they exist within an organization, a profession, or a particular geographical area (Welch, 1980). When they exist within an organization, they may or may not be officially sanctioned by the organization. Networks allow individuals to meet others who have similar professional concerns. Relationships in these contexts often provide several career or psychosocial functions; they can offer, for example, information sharing, career strategizing, emotional support, and friendship.

Finally, when a systematic diagnosis is complete, an individual may determine that while the opportunities for expanding one's relationship constellation exist, building the kinds of relationships that are envisioned appears out of reach. An individual may find it difficult to reach out to a senior colleague (a potential mentor) for coaching, or an individual may not know how to push an information peer relationship along the continuum toward greater intimacy and mutuality. These problems indicate the need for additional relationship-building skills that can be obtained through in-house or offsite educational programs (see Chapter 7).

An individual's self-diagnosis should result in a plan which will enhance the relationships that provide developmental functions. If a relationship constellation should be modified and potential additions are not apparent, one may have to look outside of the organization. Often, however, resources within the organization have not been exhausted, but are unrecognized or out of reach because of individual skill limitations or organizational features that interfere with relationship-building efforts.

The human resources or personnel department should conduct a system-wide diagnosis of the organization's effects on relationship constellations. This diagnosis would consider what training and educational opportunities already exist in the organization as well as those that could be provided. In addition, it would consider how various features of the organization encourage or interfere with relationship-building efforts.

The decision to modify features like task design, reward systems, personnel practices, etc., in order to encourage relationship-building activities depends on the fundamental values and priorities of the organization and, in particular, of senior management. If relationships are viewed as an integral part of human resource development, and if human resource development is considered an integral part of the overall business strategy, then such interventions will support other major activities of the organization.

Attention to people development is sometimes considered a luxury in periods of economic decline or scarcity; in such times, relationship-building efforts may be considered unessential and, perhaps, superfluous. Yet it is precisely in these times that individual and organizational stresses increase, anxiety and uncertainty increase, and the need for emotional support, coaching, guidance, and friendship grow rather than decline. When efficiency and productivity become extremely important, so does the quality of relationship constellations; these constellations enable individuals to maintain high performance levels as well as a continued sense of well-being.

Educational and organizational interventions designed to encourage effective mentor and peer relationships should be systematically tested and evaluated. While the desired results are becoming clearer in terms of the variety of possible developmental relationships, the educational strategies and organizational processes needed to make these relationships available to individuals at every career stage remain a subject of speculation.

# Creating Conditions
# That Encourage
# Mentoring

Mentoring can significantly benefit both individuals and organizations. *Benefits*
For individuals in early career, mentoring can reduce the shock of
organizational entry and help prepare for advancement (Levinson, et
al., 1978; Dalton, et al., 1977). For individuals at midcareer and
beyond, mentoring can help them meet generative needs, stay in touch
with their youthful sides, stay abreast of technological advances, and
attain confirmation by passing on wisdom and experience (Levinson, et
al., 1978; Hall & Kram, 1981; Dalton, et al., 1977). The potential to
enhance individual development at every career stage is impressive, yet
this potential is rarely realized.

From an organization's perspective, mentoring has significant benefits as well. While reducing the shock of entry for the newcomer and
facilitating preparation for advancement, mentor relationships provide
a socializing forum for the organization (Levinson, 1976). Members
learn the ropes of the organization and are less likely to leave because
of confusion and frustration. Thus, these developmental relationships
help the organization nurture good talent (Digman, 1978), pass on central values and practices, and reduce turnover in the early career years

(Dalton, et al., 1977; Levinson, 1976; Missirian, 1982). But usually, these benefits are only partially realized.

In addition to responding to the predictable dilemmas of each career stage, mentoring addresses special interest concerns as well. For example, in organizations where there is a signficant plateauing among mid-career individuals, encouragement to assume the role of mentor for younger colleagues can turn plateauing problems into growth opportunities (Hall, 1980; Hall & Kram, 1981). Secondly, in settings where Affirmative Action is an important objective, mentoring can counteract the disadvantages of not being a member of the dominant group and give minority group members important coaching, modeling, and career counseling opportunities (Phillips-Jones, 1982; Missirian, 1982). These special interest group applications have also not been fully explored.

Certain conditions must exist in an organization in order for the potential benefits of mentoring to be realized. First, organizations need opportunities for frequent and open interaction between managers at different career stages and hierarchical levels. Individuals can then initiate and cultivate the kinds of relationships that respond to current developmental needs. Second, organizational members must have the interpersonal skills to build supportive relationships, as well as the willingness and interest in doing so. Third, the organization's reward system, culture, and norms must value and encourage relationship-building activities (Tichey, 1983; Deal & Kennedy, 1982; Peters & Waterman, 1982). These conditions are not easily achieved, and there are a number of individual and organizational obstacles that interfere with them.

## MAJOR OBSTACLES TO MENTORING _____

Features of an organization can either create or interfere with conditions that support mentoring. Similarly, individuals in an organization may have the attitudes and skills to promote mentoring, or, alternately, they may be inclined to discount the importance of work relationships or not have the requisite skills to build supportive alliances. Studies of mentoring, superior-subordinate, and peer relationships in public utilities, high-tech firms, financial institutions, and traditional manufacturing firms highlight several features that interfere with the optimal conditions (Kram, 1980; Kram & Isabella, 1985; Clawson, 1980; Levinson et al., 1978). Many of these individual and organizational features have also been suggested by those who have attempted to set up formal mentoring systems (Phillips-Jones, 1982; Klauss, 1981; Lean, 1983).

**Obstacle 1:** *A reward system that emphasizes bottom-line results and does not also place a high priority on human resource development objectives creates conditions that discourage mentoring.*

The reward system of an organization has tremendous impact on behavior because pay and promotion are so important to people (Lawler, 1977; Beer, 1980). In most organizations, this system rewards and recognizes performance and potential related to bottom-line results; as a consequence, efforts to build supportive relationships with senior colleagues, peers, or subordinates remain unrecognized by this formal system. In this instance, the reward system discourages mentoring. Coaching, counseling, and seeking relationships with potential mentors and peers are viewed as distractions from task-related activities that lead to pay increases and advancement opportunities. Any mentoring that does occur results from personal satisfaction, not because of recognition by the organization.

Another aspect of the reward system that affects mentoring concerns the nature of rewards available to those at midcareer who will advance no further. For example, in one organization individuals indicated that taking the time to coach is not rewarded and distracts from the time that could be devoted to production-related activities (Kram, 1983a). Criteria for promotion were perceived as related only to technical performance, not to how well a manager developed subordinates or related to colleagues. Most individuals were unwilling to embrace the role of mentor when there were no organizational rewards for doing so.

This common emphasis on bottom-line results impairs the quality and availability of mentoring in an organization unless developmental objectives are simultaneously defined. When recognition and rewards are tied to efforts to coach and mentor, individuals are more likely to seek out opportunities to mentor. Research on well-managed companies confirms that rewards for subordinate development result in more attention to coaching and mentoring activities and, finally, in an increase of talented managers for the organization (Digman, 1978; Peters & Waterman, 1982). If there are no valued alternatives to advancement, then individuals who reach a plateau feel discounted, resentful, and pessimistic about their continued growth (Hall, 1980). This psychological condition contributes to self-doubt and a lack of interest in supporting others' growth. Mentor relationships frequently become destructive when the mentor does not advance further and receives no other rewards for continued service and contributions to the organization (Kram, 1983b). Only when such individuals find job enrichment opportunities and rewards for their skills and experience will they assume the role of mentor or coach.

Finally, while a reward system may encourage mentoring by promoting those who develop talent for the organization, this practice can encourage developmental relationships only for those who have been labeled as high potential candidates, rather than for a wider range of organizational members. Coaching and mentoring are sometimes explicitly assigned as responsibilities to those two levels above those managers labeled "fast trackers." This makes mentoring available only to those who demonstrated high potential early in their careers.

**Obstacle 2:** *The design of work can interfere with building relationships that provide mentoring functions by minimizing opportuntities for interaction between individuals with complementary relationship needs.*

In organizations where work is highly individualized, and there is little contact with others at different hierarchical levels, the opportunity to initiate relationships that can provide mentoring functions is minimal. In contrast, in organizations where work is designed to be accomplished by project teams, the job itself provides frequent opportunities for coaching and mentoring. These variations in work design have significant effects on newcomers who are often cautious in their attempts to make contact with those in more senior positions. Uncertainty about competence, potential, and organizational norms at this early career stage contribute to their uneasiness. Thus, unless jobs are structured to promote interaction with colleagues in other departments and at other levels, initiating relationships that could provide a variety of mentoring functions is difficult.

For example, in a research and development organization, the mentoring available to young engineers and scientists was not sufficient. Turnover of individuals with potential was high, and newcomers found it difficult to learn how to get the resources that they needed to do their work effectively. Here, the highly individualized nature of the work provided little opportunity for novices to benefit from the experience of older engineers and scientists. The technology was such that it was possible to design the work so that juniors and seniors worked together on projects. This change enabled the more experienced engineers and scientists to coach their junior colleagues on how to get the job done, how to navigate in the organization, and how to prepare for advancement. Over time, relationships evolved that provided a range of mentoring functions.

Structuring work in teams invites mentoring and coaching activities. It does not, however, ensure that such developmental relationships will emerge. If the senior colleagues are viewed as evaluators rather than coaches, or if the juniors must prove competence rather than ask for guidance, then attaining effective mentoring alliances will be difficult. Job responsibilities must include the expectation that learning and development will occur through work on the team in order for the benefits of this work design to be realized.

Task design also shapes the way individuals find alternatives to a mentor relationship in their relationships with peers (see Chapter 6). The mutuality and reciprocity of a peer relationship are enhanced by work that fosters collaboration rather than competition. When work is highly individualized and there is little reward for interacting with others about it, individuals are not likely to build supportive alliances with their peers.

**Obstacle 3:** *Performance Management Systems can encourage mentoring by providing a forum and specific tools for coaching and counseling — however, these systems are often absent, or introduced in a manner that causes individuals to avoid their use.*

*Performance management systems* have the potential to help develop relationships that provide mentoring functions. *Management by objectives* is a process in which manager and employee regularly set and review achievable goals that are consistent with organizational objectives (Ordione, 1965). *Performance appraisal* is a process in which a subordinate's performance is reviewed, and feedback is provided on performance and potential. Finally, in *career development systems* (sometimes referred to as employee development or career planning systems), the subordinate and supervisor jointly assess strengths and weaknesses of the subordinate and then develop a plan for his or her development. When carried out effectively, all these activities involve a range of mentoring functions, including coaching, counseling, role modeling, and feedback.

In many situations these systems are either not carried out effectively, or the opportunities to build mentor relationships are not seized. When the systems are not operating effectively, they have often been introduced in a manner that has created resistance, resentment, decreases in autonomy or a sense of competence, or even in an increase in employee turnover (Beer, 1980).

If managers lack confidence or fear the consequences of holding career discussions (e.g., if they have to deal with a dissatisfied employee or a low performer), then they are likely to avoid these responsibilities. Similarly, if employees feel the system is ineffective, they are not likely to do the personal work that makes these activities beneficial.

The introduction, design, and implementation of performance management systems largely determine whether or not they will foster meaningful performance feedback, career planning, and career development. If the systems respond to members' needs, if individuals feel prepared to carry out their responsibilities, and if the organization rewards use of the systems, then members will embrace them. However, this is often not the case; if managers feel anxious in the role of advisor or career counselor or that the program has no real value, then meaningful developmental discussions will not occur.

*Career development, performance appraisal,* and *MBO* systems rarely achieve their potential benefits and, thus, do not create conditions for mentoring. Often the lack of skills, confidence, and motivation makes these systems burdens rather than assets. Not everyone will embrace such systems, but with adequate training and a responsive system, resistance is reduced and potential benefits realized. Performance management systems can provide the structure and tools for a range of mentoring functions; too often they fail to do so.

**Obstacle 4:** *The culture of an organization — through its values, informal rules, rites, rituals, and the behavior of its leaders — can make mentoring and other relationships unessential.*

An organization's culture shapes people's behavior by defining what behaviors and attitudes are valued and what will be punished or discounted. Like the reward system, the culture impacts on whether individuals will invest time in developing relationships that support personal and professional growth. Shared values, rites and rituals, the heroes of an organization, and the informal network all define the culture of an organization (Deal & Kennedy, 1982). For example, an organization whose leaders provide mentoring functions and reward subordinates for developing their subordinates, both modeling and reinforcing mentoring behaviors, establishes a culture that encourages mentoring. Similarly, an organization which has effective career development processes, a system that rewards relationships and developmental activities, and other routines that enhance relationship-building efforts, will support mentoring far more than one that does not.

Equally important are the culture's values about the kinds of communication, the degree to which individuals can trust each other (particularly at different hierarchical levels), and the extent to which openness and trust are valued. When the culture perpetuates closed and superficial communication, and when a lack of trust for those in authority prevails, it is difficult to provide mentoring functions. Meaningful coaching, counseling, friendship, and role modeling are almost impossible in a situation characterized by low trust and minimal communication.

Most organizations have not examined how their culture (and particular practices) affect the nature of mentoring for members at each career stage. Those that have cultivate a culture that emphasizes the importance of sponsorship and mentoring for those identified as having high potential to assume managerial positions (*Business Week*, May 8,

1978; Collins & Scott, 1978). Organization leaders consciously model what they consider appropriate sponsor behavior, and newcomers with MBAs and high potential are linked with senior managers who are expected to provide mentoring functions. While these efforts create a culture that encourages mentoring, it is mentoring for an elite group rather than for a wide range of organizational members. Thus, the full potential of mentoring is not approached, and those who are not chosen experience a significant loss.

The culture that most severely discourages mentoring activities is the one that is so short-term results-oriented that attention to employee development and relationships is considered a distraction from important work. Leaders model a results orientation, inquire only about the bottom line, and invest little time in talking with members about their job or personal dilemmas. In addition, rites and rituals center around organizational efficiency, high production, and maximum use of technical resources, without concern for the quality of worklife or the development of human resources. Activity and results are valued, not people and development. Thus, individuals feel discounted, the quality of communication and the level of trust are low, and supportive relationships become nonexistent. While this context is extreme, many organizations with high turnover and poor performance or morale approximate this kind of culture. Here, mentoring is almost entirely absent.

**Obstacle 5:** *Individuals' assumptions, attitudes, and skills can interfere with developing relationships that provide mentoring functions—if juniors assume that seniors do not have the time to coach, if individuals at every career stage are unaware of the value of developmental relationships, or if individuals lack the interpersonal skills to manage relationships.*

A major obstacle to building relationships which provide mentoring functions is the lack of awareness of the important role that relationships play in career development. Individuals, particularly early in a career, are most concerned with mastering technical competence; the notion that relationships might help them advance their careers is frequently a foreign one (Louis, 1980; Webber, 1976; Dalton, et al., 1977). Without this recognition, juniors will probably not seek out senior colleagues for support and guidance, nor will they see the value in building relationships with peers who are experiencing similar challenges.

Similarly, individuals in midcareer and beyond frequently do not understand how they might contribute to others' growth and advancement or how guiding others would support their continued development. Without this recognition, any mentoring that does occur is a result of intuitive action, rather than conscious intention. These individuals are often unaware of how they contribute to their junior colleagues' development. And for individuals in technical careers, getting involved in junior colleagues' development frequently seems irrelevant to their current responsibilities or their career futures.

This lack of awareness and understanding can be traced to earlier socialization experiences and recent organizational experiences. Individuals are rarely educated about the predictable dilemmas that most face over the course of life and how relationships in a work setting might facilitate managing these. Most formal education programs emphasize technical training, not human relations training. It is not surprising, therefore, that individuals do not make relationship building a primary objective.

Basic attitudes and assumptions can also interfere with establishing relationships that provide mentoring functions. Attitudes toward one's competence and career potential, assumptions about those in authority, and attitudes toward the organization in general can significantly affect the extent to which individuals will take the initiative to build relationships (see Chapters 4 and 6). Optimism about one's own career and competence, a positive disposition toward those in authority, and confidence in the integrity of the organization are prerequisites for positive experiences in work relationships.

For example, individuals in early career who do not have much confidence about their competence and potential may be reluctant to ask questions or invite coaching. They assume that they will make a negative impression or that they are not worth the valuable time of senior colleagues. If, in addition, they assume that those in authority are relatively unavailable and disinterested in juniors' development, they will not be inclined to initiate contact with a potential mentor. Finally, they may misread those signals that indicate that a more senior colleague would like to provide coaching and counseling.

Individuals further along in their careers who encountered blocked opportunity or the threat of obsolescence develop assumptions and attitudes that leave them psychologically unavailable to provide mentoring functions. Their competence is called into question and self-doubts develop. This may be followed by anger and resentment toward the organization for the lack of recognition and continued challenge or toward younger colleagues who still face a variety of opportunities for growth and advancement. Only in rare instances can individuals continue to mentor others when their value to the organization is questioned. Thus, an organization's response to this predictable midcareer problem determines whether individuals will have attitudes that embrace mentoring responsibilities. Frequently, organizations' lack of attention to this problem reduces the pool of potential mentors.

Finally, lack of interpersonal skills can interfere with building supportive relationships that provide mentoring functions, even when attitudes and assumptions are positive. Skills in active listening, communication, building trust and empathy, providing coaching and counseling, and managing conflict and competition are essential to these developmental alliances. Relationships are frequently curtailed or avoided precisely because individuals do not have the skills to manage them effectively.

## ALTERNATIVE STRATEGIES

The obstacles to achieving conditions that encourage mentoring are not insurmountable. Systematic diagnosis and planning can result in actions that modify features of the reward system, the culture of an organization, elements of performance management systems, task design, or individual skills and attitudes. Indeed, an open systems perspective suggests that any change in one feature of an organization will affect other parts of the system as well (Nadler & Tushman, 1980; Beer, 1980; Rice, 1969; Alderfer, 1976). In addition, this perspective suggests that there are several ways, rather than only one right way, to achieve a desired objective. Thus the appropriate strategy for a given situation will depend on which features should be modified, where the readiness and motivation for change is located, the extent to which top management supports the objective, and what resources are available for the effort (Beckhard, 1969).

There are two types of strategies that can encourage mentoring. One strategy is *education*, which includes training and development efforts that create awareness and understanding of mentoring and its role in career development. These efforts also provide a learning context in which relationship skills are developed. The other strategy is *structural change*. This is a systematic effort to modify existing structures in the organization (including the reward system, performance management systems, or task design) in order to elicit different behaviors from employees. Each type of strategy has advantages and limitations. The open systems perspective indicates that, in most cases, educational and structural change strategies should be designed and implemented simultaneously or in sequence in order to reinforce each other.

## Educational Strategies

Educational programs can increase understanding of mentoring and its role in career development and create a learning context in which relationship skills and attitudes are developed. In addition to increasing knowledge, skills, and positive attitudes, such strategies can change the culture of an organization by reinforcing new values that give priority to building supportive relationships.

Many educational programs are possible, and the appropriate mix depends on the particular setting and objectives that have been defined. For example, when career development systems are functioning well, education related to mentoring could be incorporated into training that supports this performance management system. Alternately, when training and development programs are offered, a specific program on "Mentoring, Careers, and the Life Course," for example, could be tailored to the particular training population. Or, when higher quality and greater availability of mentoring for women and minority groups are needed, specialized training events for these groups as well as for the potential mentors would be appropriate.

It is possible to outline the predictable issues, topics, and concerns that are relevant for target groups at different career stages. Research on mentoring and on life and career stages indicates that different agendas would be appropriate for each major age group or career stage (Hall, 1976; Phillips-Jones, 1982; Levinson, et al., 1978; Baird & Kram, 1983).

**Individuals in Early Career.** This group is concerned with learning the ropes of the organization and preparing for advancement (Schein, 1978; Hall, 1976; Dalton, et al., 1977; Webber, 1976). Here, the primary agenda should be to educate individuals about the importance of relationships with senior colleagues who can coach, guide, and sponsor as one builds competence in a new career. Input about mentoring and how it helps one address primary developmental tasks encourages these individuals to consider, systematically, how they might develop supportive relationships in their work settings. In addition, these educational inputs alleviate any uncertainty about competence or potential, and periodic ambivalence or confusion about career identity.

Topics including predictable dilemmas at each career stage, as well as the role of mentoring and peer relationships in career development, heighten awareness of the value of relationships in supporting individual growth and development. It is important to highlight how individuals in early career contribute to the development of their senior colleagues when they build mentor relationships with them. This perspective eliminates any concern that benefits of such relationships are one-sided (see Chapter 4).

These agenda items serve to increase awareness, knowledge, and positive attitudes toward relationship-building activities. However, this alone is not sufficient. Self-assessment and skill development activities are necessary so that individuals leave the educational program able to take action in their work situations. Systematically assessing their own developmental needs, their current relationship constellation, and setting goals for their development and for supportive relationships transfers new learnings to their own situations. Equally important is developing interpersonal skills through experiential methods that strengthen their abilities to initiate and build supportive alliances.

**Individuals in Middle Career.** This population may vary considerably in terms of age and career experiences. Ranging in age from 35 to 55, they may be at a plateau in terms of future advancement opportunities or they may still be on an advancement track. What these individuals do have in common is a substantial history in the organization or in a particular career, as well as history of relationships. Midcareer is a period of reassessment and redirection (Levinson et al., 1978; Osherson, 1980). The primary agenda for this population should include a review of life and career stage models and a perspective on the role of mentoring in development for individuals in both early and midcareer stages. Relating their own experiences in an educational context allows them to discuss concerns about assuming the role of mentor in relationships with junior colleagues. In addition, the models of life and career stages legitimize concerns about competence and value to the organization. The loneliness frequently encountered at midcareer, particularly from the threats of obsolescence and aging, can be addressed by considering these perspectives.

In this population there are variations in the degree to which individuals have positive attitudes toward mentoring. This is a function of personal experiences as well as the organization's current treatment of individuals at this career stage. The opportunity to explore these in a supportive, educational context increases the likelihood that individuals will leave the educational process wanting to provide mentoring functions in a manner that is also self-enhancing. Some, though not all, will embrace the role of mentor with enthusiasm; when midcareer employees are treated poorly in terms of rewards and recognition, fewer are likely to want to actively coach and guide younger colleagues.

Opportunities for self-assessment and skill development are critical for this population as well. Through self-assessment activities, individuals examine relationships in their careers and how mentoring either played a significant role or was missed at critical points along the way. Within a supportive educational context, individuals share their experiences and learn about alternatives to their own perspectives. Insights into past relationships may improve future relationships. Skill development activities enable individuals to develop confidence and competence in providing mentoring functions to junior colleagues and in building alliances with peers and superiors who might provide developmental functions needed during middle career years.

**Individuals in Late Career.** This population is likely to be anticipating retirement or anxious about how much to invest in the organization and how much to invest in other areas of life (Levinson, et al., 1978; Kram & Jusela, 1978). Concerns about what one will leave behind are suddenly important, and awareness of one's mortality is high. For this group, mentoring can allow one to pass on one's wisdom and experiences to a younger generation. In doing so, both psychological and organizational benefits are derived.

Educational input should include a review of life and career stage perspectives in a manner that encourages individuals to review their pasts, to identify positive and negative experiences, and to define opportunities to provide mutually enhancing mentoring functions. With this group, cognitive input and skill training are not as critical as identifying ways to create a consultative role for themselves (Hall & Kram, 1981).

There is probably much variation in this population, with some individuals already engaged in mentoring activities. Those with positions of authority and power may be providing sponsorship, coaching, and role modeling to junior colleagues. In addition, those with the personal desire to teach and pass on values may be taking the initiative to coach and counsel on a regular basis. Finally, those who are already leaving the organization in a psychological sense may be detached from relationships in the work setting. In a supportive educational program, discussing personal experiences offers new alternatives to individuals who have not realized their potential in relationships.

Educational programs for homogeneous populations by age or career stage may not be practical in many instances. While these have the advantage of bringing together individuals who share similar developmental concerns and opportunities (so that empathy and peer support are easily achieved), heterogeneous groups have advantages as well. With populations that include individuals at every career stage, participants learn from those in a different generation. As a consequence, they develop greater empathy for those with whom they are likely to develop mentor relationships and insight into their personal dilemmas by listening to those who may be further along in their careers. Finally, in a heterogeneous training group, potential mentoring relationships between juniors and seniors may get started.

The agenda for educational programs designed for a more heterogeneous population would have to be more generalized. "Perspectives on Life and Career Stages," and the role of "Mentoring in Careers" would be the appropriate topic areas. At the same time, however, it would be valuable to address special interest topics with the group as a whole, or in smaller discussion groups. For example, individuals in early career could discuss difficulties with initiating relationships that might provide mentoring functions. In addition, women and men might discuss the complexities of cross-gender relationships and strategies for managing these. Or midcareer individuals might consider personal resistance to assuming the mentoring role. Clearly, particular groups will have concerns unique to their histories in the organization; an opportunity to explore these in an educational context helps build awareness, attitudes, and skills necessary for achieving supportive alliances.

The appropriate objectives, design, and target populations for education of this kind depend on what programs exist, the role of training activities, and the needs of organizational members. For example, some organizations integrate education on mentoring into career planning workshops that contain both cognitive input and skill training elements (Lewis, 1981–82; 1983). Separate programs on mentoring are not necessary, and integration with career planning programs gives wider acceptance to the topic and its relevance for individuals at all career stages. Regardless of the target population or special interest objectives, however, certain principles of laboratory education are important for reorienting attitudes and developing new behavioral skills (Bass & Vaughn, 1966; Hall, 1970; Porter, Lawler & Hackman, 1975; Beer, 1980).

The principles in Figure 7–1 stress the importance of focusing on behavior and attitudes rather than on cognitive learning, although cognitive learning on the topics outlined previously should be provided to support skill development. The design should allow participants to practice the interpersonal skills needed in order to provide mentoring functions or to initiate relationships with senior colleagues. This can occur through role-play situations as well as through examination of job-related experiences. In addition to skill practice, the opportunity to obtain constructive feedback, to experiment with new behaviors, and to see modeling of effective coaching in action, reinforces the development of new skills and attitudes. Finally, the opportunity to plan for implementation of new knowledge facilitates the transfer to relationships in the immediate work setting.

Educational strategies have a number of limitations. First, not all potential participants are interested or open to learning about mentoring; prior experiences in relationships as well as current organizational status and prospects for the future shape the extent to which individuals will embrace the opportunities offered in an educational context. Second, unless the educational program is introduced with a clear rationale about how it fits with participants' job situations and broader organizational objectives, it may be viewed as interesting but superfluous. Finally, if organizational structures and systems do not support the attitudes, knowledge, and skills developed in the educational context, new knowledge will fade rapidly (Argyris, 1970).

Since all eligible participants are not likely to embrace the new attitudes, knowledge, and skills, educational programs of this kind should be voluntary. Research has indicated that some individuals are more inclined to provide mentoring functions than others (Kram, 1980; Alleman, 1982; Levinson, et al., 1978). While we don't know whether educational intervention can significantly improve individuals' relationship skills and attitudes, providing educational opportunities to those who want to learn offers the most benefits for both the individuals and the organization. At a minimum, it is important to acknowledge and address individuals' reluctances and anxieties about building mentor relationships.

Coaching and counseling individuals as they build supportive relationships with peers, superiors, and subordinates subsequent to participation in an educational program facilitates the transfer of new attitudes and skills in the immediate work situation. If possible, talking with a third party about experiences with providing mentoring functions or initiating discussions with potential mentors will give the support individuals need as they venture into new relationship behaviors. A

---

**Figure 7–1.**    Principles for Designing Education on Mentoring.

1. Define learning objectives for a specific target population.

2. Emphasize exploration of *attitudes* toward mentoring and the *behavior* required to initiate and manage relationships that provide mentoring functions. Supplement skill training and self-reflection with cognitive learning about life and career stages and the role of mentoring in career development.

3. Provide opportunities to *practice the interpersonal skills* of active listening, communication, building rapport, managing conflict, collaboration, coaching, counseling, etc., in role-play situations and/or in discussion of on-the-job relationships.

4. Provide opportunities for *constructive feedback* from instructors and participants on interpersonal style and on specific strategies for initiating relationships that provide mentoring functions.

5. Provide opportunities to *experiment with new behavior*, and to see models of effective coaching and counseling.

6. End with *planning for back-home application* of skills to current and future relationships.

good alternative to this staff resource is structuring peer counseling agreements among program participants so that they can serve as a sounding board for each other as they implement knowledge back on the job.

Senior management is critical to insuring that education to encourage mentoring is viewed as legitimate and important. They should actively articulate how mentoring efforts contribute to organizational objectives; this should occur at the outset of formal educational events, as well as in meetings with organizational members. In addition, senior managers should model effective mentoring behaviors in their relationships with subordinates. They should provide strong role models so that organizational members will find the skills and attitudes acquired during training to be consistent with organizational norms and practices. Finally, senior management must insure that the structural changes needed to encourage mentoring are implemented; the reward system, aspects of task design, the culture of the organization, and features of performance management systems will not change significantly without the active support of this group (Argyris, 1970; Beckhard, 1969; Beer, 1980).

In order to insure that educational strategies have impact, organizational structures, norms, and practices must support the skills and attitudes developed during participation in a program. Without this support, individuals will quickly revert to former attitudes and behaviors. For example, if organizational conditions contradict new attitudes, and more specifically, if the reward system only values bottom-line results and task design does not allow for frequent interaction among colleagues who might have complementary relationship needs, then those who have participated in an educational program on mentoring are likely to become frustrated or angry and ultimately fail to use newly acquired skills.

## Structural Change Strategies

While education focuses on changing knowledge, attitudes, and skills of organizational members, *structural changes* focus on changing existing systems of the organization or introducing new ones in order to shape employees' behaviors in new directions (see Figure 7–2). Structural changes stimulate and reinforce new behaviors in members. Thus, changes in the reward system encourage mentoring activities, and changes in task design encourage relationship building by facilitating interaction among individuals with complementary needs.

Ideally, educational and structural interventions should be implemented simultaneously or in sequence to reinforce each other. One

**Figure 7-2.** Structural Changes.

| Strategy | Alternative Methods | Major Advantages | Major Disadvantages |
|---|---|---|---|
| **Modify the Reward System** | Base decisions about pay and promotion on both bottom-line results and how well individuals develop subordinates and build relationships with senior colleagues and peers. | Has a high impact on individuals' behavior at all career stages. | Likely to encounter significant resistance. |
| | Develop a human resource accounting system to provide data for evaluating performance related to developing people. | Rewards developing relationships and people. | Difficult to define specific measures that reflect quality of relationships. |
| | Develop a formal process for soliciting feedback from peers and subordinates to be utilized in performance appraisal, development planning, and decisions about pay and promotion. | Provides rich qualitative data that can improve performance and offer rewards for relationship-building efforts. | Likely to encounter significant resistance from organizational members who want to maintain one-way communication and feedback. |
| | Develop explicit rewards at mid-career for providing coaching and counseling to junior colleagues. | Reduces stagnation and withdrawal of individuals at mid-career, while developing human potential to provide mentoring to juniors. | Difficult to define what rewards would have value and be consistent with ongoing systems. |

| | | |
|---|---|---|
| **Modify the Design of Work** | Modify space arrangements to encourage frequent interaction among juniors and seniors. | Affects daily interaction patterns and easy to do. | Not likely to change quality of interaction, only frequency. |
| | Modify juniors' jobs to require more contact with clients and senior colleagues. | Legitimizes regular contact with potential mentors. | Individuals may not have the requisite interpersonal skills. May violate norms of interaction. |
| | Modify seniors' jobs to include coaching and counseling younger colleagues. | Legitimizes role of mentor or coach. | Some individuals may not want to assume the responsibilities, or they may not have the interpersonal skills to do so. |
| | Create project teams that include individuals at different career stages. | Provides ongoing mentoring activities through the work itself. | Individuals may not have the requisite interpersonal skills. Work technology may prohibit the change. |
| **Modify Performance Management Systems** | Introduce performance appraisal, MBO, and development planning processes. | Provides a forum for mentoring activities. | Frequently encounter considerable resistance, particularly without adequate skill training. |
| | Offer educational programs on the rationale and skills required for each system. | Changes attitudes and builds requisite interpersonal skills. | Will be viewed with skepticism unless formal systems are endorsed by senior management. |
| | Allow other than immediate supervisors to provide mentoring functions. | Insures a positive interaction since participation is voluntary. | May threaten immediate supervisor's turf. |

(continued)

**Figure 7-2.**   Structural Changes. (continued)

| Strategy | Alternative Methods | Major Advantages | Major Disadvantages |
|---|---|---|---|
| **Introduce A Formal Mentoring Program** | Set up pairs of junior and senior colleagues who are expected to build a mentoring relationship. | Insures that juniors and seniors find each other and that relationships are readily available. | Individuals may feel coerced and confused about relationship responsibilities; destructive dynamics emerge. |
| | Define a population for whom relationships should be established and identify and match potential juniors and seniors. | Increases the likelihood that matches will be good ones. | Those who are not matched feel deprived, resentful and pessimistic about their futures. |
| | Set up procedures for monitoring the pairs and for providing feedback to the organization. | Provides support to the pairs and helps end relationships that don't work. | Sets up an evaluation agenda which puts individuals in the program on the defensive. |
| | Offer educational opportunities to enable juniors and seniors to participate effectively in the program. | Changes attitudes and builds requisite interpersonal skills, preparing individuals to initiate and manage the new relationship. | Assumes that all volunteers can learn the requisite interpersonal skills; some may be ill suited for the new responsibilities. |

without the other produces negative consequences. For example, if educational programs are implemented without attention to the reward system, task design, and performance management systems, organizational members are likely to become frustrated, angry, and resentful when they attempt to implement newly acquired skills in building relationships that provide a greater range of developmental functions. In turn, new attitudes and skills are likely to fade out if relationship-building efforts are disconfirmed by existing systems and practices. Alternately, if the reward system is modified to encourage members to provide mentoring functions, or if performance management systems are modified to incorporate mentoring functions into performance appraisals, managers may become anxious and insecure about their abilities to adequately meet expectations unless education in the requisite knowledge and skills is provided (Tushman, 1974). The primary advantage of structural interventions is that they produce rapid changes in behavior (Beer, 1980). If these changes are supplemented with appropriate educational programs, they can alter organizational norms and practices to encourage mentoring for members at all career stages (see Figure 7-2).

**Modifying the Reward System.** There are several ways a reward system can be modified to encourage relationship-building activities and to make these activities essential and valued efforts in the workplace. First, decisions about pay increases and promotions can be based not only on financial results but also on how well individuals develop subordinates and build relationships with peers and senior colleagues. Second, feedback from peers and subordinates concerning how well an individual provides developmental functions can become part of the data on which pay and promotion decisions are based. Finally, individuals at midcareer can be given rewards other than promotion and pay that are valued alternatives to advancement. Individuals at this career stage would then find encouragement and incentive to assume the role of coach or mentor in relation to their less experienced colleagues.

Rewards for developing subordinates and for building supportive relationships can be reflected in promotional decisions as well as in performance appraisal and development discussions. As organizational members see those who have actively provided mentoring functions advance, perceptions of the reward system change, and mentoring skills become a prerequisite for advancement. A clear statement from senior management regarding the importance of mentoring for developing the human resources of the organization facilitates this change as well.

However, it is difficult to measure how well members assume the role of mentor and coach. Indeed, this may be one reason rewards have focused on tangible bottom-line results; these results are easier to measure and evaluate. Several organizations are now attempting to develop human resource accounting systems, which is a method for measuring the costs incurred by organizations to recruit, train, and develop their human resources (Flamholtz, 1974). With varied success, these methods provide some basis on which to account for the time individuals spend on coaching and counseling subordinates or other developmental activities.

A human resources accounting approach enables individuals to report the time they spend in mentoring activities. As a consequence, this time does not go unrecognized, and is less likely to be viewed as a distraction from work. However, such an approach does not measure the quality of relationship time, that is, how well interpersonal transactions provide support and developmental opportunity. If a reward system truly acknowledges the importance of developmental relationships, subjective data concerning the quality of mentoring or coaching experiences must be considered.

Feedback from peers and subordinates on how well an individual manages relationships and provides developmental functions is an important source of information. This is a major departure from most performance appraisal systems and may be difficult to implement in authoritarian organizations. However, in settings where there is a clear desire to encourage mentoring processes and where two-way communication is valued, feedback helps individuals learn about their skills in providing developmental functions and produces data that can be used in decisions about pay and promotion.

Blocked opportunity can significantly affect individuals' motivations, involvement, commitment to work, and willingness to support junior colleagues' development (Kanter, 1977). Indeed, individuals who have reached a plateau in their careers frequently enter a phase of withdrawal from the organization or a period of self-doubt and resentment about their competence and value (Hall, 1976). However, those who reach a plateau are also likely to be at an age and career stage when the desire to meet generative needs and to teach others increases (Levinson, et al., 1978; Dalton, et al., 1977; Hall, 1976). Rewards and recognition for embracing the role of mentor or coach make use of a relatively untapped resource and meet primary developmental tasks of this life/career stage. Depending on the organization's culture and practices, the mentoring role may take the form of specific jobs with explicit responsibilities to coach, or it may remain a less tangible expectation rewarded with pay and public acknowledgments.

Changing the reward system is a complex task. The first step is to begin to recognize and value relationship-building efforts and capacities to provide developmental functions for subordinates. In a modified system, members must be informed about changes in expectations and encouraged to make mentoring activities a higher priority. They must also be given the educational support to do so. If this is not done, members become anxious and resentful about the change in the rules of the game (Tushman, 1974).

Resistance to changes in the reward system is predictable. Whenever change is introduced, it creates some fear and anxiety about what life in the organization will be like (Watson, 1969; Zaltman & Duncan, 1977). And with a change that has a significant impact on people's careers and life-styles, it is not surprising that there would be considerable concern, particularly for those who are not interested in assuming the role of mentor.

There is no clear procedure for modifying the reward system to encourage mentoring. There are, however, several alternatives, particularly in organizations where attention to developing subordinates and relationship-building efforts are considered a distraction from work. Perhaps the best way to discover which alternative is most appropriate in a given setting is to involve organizational members in changing the reward system. This not only insures modifications that are relevant to those who will be most directly affected, but it also reduces some of the resistance (Lawler, 1977; Beer, 1980).

**Modifying the Design of Work.** Opportunities for interaction are essential for encouraging relationships that provide mentoring functions. Mentor relationships frequently begin when two individuals collaborate on a task and discover a mutual liking and trust which pushes the relationship further (see Chapter 3). While modifications in the reward system are usually significant and therefore subject to resistance and scrutiny, modifications to the design of work in order to foster interaction can range from minor changes to major reorganizations.

First, the impact that physical space of an organization has on frequency and quality of interactions among organizational members is often overlooked (Steele, 1973; Steele & Jenks, 1977). Conditions that encourage relationship-building efforts can be enhanced by making it easier for individuals to have informal dialogues with those who might have complementary developmental needs. For example, newcomers could be located close to more senior colleagues who might offer guidance and coaching. In some organizations, a conscious decision is made to have junior and senior engineers share office space, particularly during the newcomer's first six months of employment (Phillips-Jones, 1982). Similarly, organizational members committed to fostering mentoring processes can model effective management of physical space by creating an "open door" policy through their own actions. Perceptions of availability have a tremendous effect on juniors' willingness to seek out guidance from their senior colleagues.

Individual jobs can also encourage contact with organizational members who have the potential to meet important relationship needs at a particular career stage (Levinson, 1976). Thus, technical jobs for newcomers can be expanded to require contact with employees in other parts of the organization or contact with senior colleagues who might provide feedback on one's performance. Establishing contact with clients and opening feedback channels not only offer an enriched job (Hackman, et al., 1975; Hackman & Oldham, 1980), but also increase opportunities for interaction with people who can provide mentoring functions. This kind of modification in the design of work can be accomplished without major organizational changes, particularly in settings where there is some degree of autonomy in how work gets done.

Similarly, individuals in midcareer can be encouraged to incorporate coaching and mentoring into their ongoing job activities. In one organization, for example, an individual in each work unit would volunteer to coach and counsel other members of the department, and this would become a recognized work responsibility (Phillips-Jones, 1982). Not only does this provide a valuable resource for those who need support and guidance, but the individual assuming this responsibility expresses generative needs and is rewarded for doing so.

A more radical modification in the design of work involves creating project teams comprised of individuals at different career stages who have complementary needs. When task requirements necessitate and benefit from collaboration, this intervention enhances productivity as well as the quality of relationships that can provide mentoring functions. In several R & D organizations, project teams have been formed primarily to create a more synergistic work process. Not only does this new form result in higher quality work, but it requires frequent interaction among junior and senior scientists and engineers. As a consequence, coaching and counseling functions are provided more frequently than they were when engineers and scientists at different career stages had few task-related reasons to get together.

Modifications in the design of work that contribute to conditions that encourage mentoring can take a variety of forms. The appropriate change strategy depends on the nature of the work and technology, the nature of other systems, and the skills and attitudes of organizational members. Project teams are excellent for both task and relationship-building objectives. However, if individuals do not have the interpersonal skills to work effectively in a team setting, this modification could result in poor task performance and considerable frustration and anger.

A careful diagnosis should determine what modifications to task design are possible and needed. As with the redesign of the reward system, involvement of those affected by the change is most likely to result in solutions that are acceptable to those who will implement them.

Unlike modifications to the reward system, however, changes in the design of work do not have to be system-wide; they can be individually based. Thus, in a discussion between a supervisor and a subordinate it may be decided that the latter would benefit from more regular contact with senior colleagues and/or clients who might provide feedback and guidance in particular areas. Or, in the context of a career planning workshop, an individual might decide to initiate changes in the way he or she carries out the job in order to have more contact with potential mentors or proteges.

When modifications in the design of work are made on an individual basis, they can have a significant impact on relationship-building opportunities for that particular individual. When they are made on a departmental or organization-wide basis, they can have a significant impact on the general quality of interpersonal relations, the level of trust across hierarchical levels, and the culture of the system. System-wide change of this kind, however, also has an impact on other structures and systems. Participation of those affected by the change, and systematic consideration of how other systems must be modified to maintain a good fit among organization components are both essential for effective implementation (Nadler & Tushman, 1980; Hackman, 1977; Beer, 1980).

**Modifying Performance Management Systems**. Strategies for modifying these systems so that they encourage mentoring can take several forms. If no formal systems are yet in place, introducing them should involve a planned step-by-step process which includes top management support, successful pilot projects which are evaluated, and education to provide knowledge, attitudes, and skills to carry out the systems effectively. Within this context, mentoring can be incorporated as an integral element in all three systems. During the education process, organization members can learn about mentoring functions, their role in MBO, performance appraisal, and career development, and can develop the interpersonal skills to employ them.

Sometimes the systems are already in place, but they are not highly valued. Managers and employees may go through the motions of completing the forms with little exchange of value to individuals' development or to the relationship between manager and employee. Here, a systematic diagnosis is needed to determine why these systems have not been established as useful tools for employee development and human resource management. If organizational members lack the skills to implement the systems, then education may be warranted. However, if the systems' designs are inappropriate for the employee population, then changes in the systems must be considered before education will have a positive impact.

Performance management systems demand considerable commitment and skills from organization members. Too often this commitment is overlooked in designing and implementing them, and organizational members become resentful and unwilling to embrace responsibilities. In addition, these responsibilities span a wide range and are complex; individuals must assume the roles of evaluator, coach, friend, and counselor, and these often conflict with each other (Meyer, Kay & French, 1965). Clearly, not everyone who is expected to carry out these roles will be able to do so.

Recognizing that not all members can carry out the conflicting roles required by these systems is an important first step toward modifying performance management systems in a positive direction. For example, some supervisors cannot carry out mentoring functions with particular subordinates because they are at a career stage when concerns about their own competence and potential make supporting junior colleagues difficult (Baird & Kram, 1983). If performance management systems are to encourage mentoring functions for organization members, someone other than the self-absorbed immediate supervisor will have to carry out discussions about performance and plans for developing subordinates. In one engineering organization, for example, the role of "alternative advisor" was introduced in the context of a new career development program (Lewis, 1981–82, 1983). The alternative advisors were a group of managers who volunteered to be available for career discussions with employees who did not feel comfortable talking with their immediate supervisor about personal and professional development issues. In essence, this enabled the mentoring functions inherent in such a system to be provided by those who were interested in doing so and who were respected and trusted by employees.

Performance management systems can encourage and reinforce mentoring behaviors. Modifying these systems to incorporate mentoring functions and providing the educational support for members to implement their responsibilities effectively increases the quality and availability of mentoring. As with other structural interventions, acceptance depends on how the changes are introduced.

**Introducing a Formal Mentoring Program.** A formal mentoring program consists of an explicit goal and set of practices for pairing junior and senior organizational members in order to welcome newcomers and to help them prepare for career advancement (Phillips-Jones, 1982). Generally, such a program establishes a set of required or optional activities that should occur in these relationships. The purpose of these activities is to encourage mentoring by arranging relationships between juniors and seniors that will provide a range of developmental functions for both individuals.

A number of formal mentoring programs have been used in both the private sector and the federal government. These programs vary in terms of the target population served, the degree of structure and formal requirements, how mentors and proteges are assigned to each other, and the extent to which education is offered to help individuals learn how to carry out mentoring responsibilities. In the federal government, for example, the IRS, the Federal Executive Development Program, the Presidential Management Internal Program, and the U.S. Department of Agriculture have a formal system in which the training and development staffs assign coaches or mentors to junior level employees (Klauss, 1979). In the private sector, the Jewel Companies assign each new MBA to a senior manager for coaching and mentoring when they join the organization (Collins & Scott, 1978). AT & T Bell Labs have junior and senior engineers share the same office for several months, the Glendale Federal Savings and Loan has volunteer leaders in each unit counsel employees, and Merrill Lynch and Company have bosses nominate junior managers who are then assigned to seniors who act as mentors (Phillips-Jones, 1982). Finally, Federal Express has a structured mentoring system which also includes education and involvement of immediate supervisors, as well as an advisory board that monitors the system's effectiveness and any problems that might occur (Lean, 1983).

While no systematic evaluation of these formal mentoring programs has been completed, a partial assessment of their impact raises a number of questions about their value in creating conditions that encourage mentoring. The primary objective is to effectively incorporate newcomers (and, in some instances, particular groups of newcomers, such as women, minorities, and/or high potential candidates). However, assigned mentors and proteges are not accomplishing this goal and, in some instances, these relationships have destructive consequences. Some of these negative by-products of a formal program may be avoided through careful design and implementation; others are inevitable consequences of engineering relationships that must evolve through mutual attraction and interpersonal chemistry (Kram, 1980).

First, when mentors and proteges are assigned to each other, the likelihood of the relationship evolving into one that provides a variety of developmental functions is small. Both juniors and seniors may feel mismatched or coerced into a relationship that they do not particularly want to cultivate; yet the organization pressures them to continue their interaction. In these instances, seniors may resent their responsibilities as mentors, and juniors are likely to grow pessimistic about the value of relationships with senior colleagues.

Even if the match is not a poor one—that is, mentor and protege like each other and want to build a relationship—both individuals can become anxious and confused about their new responsibilities as mentor or protege. Seniors, when asked to mentor or coach, frequently have an idealized image of what this may entail. This image may cause considerable self-doubt and concern about their abilities to be successful. Education can alleviate some of this anxiety and confusion by defining mentoring functions and by providing interpersonal skill training.

Even with education, however, there are some individuals who will not be able to assume the role of mentor or coach effectively. Individuals at midcareer who are concerned about their own advancement potential (and who are not pleased with their prospects) are likely to be unavailable to provide mentoring functions (see Chapter Four). Similarly, individuals who have not experienced developmental relationships earlier in their careers are unlikely to have the intuitive and interpersonal skills to cultivate supportive alliances with junior colleagues. Relationships in which either individual feels uncomfortable and inadequate evolve into destructive experiences where resentment, anger, and frustration, or, at best, superficial interaction develop.

Negative mentoring experiences, in which either colleague feels undermined, smothered, or abandoned, can be minimized by making participation in a formal mentoring system voluntary. Screening procedures can help individuals think through a decision to participate, and data can be collected to facilitate a good match between potential mentors and proteges (Phillips-Jones, 1982). However, the formal system that is endorsed by an organization's management makes it unlikely that such a program will be completely voluntary. Subtle pressures will exist for individuals to participate regardless of their private reservations; these reservations can lead to destructive experiences.

Voluntary participation in a mentoring program reduces the risk of a destructive relationship; it cannot, however, eliminate the negative reactions from those who were not selected to participate or from those who are affected by the arranged relationships. For example, in a mentoring system designed for high potential candidates, juniors who are not labeled as such may feel deprived, resentful, and pessimistic about their own opportunities for development. Similarly, in a mentoring program designed to facilitate affirmative action goals, majority group members may become resentful of the guidance and support offered to special interest group members. These side effects affect relationships among peers as well as individuals' long-term commitment to the organization.

Even if a formal mentoring system is available to all employees, immediate supervisors of the juniors may become uncomfortable and threatened by these new alliances. The risk of losing influence over the performance and career decisions of a subordinate increases as the bond between mentor and protege strengthens. It is essential to involve the immediate supervisor in the process of arranging the pairs so that a sense of powerlessness and resentment does not evolve. At the same time, the arranged relationship may not ever be entirely acceptable to an immediate supervisor since, in practice, some of his or her responsibilities are infringed upon with the explicit mentor relationship.

The risks of a formal mentoring system are high, and the potential benefits have not been clearly demonstrated. However, certain conditions can reduce some of the risks. First, participation should be voluntary, and some systematic screening procedure should be used to enhance the decision to participate as well as to match mentors and proteges. Second, top management support is essential to convey the serious intent of the program and its importance in developing human resources for the organization. Third, education should be provided in order to increase individuals' understanding of mentoring functions and interpersonal skills so that self-confidence is strengthened. Finally, flexibility is necessary so that mismatches can be gracefully ended, and pairs can continue relationships only as long as they fulfill needs.

These conditions are feasible but not easily achieved. Efforts to set up a formal mentoring program within the context of a career development program or a human resource development process should be monitored to insure that destructive consequences do not occur, and the potential benefits for both juniors and seniors are evident. The costs of a formal system are high and are only justifiable if juniors find guidance and support, seniors do not feel coerced or incompetent, and those who are not part of the formal arrangements do not feel resentful or deprived.

Aside from the practical difficulties inherent in creating an effective formal mentoring system, the premises on which this kind of structural intervention is based are of questionable validity. First, research to date indicates that mentoring relationships cannot be engineered but must emerge from the spontaneous and mutual involvement of two individuals who see potential value in relating to each other (Levinson, et al., 1978; Kram, 1980). Second, individuals are more likely to develop a variety of relationships that provide some mentoring functions, rather than meet all their developmental needs in one (Shapiro, et al., 1978; Rowe, 1980, Chapter 6). Thus, expecting that a formal relationship should provide most or all of the mentoring functions for a junior person is unrealistic and may be destructive for both junior and senior colleagues.

The basic intent of a formal mentoring program has value for both individuals and for organizations. However, in examining the potential risks and benefits, it appears that alternative structural change and educational strategies may ultimately have greater positive impact. Opportunities for interaction and pairing of juniors and seniors can be created through appropriate task design, reward systems, and performance management systems, and individuals can be offered the education that will help them develop the requisite interpersonal skills. These strategies increase the likelihood that juniors and seniors will find each other, and decrease the risks associated with formalizing such developmental alliances.

The discussion of educational and structural change strategies designed to encourage mentoring highlights the potential benefits and limitations of each type. While education can increase knowledge about and positive attitudes toward mentoring and develop interpersonal skills, these will not have much impact if organizational conditions do not support changed attitudes and behaviors back on the job. At the same time, structural changes can influence behavior by establishing new stimuli and reinforcements that encourage relationship-building activities. However, individuals resist these interventions without adequate understanding of or skills for the proposed changes. Thus, both types of strategies are necessary. The combination and sequencing of alternatives can only be chosen through systematic diagnosis of the particular context in which mentoring is desired.

## CHOOSING A STRATEGY

Since effective mentoring requires considerable personal involvement and commitment of time, energy, and human resources, a strategy to create conditions that encourage developmental alliances must be based on a thorough understanding of organization members' attitudes, knowledge, and skills, as well as the nature of systems, structures, and procedures which promote or interfere with relationship-building efforts. With this understanding, it is possible to define which educational programs and/or structural changes will remove major obstacles.

The value of an *organizational development* approach for determining and implementing the strategy cannot be overstated. Beer (1980) offers a definition of *organizational development* which illustrates how this approach leads to effective intervention.

> Organizational Development is a system-wide process of data collection, diagnosis, action-planning, intervention, and evaluation aimed at: 1) enhancing congruence between organizational structure, process, strategy, people, and culture; 2) developing new and creative organizational solutions; and 3) developing the organization's self-renewing capacity. It occurs through collaboration of organizational members working with a change agent using behavioral science theory, research, and technology. (p. 10)

Systematic diagnosis of the situation defines the obstacles to mentoring as well as the lack of fit between structure, process, strategy, and people that contributes to these obstacles. A collaborative approach among organization members suggests that data collection, diagnosis, and action planning will involve the target population for whom mentoring is desired, the management group who must commit resources and support, as well as the internal and/or external change agents who have the behavioral science knowledge and skill to orchestrate this process (see Figure 7–3).

## Data Collection

This approach to defining a strategy requires that individuals at all career stages be consulted about the factors that encourage or interfere with establishing effective relationships and that features of the organization, including the reward system, performance management systems, task design, and the organization's culture be examined as well. Only then will it be possible to identify which sequence of interventions is most feasible and most likely to have positive impact.

By systematically interviewing members of relevant groups, data can be collected to determine the appropriate objectives and systems. Some objectives include, for example, providing mentoring for women and minorities, enhancing mentoring for all employees, and expanding career development processes in the organization. The systems involved may include one department, the entire organization, or one division. It is also important to analyze the willingness and capability of members to support the proposed objectives and required change and the resources available to support the established goals and strategy (Beckhard, 1969).

**Figure 7–3.**    Creating Conditions That Encourage Mentoring. Guidelines for Developing a Change Strategy.

1.  ESTABLISH THE OBJECTIVES AND SCOPE FOR THE PROJECT.

    What is the population in need of mentoring?
    What population can provide mentoring?
    Are resources available for a system-wide change or a smaller-scale departmental change?

2.  COMPLETE A DIAGNOSIS OF THE FEATURES THAT ARE CREATING OBSTACLES TO MENTORING, AND IDENTIFY ALTERNATIVE METHODS FOR ALLEVIATING THESE.

    Which features are discouraging relationship-building efforts? The reward system? The design of work? The culture? The absence of effective performance management systems? Individuals' attitudes, assumptions, or skills?
    Which educational and structural change strategies are feasible? Which would address the obstacles identified?
    Are there other change efforts, or established programs, underway in which a strategy to encourage mentoring could be incorporated?
    Who needs to be involved in choosing the appropriate strategy so that requisite management support is provided and resistance is minimized?

3.  IMPLEMENT THE STRATEGY.

    Which should happen first, education or structural change(s)?
    Who should be consulted and involved in implementation?
    What depth of intervention is required in order to accomplish the objectives?

4.  EVALUATE THE IMPACT OF THE INTERVENTION AND ASSESS APPROPRIATE NEXT STEPS.

    How did individuals respond?
    What other interventions are needed to support the desired changes in attitudes and behavior?
    Who needs to be informed of the impact of intervention in order to insure long-term support for the change?

The data collection phase of an organizational development approach lays the foundation for a collaborative approach. Organization members develop a sense of responsibility for the proposed changes and actually manage the definition and implementation of both educational and structural change strategies (Beckhard & Harris, 1976; Beer, 1980). Resistance to change is then minimized because organization members participate in creating the objectives, design, and implementation (Alderfer & Brown, 1975). One cannot sit in a private office and decide whether to change the reward system or provide training on mentoring; rather, one must interview organization members and policy makers in order to produce a strategy that responds to the situation and is acceptable to those who must support implementation.

## Diagnosis and Action Planning

These phases include synthesizing the information gathered and then identifying possible alternative actions. For example, if the data suggest that bottom-line results are rewarded and people development activities are perceived as unimportant then changes in the reward system are necessary. Similarly, if individuals have no understanding or experience with developmental relationships and how they can support career advancement and personal growth at each career stage, then educational programs are needed. Finally, the data may suggest factors that already encourage mentoring behavior. Task design may already foster frequent interaction between juniors and seniors, or performance appraisal systems may already enable managers to provide some mentoring functions to their subordinates. These supporting factors should be acknowledged during the diagnosis and built upon during the action planning process.

It is essential to assess alternative strategies in light of other change processes and developmental efforts. Are there programs already underway, such as a management development program, in which a strategy to encourage mentoring could be incorporated? Who needs to be involved in choosing the appropriate option for the requisite management support? Is the objective to encourage mentoring a realistic one given current business conditions and the culture and practices of the organization? As these questions are answered, the appropriate intervention becomes evident.

## Intervention

There is no one way to intervene in any situation, but a number of strategies can lead to the same end (Nadler & Tushman, 1980). The choice and sequencing of educational and structural change strategies has to be made on the basis of predicting the potential costs and benefits of each alternative. It is always useful to anticipate possible resistance and how it could be addressed (Watson, 1969; Zaltman & Duncan, 1977; Kotter & Schlesinger, 1979).

In creating conditions to encourage mentoring, resistance could be encountered among the group of potential mentors, potential proteges, or senior management staff. The potential mentors may be resistant because they have never received mentoring and/or they are experiencing such blocked opportunity that the desire to support junior colleagues has been extinguished by poor career development prospects for themselves. The potential juniors may be resistant because they do not trust senior managers to have their interests at heart, or they do not respect the competence and advice of senior colleagues, or they do not have the attitudes and skills required to initiate relationships with potential mentors. Finally, senior management groups may be resistant because of a results orientation that overrides any energy directed to people development objectives. Each of these sources of resistance must be considered; if they are evident in the diagnostic phases, then they must become a focus for intervention (Lewin, 1951; Benne, Bennis & Chin, 1969).

Education frequently minimizes resistance to change (Beer, 1980). For example, if senior management is dominated by a results orientation, it is useful to begin a strategy with a presentation on the role of mentoring in career development of organization members and data that indicate the need for attention to this matter. Similarly, if juniors and/or seniors are uninformed or skeptical about the value of mentoring, a similar presentation at an established educational program increases knowledge and modifies attitudes toward the importance of relationship-building activities.

If resistance is due to infrequent interaction between juniors and seniors or poor career prospects and declining attitudes about self-worth, then structural interventions are warranted. If situational factors contribute to a sense that relationships and people don't count or to resentment and self-doubt on the part of potential mentors because they are stuck (Kanter, 1977), then the only way to reduce this resistance is to modify key systems and practices. And if these poor conditions cannot be changed, then fostering effective mentoring should be postponed until the situation improves.

Harrison (1970) has suggested that the depth of intervention should be no deeper than required in order to achieve the objectives for change, nor should the depth of intervention go beyond the energy and resources that can be committed by system members. Since relationships

that provide mentoring functions require that individuals have particular interpersonal skills, educational programs will be necessary
unless the organization's members are unusually skilled and knowledgeable. At the same time, however, if limited resources make it impossible
for education to be offered or attended, or if a change in the design of
work or the reward system requires more study and human effort than
can be allocated, then consideration should be given to the decision of
not intervening at all.

## Evaluation

The process of organizational development and change is a dynamic
one, and major phases of data collection, diagnosis, action planning,
intervention, and evaluation do not unfold one by one but are reiterated
over time (Kolb, 1979). As each strategy is implemented and evaluated,
data are generated, a new diagnosis evolves, and ideas for further
intervention can be defined. For example, a decision to begin with an
educational program might result in data from participants that new
behaviors are difficult to implement within the current organizational
context. As a consequence of this evaluation, the reward system may be
modified or performance management systems may be strengthened in
order to create ways to provide mentoring functions. If these structural
changes are implemented, a subsequent evaluation and further
diagnosis may point to further education or modifications in other
systems in order to insure congruence between structure, people, process, strategy, and culture (Beer, 1980; Nadler & Tushman, 1980).

The steps involved in defining a strategy highlight the complexities of
creating conditions to encourage mentoring. Often organizations want
to find a solution which can be implemented quickly and efficiently; yet
this approach guarantees resistance from those who are affected by the
change and will fall short of achieving the desired objectives. For example, the introduction of a formal mentoring system without careful data
collection, diagnosis, and action planning, produces superficial relationships that provide no mentoring functions, destructive interactions
that hurt both juniors and seniors, and resentment and anxiety about
what is expected of managers.

## IMPLICATIONS

An organizational development approach to encourage mentoring
insures that efforts to alleviate obstacles to relationship-building
activities are relevant, acceptable, and have the intended impact (Beer,
1980). In addition, this approach requires a systematic process of data

collection, diagnosis, action planning, and evaluation. This implies that strategies which are effective in one setting may be inappropriate in another and that an organization must consider its objectives and resources carefully when choosing among educational and structural change possibilities. Frequently, organizations choose the intervention that appears most efficient in order to conserve resources. Yet, this same alternative is inadequate in altering the systems that create the most significant obstacles.

One example of an inappropriate strategy is the instance where an organization decides to set up a formal mentoring system for women and minority engineers in an attempt to support affirmative action objectives. While setting up formal relationship pairs appears to address the fact that these special interest group members do not have access to senior colleagues as much as majority groups members do, it fails to facilitate relationships that provide mentoring functions. First, senior engineers resent the new responsibility and feel inadequate for the task. Second, the reward system does not recognize energy directed toward subordinate development. Finally, those who have not been matched with a mentor, the white males in particular, become resentful and angry. What appears to be a good answer to the obstacles to cross-gender and interracial mentoring creates a number of negative consequences.

The introduction of a formal mentoring system, while a solution to the lack of effective mentoring, is a high risk strategy. Those who are matched may resent the formalized relationship, and those who are not matched may feel deprived. Without skill training and a reward system that encourages mentoring alliances, participants become frustrated even if they are initially enthusiastic about the program.

A systematic diagnosis of the situation is needed, as is an identification of the sequence of educational interventions and structural change strategies that will create conditions for effective mentoring. For example, if opportunities for interaction among those who might build relationships is lacking, then changes in task design, performance management systems, or cross-hierarchical contact may be needed. If organizational members do not understand the role of mentoring or if they do not have the requisite interpersonal skills, then education is warranted. Finally, if people development and relationship-building activities are unimportant in promotion decisions, then changes in the reward system will have to be made.

An organizational development approach points out the need to involve individuals at all levels and career stages in the diagnosis and action planning and evaluation phases. Each phase of the process is enhanced by having representatives of major interest groups involved.

Thus, senior management, junior members, and senior members should be consulted, and a pool of representatives should participate in the planning and implementation of educational and structural change strategies. A temporary project team, with the primary objective of proposing and managing the strategy designed to create conditions that encourage mentoring, should be designated (Beckhard & Harris, 1976; Alderfer, 1976; Beer, 1980).

The discussion of strategies designed to encourage mentoring has been aimed, primarily, at the human resource staff specialist or the line manager who wants to foster career development. From either position, an organizational development approach can define what sequence of education and structural changes is best. The human resource specialist must elicit the support and involvement of line personnel and, similarly, the line manager requires assistance from staff members who have the behavioral science knowledge and technology to facilitate diagnosis and intervention. Multiple perspectives from organization members representing different groups contribute to a comprehensive understanding of the obstacles that must be addressed in order to nurture mentoring processes.

Finally, individuals can use this framework to enhance their own relationship-building opportunities as well. If one is lacking the interpersonal skills to initiate relationships with senior colleagues, then steps to enroll in either in-house or public educational programs that enhance skills and knowledge in this area are useful. If, on the other hand, one finds few opportunities to meet with potential seniors then steps to redesign the work should be explored. Similarly, if there is uncertainty concerning the extent to which relationship-building activities will be rewarded, questions should be asked about the reward system. Such actions for one's own development can also serve as a catalyst for change in the organization by heightening others' awareness of the factors which inhibit quality relationships and effective career development.

8

# Mentoring in Perspective

Managers' personal accounts have made it possible to develop a comprehensive understanding of mentoring at work. These case histories have also prompted consideration of a wide range of relationships in organizations that have the potential to support psychosocial and career development. With each successive study, a clearer definition of mentoring has evolved, and the individual and organizational factors which shape developmental relationships have been identified.

Five commonly shared misconceptions about mentoring have been clearly dispelled in this book. Following is a realistic view of mentoring that accounts for its potential benefits, limitations, and variations. Then, in summarizing several guidelines for action are specific steps that can be taken to improve the quality of relationships and career development practices in organizations. Finally, the chapter ends with a proposed future agenda that employees, managers, human resources specialists, and organizational researchers are urged to pursue.

## MISCONCEPTIONS ABOUT MENTORING _____

Research clearly indicates that mentoring has been aggrandized by trade media and by the popular press. It has been presented as the answer to all career development problems, it has been oversimplified as a relationship that is easily created and maintained, and it has been viewed as the solution to sometimes unrelated career problems or obstacles. A more realistic and complex view of this kind of developmental relationship makes it a more valuable resource. If the potential benefits and limitations are understood, individuals and organizations will create conditions so that mentoring can help in the socialization of newcomers, as well as allow for creative expression of those with experience and wisdom to share.

**The first misconception is that the primary beneficiary in a mentor relationship is the junior person.** It is easy to recognize the benefits to the individual who is launching a new career and entering the adult world of work (Levinson, et al., 1978; Dalton, et al., 1977; Hall, 1976; Schein, 1978). A relationship with a senior colleague that provides a range of developmental functions including sponsorship, coaching, exposure-and-visibility, protection, challenging work, role modeling, counseling, acceptance-and-confirmation, and friendship, enables the novice to learn the ropes of organizational life, to prepare for advancement, and to develop competence and self-confidence. It is less obvious how these functions benefit the senior colleague as well.

The study of relationships between junior and senior managers identified significant benefits for the more senior colleagues (see Chapters 2, 3, and 4). These individuals, generally in midcareer, found in a mentor relationship technical and psychological support from loyal subordinates. They were recognized by peers and superiors for effectively developing talent. Finally, they received internal satisfaction from passing on wisdom, thus helping younger colleagues grow while leaving a mark on the next generation of managers.

Mentor relationships respond well to the developmental tasks of midlife and midcareer. They meet generative needs that are likely to become important at this stage, and provide an alternative purpose or project for those who are no longer focused on advancing their own careers. Thus, this kind of developmental relationship is a reciprocal one; it satisfies the needs of both individuals.

The mutuality and reciprocity of a mentor relationship has several implications. First, juniors should not assume that they are the only ones to benefit from these relationships; this understanding may alleviate guilt about requesting coaching from a mentor figure. Second, seniors who have not experienced the mentoring role may want to experiment with it, particularly if they are searching for new areas of involvement at work. Finally, organizations should realize that both newcomers and midcareer employees benefit from these developmental relationships.

**The second misconception is that a mentor relationship is always a positive experience for both individuals.** While this kind of developmental relationship benefits both juniors and seniors, it is limited in its duration and value as individual needs and organizational circumstances change. A mentor relationship generally lasts from two to five years and, under certain conditions, it can become destructive for one or both individuals (see Chapter 3).

Several factors can cause a mentor relationship to evolve into one that interferes with career advancement or contributes to a negative self-concept or lack of well being. For example, when a junior manager enters a stage of development in which testing independence is important, she may no longer welcome or even tolerate coaching from a mentor. Or, if a junior manager wants but doesn't get a promotion out of the mentor's department or to the mentor's organizational level, he may resent and feel smothered in the relationship.

Alternately, if a senior enters midlife and has a crisis of esteem or internal conflict, he may become so self-absorbed that no energy remains for coaching and counseling. If a senior is passed over for a promotion, or reaches a career plateau, she may feel angry, resentful, or depressed and may take it out on the junior colleague who faces unlimited opportunities. Finally, the senior colleague may feel unappreciated and threatened by the junior colleague's increasing competence and self-confidence, since he may be surpassed or no longer valued as a mentor.

Organizational factors can cause a mentor relationship to become destructive as well. If, for example, the reward system in an organization does not value people development and relationship-building activities, mentors will be less inclined to provide developmental functions and may even feel burdened by the responsibility of the relationship. Or, a senior who is passed over for a much wanted position may become depressed, hostile, and disinclined to counsel a younger colleague. Other promotion or transfer decisions can separate a junior and a senior so that continuing developmental functions becomes difficult. Then, either individual may feel abandoned or let down by the other.

In general, external events can distract either individual from it. In a slow economy, the lack of opportunity for movement creates feelings of resentment, smothering, or undermining, particularly for a junior seeking advancement. Or public scrutiny of a relationship by one's peers can cause either or both individuals to withdraw from a previously enhancing connection. This frequently occurs in cross-gender mentoring relationships where rumors of sexual involvement or favoritism cause distancing in the relationship (see Chapter 5). Changes in a mentor relationship that are due to organizational factors are often interpreted as a lack of interest or commitment, and this generates a lack of trust in a previously solid alliance.

**The third misconception is that mentor relationships look the same in all work settings.** While it is true that there is a common set of mentoring functions (see Chapter 2), mentor relationships vary across organizational settings in terms of the range of the functions provided, the length of time a relationship endures, and the level of intimacy and commitment achieved. Some of the variances can be explained.

The organization's culture either facilitates or inhibits the development of connections that allow for the widest range of career and psychosocial functions (Deal & Kennedy, 1982). For example, in very open systems where communication across hierarchical levels is valued and encouraged and where relationship-building activities are considered important, mentor relationships develop into close friendships. In contrast, in more closed systems where communication across hierarchical levels is limited in both frequency and depth, distance characterizes relationships and developmental functions are limited to career functions and perhaps some role modeling.

While we know that mentor relationships go through phases of initiation, cultivation, separation, and redefinition (see Chapter 3), the length and character of these phases will differ across work settings. For example, job rotation policies may push a relationship on to the separation phase so that in organizations where movement is frequent, relationships will be of shorter duration or of limited intimacy. Similarly, career pathing may force a junior colleague and a senior colleague to separate when otherwise critical developmental functions would emerge during the cultivation phase of their relationship. In growing organizations, advancement is more likely than in stable or declining organizations. In the latter, it may be difficult for individuals to enter the separation and redefinition phases of a mentor relationship without achieving a structural separation through job changes.

Whether mentor relationships are available to the average performer or only to high potential candidates also varies from setting to setting. If, for example, the reward system values development of all employees, not just those with high potential, mentoring will be available to a wider range of an organization's employees. Alternately, if the reward system values development of only those who have been labeled as high potential candidates, a wide range of employees will find it difficult to attain the mentoring they need.

Job designs also affect what developmental relationships look like, how they begin, and how they evolve over time. If jobs encourage collaboration between juniors and seniors, for example, mentor relationships will emerge easily around work tasks. On the other hand, if contact with seniors is possible only outside of regular work assignments, special events must be offered in order to create opportunities for interaction.

**The fourth misconception is that mentor relationships are readily available to those who want them.** It is sometimes presumed that if we define mentoring, people will then be able to build relationships that provide mentoring functions. In other words, mentor relationships in organizations are absent because individuals are unaware of the value of mentoring in career development. This is partly true; however, even with increased awareness there are still many obstacles that perpetuate the unavailability of mentoring to most individuals.

A significant obstacle is created because of the way an organization treats individuals at midcareer. For if managers at this stage are treated poorly in terms of continued growth and recognition, the number of potential mentors will decline. While individuals at midcareer appear to be the most likely candidates to provide mentoring functions in terms of their age and organizational experience, resentment and frustration in response to blocked opportunity may make them unavailable. And, as the organizational pyramid narrows, it becomes a challenge to continue to offer rewards and growth opportunities to individuals in midcareer. Only when creative responses that convey recognition and support to this population are implemented will this obstacle be alleviated.

More generally, the reward system can hinder the availability of mentoring. It frequently discourages attention to people and relationship development. The emphasis on short-term, bottom-line results causes many managers to ignore developmental responsibilities. In addition, the reward system that encourages mentoring may only do so for fast trackers; senior managers may be rewarded for coaching those already identified as having the potential for rapid advancement. A consequence of this is that many individuals are left out of the mentoring process.

Similarly, other organizational characteristics, including task design, the culture, and performance management systems, can create obstacles to relationships (see Chapter 7). Figuring out why mentoring is relatively unavailable to organizational members involves a systematic diagnosis of the obstacles to juniors and seniors building supportive alliances. Once these obstacles are identified, structural changes can be implemented to alleviate them.

The lack of self-awareness and interpersonal skills limits the availability of mentor relationships as well. If individuals do not understand what they need for relationships and developmental opportunities, they will be unable to actively manage their careers. Too often, for example, juniors do not have the skills to seek out the kinds of relationships they need. They take a passive stance toward potential mentors, hoping that someone will take an interest in their careers. Similarly, senior colleagues may also lack self-awareness and interpersonal skills. Educational programs that promote awareness and interpersonal skill development allow individuals at both early and midcareer stages to alleviate personal obstacles to building effective relationships.

These multiple influences are vividly illustrated in cross-gender relationships where psychosocial functions are frequently more limited than in same-gender relationships. While male mentors intend to aid young females' growth and advancement and the junior women want to find mentors who will provide guidance and support, both men and women encounter obstacles to creating developmental relationships. Collusion in stereotypical roles puts both in the position of discounting the junior's competence and strengths. Fears of intimacy and sexuality cause both to maintain distance so that an informal forum for counseling and friendship is prevented. Junior women find inadequate role models in their male mentors since the latter have not experienced similar personal and professional dilemmas. Or the stress associated with public scrutiny of these alliances causes both to proceed with caution (see Chapter 5). Even with an organizational commitment to Affirmative Action, it is difficult to achieve the full range of developmental functions in these relationships.

Cross-gender dynamics are one example of the added complexities of developmental relationships that involve individuals with significantly different historical group memberships (Alderfer, 1977; Babad et al., 1982). Differences in sex, race, ethnicity, socioeconomic background, or educational background can thwart the initial expectations of a mutually beneficial alliance and the unconscious identification process that frequently sets a mentor relationship in motion. Self-awareness and a repertoire of interpersonal skills are prerequisites for overcoming these additional barriers. It is not surprising that sponsorship, coaching, and counseling have been more readily available to white males, since those who can provide these developmental functions have historically had similar background characteristics (Kanter, 1977).

**The fifth misconception is that finding a mentor is the key to individual growth and career advancement.** As a result of recent attention to mentoring in both academic and trade journals, individuals launching careers often believe that they must find a mentor in order to be successful. Indeed, many look for specific guidelines on how to conduct an effective search. However, such an endeavor is an unwise use of personal energy and time. Individuals in early career should consider several relationships that can provide some of the mentoring functions they need. Similarly, individuals beyond the novice stage should consider how providing mentoring functions to junior colleagues might enhance their own growth and career satisfaction.

Given the limitations of mentor relationships, the fact that they are relatively unavailable to most individuals in organizations, and their potential destructiveness in certain situations, it is risky to rely on one individual for all developmental functions. Relationships with peers can also offer developmental functions, and individuals should develop a relationship constellation that consists of several relationships, each of which provides some career and/or psychosocial functions (see Chapter 6).

It is no longer disconcerting to encounter so many variations in developmental relationships. Shapiro, Hazeltine, and Rowe (1978) had, perhaps, the most foresight when they defined a continuum of support relationships, including peerpal, guide, sponsor, and mentor. And Phillips-Jones (1982) defined primary and secondary mentors, while Clawson (1979) illustrated how effective superior-subordinate relationships also provided a variety of developmental functions. These conceptualizations acknowledged that relationships vary in terms of their level of intensity, commitment, and exclusivity.

It is self-limiting to search for a mentor when one could build a relationship constellation. This nexus of relationships can support both psychosocial development and career advancement. It can include relationships with peers, mentors, bosses, friends, and family members. When an individual experiences stress, alienation, or disaffection at work, it is possible that his or her relationship constellation is not adequate in terms of the range of developmental functions that it provides. And, when relationships no longer provide critical functions, or as individuals transfer or leave, new relationships can be cultivated; no one person becomes essential to career advancement or to a sense of well-being.

## GUIDELINES FOR ACTION

A more complex and realistic view of mentoring offers a number of practical guidelines for both individuals and organizations. Individuals can use this perspective to identify strategies for building relationships that provide critical career and psychosocial functions. Those in managerial positions can use the framework to identify major obstacles to mentoring and then choose appropriate strategies for alleviating them. Finally, senior managers and human resources staffs with a system-wide concern for employee development can use an organizational development approach to determine which factors prevent individuals from developing relationships that support performance and growth.

An active stance toward managing relationships insures that individuals do not have to experience ongoing deprivation or resentment for not having the kinds of relationships that they need. If one's relationship constellation is still inadequate after identifying developmental tasks and relationship needs, assessing individuals who might provide critical developmental functions, and attempting to initiate relationships with senior colleagues and peers, the need to change jobs may be indicated. Frequently, however, this process will result in forming new relationships that are responsive to current personal and professional concerns.

Perhaps most empowering is the recognition that a variety of psychological and organizational factors shape relationships over time. This insight helps individuals understand and not assume blame when a relationship becomes less satisfactory or destructive due to forces outside of his or her control. For example, when a senior colleague enters a crisis of esteem after being passed over for a promotion, a younger colleague will not interpret withdrawal from a previously enhancing relationship as a personal rejection but as a consequence of organizational circumstances and a difficult transition in the senior's career.

Individuals at every career stage face complexities in managing relationships with those of different gender, race, or ethnicity. Women and minority group members sense the need for attention to these challenges because they are confronted with them daily. Female managers interviewed generally found mutual problem solving with their female peers extremely helpful in overcoming obstacles created by male-female dynamics. This kind of collaboration among peers who share group memberships will strengthen individuals' relationship skills. Networking inside organizations and across organizations is one way to encourage such collaboration (Metha, 1979; Welch, 1980).

Individuals with managerial responsibilities should consider how they can create conditions that encourage effective mentoring. They can do this by modeling effective relationships with subordinates and peers that provide a range of career and psychosocial functions. In addition, they can identify the organizational features that interfere with relationship building and then act to change these. Finally, they can encourage members of their departments to attend educational programs that will heighten self-awareness, understanding of the role of developmental relationships in careers, and interpersonal skills.

As role models, managers can show their departments the importance of relationship-building activities. When a manager conveys the importance of mentoring functions verbally and also provides the functions to subordinates, he or she is an example as well as a guide to others on how to do the same. Alternatively, the manager who is solely results-oriented and who pays little attention to developmental needs of his or her subordinates is unlikely to encourage others in the department to devote attention to relationships that aid psychosocial development or career advancement.

With or without the assistance of a human resources specialist, a manager can invite department members to identify existing obstacles to effective mentoring. Predictably, obstacles will involve some aspect of the reward system, task design, performance management systems, the culture of the organization, or individuals' skills and attitudes. For example, a manager with the help of his department modified the work design to create project teams that facilitate frequent interaction among junior and senior engineers who have the potential to form complementary developmental relationships. In another instance, a manager recognized how the rewards that she dispensed were entirely based on financial results and did not take mentoring activities into account. By changing the criteria for pay increases and promotions to include attention to subordinate development, she encouraged individuals to view relationship-building efforts as an important part of their responsibilities.

There are a number of situations which should prompt organizations to examine whether mentoring processes are as effective as they could be. If, for example, turnover among newcomers is high, it may be that the socialization of novices is not sufficient and that relationships with senior colleagues that aid learning the ropes are not available. Or, a low retention rate among women and minority group members might indicate that special interest group members are not receiving sufficient mentoring at critical points in their careers. Finally, several common problems among midcareer and late career individuals, including depression, anxiety, anger, or withdrawal, may indicate that these populations are not positively engaged or challenged by their work, and that there are considerable costs in their not embracing the mentor role.

These scenarios have several characteristics in common. Each creates stress and personal or professional dilemmas that can hamper individual performance and a sense of well-being. In addition, each reflects less than optimal human resources management and, thus, losses in organizational effectiveness. Finally, if the cause of these problems is related to the quality and availability of developmental relationships, strategies for improvement do exist.

An organization that has any of these symptoms must systematically assess whether they are related to the quality of relationships between juniors and seniors or among peers. A diagnostic process that collects data from the target population, and this group's involvement in analyzing the data, results in a valid understanding of the factors which are causing turnover, poor performance, or depression and withdrawal.

For example, in the instance of high turnover among newcomers, it is essential to find out what experiences contribute to alienation and disaffection. It may be that first jobs are not sufficiently challenging, or that opportunities for advancement are not apparent, or that those who leave are a poor fit with the organization (Schein, 1978; Berlew & Hall, 1966; Webber, 1976; Van Maanen, 1976). If one of the factors identified is the experience of isolation or the absence of coaching and guidance in learning the ropes, then relationships with senior colleagues and peers that provide critical developmental functions are lacking. Systematic diagnosis will indicate whether changes in initial job assignments have to be made, whether opportunities for advancement and growth have to be augmented, and whether developmental relationships have to be more actively encouraged.

Similarly, in diagnosing the problem of low retention among talented women and minority group members, systematic data from representatives of these groups will clarify whether the socialization experiences of these individuals are dysfunctionally stressful (Van Maanen, 1976; Webber, 1976). If individuals are isolated, lack information, and lack support in learning the ropes and developing competence in a new job, then the quality and availability of developmental relationships are inadequate (Kanter, 1977; Hennig & Jardim, 1977; Missirian, 1982; Phillips-Jones, 1982). This may not be the only factor, but it is certainly an important one in guiding action.

Finally, it is not uncommon for organizations to encounter mid-career employees who are plateaued and depressed or psychologically withdrawn from their work (Hall, 1980). Generally, this has been associated with the midlife transition or with the fact of blocked opportunity and no further outlets for personal growth and development (Levinson et al., 1978; Kanter, 1977). These individuals are unavailable to provide mentoring to junior colleagues and they contribute far less than their potential toward organizational objectives. Redirecting energies toward subordinate development can alleviate negative symptoms and provide more enhancing relationships for both juniors and seniors. This is accomplished by changing the reward system, job expectations, and/or the culture to encourage mentoring activities.

There are no ready-made solutions for the problems just described, but we do know that the location of the initial concern determines the appropriate strategy for action. For example, the middle manager who observes considerable depression and withdrawal among his or her peers must spark the interest of human resources staff members or senior management personnel in order to gain the leverage required for educational or structural change strategies. Similarly, the young adult just launching a career who knows that guidance, coaching and support from senior colleagues is lacking for many at the same career stage must gain the attention of the staff reponsible for socialization of new employees and, ultimately, the support of policymakers who can alter current practices. Finally, a human resources specialist who is acutely aware of personal and organizational losses created by the lack of developmental relationships must demonstrate a need to gain the resources and support to make significant changes in structures and practices that create obstacles to effective mentoring in the organization.

Currently, few systematic evaluations of change efforts designed to enhance mentoring processes have been completed. Some organizations have established formal mentoring programs only to discover a number of unanticipated consequences. This approach has considerable limitations in terms of the quality of relationships that are engineered by a formal system and the reactions of both participants and non-participants (see Chapter 7). Alternative educational and structural change strategies have been proposed to create conditions that increase the quality and availability of relationships that provide a range of developmental functions. These include education for individuals at different career stages as well as modifications in the reward system, work design, performance management systems, and/or the organization's culture. Prior change efforts indicate that a collaborative approach to choosing the appropriate strategy is most likely to succeed.

## FUTURE AGENDA

There are still a number of questions about developmental relationships and their long-term consequences, about career development for those who don't experience the traditional male model of career advancement, and about how organizational contexts can enhance development at every career stage (Hunt & Michael, 1983). These comprise a substantial agenda for future collaborative efforts among researchers, human resources practitioners, and organizations' members.

First, there are many questions that involve differences in gender, race, or ethnicity. While progress has been made in understanding the complexities of cross-gender relationships, strategies for managing them effectively have yet to be evaluated. In addition, these complexities, while somewhat relevant to interracial relationships, may not adequately describe the characteristics of relationships of individuals with different group memberships (Alderfer, 1977; Babad et al., 1982). These relationships have personal and organizational obstacles that make them less available to women and minority group members. Thus, if Affirmative Action is to be realized, and individuals are to receive developmental functions that aid advancement in early and middle career years, these obstacles must be identified and alleviated. The dynamics created by diversity in the workforce, as well as educational and/or structural change strategies should be investigated.

Similarly, it is important to consider the dynamics of mentor relationships in which the senior colleague is close in age or younger than the junior colleague. With more individuals entering the workforce or changing careers at midlife, this will occur more frequently. Competition will be more significant, particularly if the junior feels that previous experiences make him or her as competent as the senior who can offer mentoring functions. In addition, the senior colleague may feel threatened or unable to coach someone older. When career and life stages are out of sync individuals may encounter dynamics that are difficult to manage.

Progress has also been made in understanding the role of peer relationships in supporting career development and personal growth at every career stage. Both relationships between juniors and seniors and relationships among peers can provide developmental functions. The relationship constellation is the nexus of relationships that provides a wide range of developmental functions for an individual. Understanding the predictable personal and professional dilemmas at each career stage suggests that relationship constellations vary in terms of the functions provided and which kinds of relationships dominate during each stage. For example, relationships with mentors may be more important in early career, while relationships with peers more important in late career. To the extent that patterns do exist, strategies for personal career management and employee development can be identified.

Our understanding of relationships in organizations and their role in career and psychosocial development is still in the infancy stage. Though relationships providing developmental functions are important at every career stage, individual differences about the role of relationships or inclinations to engage in certain relationships have yet to be delineated. It has been suggested that women may be more relationship-oriented due to their sex-role socialization (Gilligan, 1982). This may suggest, then, that relationship constellations look different for men and women. Also, relationships in youth, including relationships with parents, teachers, and siblings, may affect inclinations toward potential mentors and peers (Levinson, 1976; Zaleznik, 1977). This may suggest, then, that some gravitate toward seniors, others toward peers, and still others operate primarily without developmental relationships.

If there are significant differences in relationship needs among individuals with different experiences, then what are the long-term consequences of experiencing or not experiencing mentoring during the early career years? Among a group of successful top officials, a large percentage had been mentored earlier in their careers (Roche, 1979). This suggests that relationships with seniors do aid advancement, but it does not explain the effect of these relationships on psychosocial development, or how those who did not reach the top differed in their relationships and other work experiences. Longitudinal studies that follow individuals through periods of stability and transition are needed.

If the consequences of different relationship constellations are clarified, then can individuals be trained to build enhancing relationships at each stage of development? What personal attributes characterize those who provide mentoring functions and benefit from assuming a generative role, and what personal attributes enable individuals to initiate relationships with senior colleagues and peers? Research indicates that mentors generally achieve self-acceptance and self-awareness and are satisfied with their accomplishments, before they assume the advisor role. Young adults who have had positive relationships with parents or teachers, and who seek out supportive relationships with those in authority positions, are likely to establish satisfactory mentor relationships. Even if prototypes are defined can adults learn the appropriate attitudes and interpersonal skills?

Destructive relationships between juniors and seniors evolved when the senior encountered blocked opportunity and entered a period of self-doubt. This finding suggested that the treatment of individuals during the midcareer years could significantly shape the extent to which this population would effectively mentor younger colleagues. The psychological and organizational forces that shape midcareer experiences should be investigated in order to prevent stagnation and self-doubt, and to insure continued growth. With this understanding, organizations will be able to create conditions that improve the quality of life at work for midcareer individuals and, at the same time, increase the availability of mentoring for those in the early career period.

Similarly, there is a need to delineate the developmental tasks that women face in adult and career stages. How do these affect their experiences in relationships as well as their long-term career development? The task of developing a professional identity is different for women in their twenties and thirties as they grapple with integrating family and work roles (Stewart, 1976; Scarf, 1980; Gilligan, 1982). In addition, women's experiences with learning the ropes and preparing for advancement are different from those of men's (Kanter, 1977). Finally, the experiences, stresses, and challenges of older, successful women need to be examined to understand the role of relationships in their development and the factors that sometimes interfere with their assuming mentoring responsibilities.

A more complete model of adult female development is an essential element in any research program designed to understand the role of relationships in career development. It would greatly enhance potential mentors' understanding of the personal and professional dilemmas women face. It would help women manage their careers and seek out developmental relationships that are most responsive to their needs. It would also show organizations how to alleviate major roadblocks to women forming alliances that facilitate career advancement and personal development. Certainly, similar investigations should be undertaken to understand the developmental issues for other special interest groups as well.

Similar investigations should be undertaken to understand the developmental issues for other special interest groups that differ from the traditional models of adult male development. Individuals of color will encounter unique personal and professional dilemmas as they attempt to establish themselves and to advance in mostly white organizations. In addition, individuals who are launching new careers at midlife will encounter unique concerns about competence and relationships with authority as they take on the role of novice with years of life experience behind them. A better understanding of these differences would offer insight into the obstacles to effective mentoring for those who don't fit the traditional male model of career advancement.

Finally, the impact of the organizational context on relationships and career development needs to be investigated further. In this research program, organizational features that affect relationship dynamics have been delineated. However, comparative studies of relationships in different organizations would provide empirical tests of the effects of different contexts on relationships. While it has been suggested that the reward system, the culture of an organization, the performance management systems, and the individuals' attitudes and skills shape the quality of relationships, it is still necessary to identify the major consequences of various organizational forms.

This suggests, too, the need to assess the value of educational and structural change strategies that have been proposed to create conditions that encourage mentoring. This would determine to what extent education enables individuals to complete the psychological work and develop the interpersonal skills required to build effective alliances at work. In addition, it would determine how changes in organizational structures and processes encourage and facilitate the formation of complementary developmental relationships. Collaboration among researchers, human resources specialists, policymakers, and organizational members would increase the likelihood that systematic diagnosis, intervention, and evaluation will contribute to both theory and practice.

Attention to the quality of relationships between juniors and seniors and among peers is critical for effective employee development, a satisfactory quality of worklife, and organizational effectiveness. This premise shaped the direction of the work reported here, and it has led to a future agenda which promises to be both challenging and fruitful.

# APPENDIX
# The Research
# Methodology

My program of research began with a study of relationships between junior and senior managers in one corporate setting. Pairs of managers were interviewed individually about their career histories and about their relationships with each other. This study contributed to understanding the nature of mentor relationships and defining a broader conception of developmental relationships. In addition, the project stimulated new questions about the role of peer relationships in career development and provided the impetus for a second study. Individuals at three different career stages in a second organization were interviewed about their significant relationships with peers in their work setting, and one or two significant others were interviewed as well. The interview methodology paralleled that used in the first study. These two studies not only produced insight and theory but also delineated a research methodology for investigating the nature of relationships in organizations and their role in adult and career development.

In these studies, methodological decisions were guided by the assumption that an appropriate research strategy emerges from considering the interaction of the problem, the method, and the researcher (Reinharz, 1979). Thus, the resolution of predictable issues was shaped by how I defined the research problem, the feasibility of alternative methods, and the skills, interests, and personal values that I brought to the research task.

First, my definition of the research problem for each study was influenced by an open systems perspective on behavior in organizations (Alderfer, 1976; Nadler & Tushman, 1980; Rice, 1965). This perspective suggested that to understand developmental relationships would be achieved only if I considered psychological and organizational factors. I set out to investigate how individuals' career histories and current situations, as well as the surrounding organizational context, contributed to these alliances with mentors, peers, or proteges. In addition, since both studies involved investigating relatively unexplored phenomena, they required an exploratory research method that would generate theory and hypotheses (Glaser & Strauss, 1967).

A flexible data collection method was needed to find unpredicted aspects of the phenomenon (Filstead, 1970). Since so little was known about the intrapersonal, interpersonal and organizational processes that shape developmental relationships, I could not predetermine exactly what questions to ask of the research population. Since I needed flexibility to explore unanticipated interesting questions, I found an in-depth qualitative interview method most appropriate (Glaser & Strauss, 1967). In addition, my interest in understanding individuals' personal experiences of significant relationships at work influenced definition of the research problem. My bias toward the importance of subjective experience guided the focus of both studies.

Finally, my choice of method helped me obtain rich descriptive accounts of personal experiences. Qualitative research helps conduct "inquiry from the inside" (Evered & Louis, 1980), and, in the interpretative tradition (Morgan & Smircich, 1980), it relies heavily on interpretation of data provided by the personal accounts of research participants. The researcher and research participant must have a mutual desire to learn, high trust, and self-disclosure, as well as the opportunity for confidential and systematic exploration of issues (Argyris, 1970). This relationship could best be established in an interview context.

In sum, the influences of problem, method, and person led first to a decision to conduct an in-depth interview study of relationship pairs in one organizational context, and then to conduct a parallel in-depth interview study of peer relationships in another organizational context. These decisions had a tradeoff of generalizability for richness and depth of understanding of the complexities of developmental relationships. Theory and hypotheses were generated for future studies. These decisions also shaped subsequent actions concerning the identification and recruitment of research participants, the design and implementation of the interview method, and the design and implementation of the descriptive analyses. A discussion of these components of the research methodology highlights how each evolved.

## SETTINGS AND SAMPLES

The location of research sites and the identification of research participants required a sequence of decisions that shaped the research methodology. Each decision clarified what I wanted to learn, and at the same time I generated hypotheses about the nature of developmental relationships. Each study, from initial entry into the research setting, involved continuous recycling over questions and hypotheses that ultimately contributed to these new theories.

After initial discussions with several human resources staffs I decided to locate the first study of mentoring in one organization. This decision reflected an important tradeoff; I had an in-depth study of relationships in one organization, and I forfeited the possibility of varied characteristics that might influence the nature of developmental relationships. The primary focus of this study was to understand the dyadic relationship. This primary focus generated the initial hypotheses concerning the influence of the organizational context on developmental relationships. Cross-organizational comparisons were left for future research efforts.

The organizational choice was based on how likely the potential research sites were to support, cooperate, and value my research (Alderfer, 1976; Alderfer & Brown, 1975). I felt that the quality of interactions with potential organizational liaisons paralleled the quality of relationships I would establish with other members of the organization. I predicted that if an organization's human resources staff was open with me, showed interest in the research topic, and offered assistance in locating research participants, then other organizational members would likely do the same. One organization emerged as the most willing to collaborate on the research.

The first study was conducted in a large northeastern public utility with 15,000 employees. My initial discussion with two liaison individuals provided me with information about the organization. These initial meetings helped me learn about the culture of the organization and to shape the interview methodology so that questions would make sense to research participants. In exchange for the opportunity to conduct the study, I agreed to provide a written report of the study to research participants and to the Organization Development staff.

Throughout the study the two liaison individuals were an important sounding board and support system. I tested initial impressions and hypotheses with them and listened to their reactions for insights into my experiences with research participants. The loneliness that often accompanies immersion in the research process was somewhat alleviated by the opportunity to have this continuing dialogue. These individuals not only provided me with information and introduced me to the organization, but also helped debrief my experience at critical points during the study.

Since the primary purpose of both studies was to develop an understanding of developmental relationships, it made sense to locate relationship *pairs* so that I would be able to interview both individuals about their career histories and their experiences in the relationship.* I estimated that fifteen to twenty relationships would provide sufficient data to understand the essential dynamics of interest. As in any exploratory research, however, the exact size of the sample would be determined as the study progressed. When recurrent patterns clearly emerged from the interviews that shaped a descriptive theory, and the amount of significant new learning in successive interviews decreased substantially, data collection would be complete (Glaser & Strauss, 1967).

In the first study, junior managers between the ages of 25 and 35 who had three or more years of tenure in the organization were the target population. Theories of adult development and career development suggested that this group represented the population with the greatest need for mentoring (Levinson et al., 1978; Schein, 1978; Hall, 1976). If developmental relationships existed at all, they would most likely exist in this group. I decided to start with junior rather than senior managers since it was easier to identify relationship pairs working upward rather than downward. Senior managers are more likely to have multiple relationships with young managers, while young managers are more likely to have only one or two such relationships.

I identified three developmental relationships through interviews with a random sample of fifteen young managers that met the selection criteria. This low frequency suggested that either such relationships were not very common, or that the interview methodology failed to effectively identify developmental relationships. Continuing a random sampling would make the study unmanageable, requiring approximately 100 initial interviews to locate fifteen relationships. Therefore, I decided to obtain recommendations from the human resources staff of

---

*Previous studies of mentor and sponsor relationships involved interviews with only one member of the relationship. They generally involved retrospective accounts of a relationship that occurred earlier in one's career. It was assumed that *both* individuals' perspectives on a *current* relationship would enhance understanding of critical relationship dynamics.

young managers with developmental relationships. These recommendations located twelve young managers with developmental relationships. Interviews with these managers confirmed the data collection methodology, since all of these individuals identified one or two developmental relationships during the first interview session.*

Data were obtained on eighteen relationships (see Table 1-1). During the interviews with the fifteen young managers, two senior managers were identified as significant others by two of the young managers. These two senior managers were interviewed about both relationships on separate occasions. In addition, each of three young managers identified two senior managers who were equally important to them; in these instances both senior managers were contacted and interviewed. Finally, one young manager did not give permission for the senior manager to be contacted. Comparison of relationships involving the same senior managers and comparisons of relationships involving the same young manager contributed to the final descriptive analysis.

After these interviews were completed I decided to interview ten officers of the organization about their career histories and relationships that had contributed to their development. These interviews provided another perspective on the role of developmental relationships in career development in this organization. They supported the emergent theory that described current developmental relationships. This supplementary sample was similar to previous studies of mentoring that involved retrospective study of such relationships with successful top managers (Dalton et al., 1977; Phillips-Jones, 1982; Missirian, 1982). It was therefore possible to compare relationships in process (the primary research sample) with retrospective accounts in other studies.

From the participants in this study of mentor relationships I learned that relationships with peers frequently provide an important alternative to a primary developmental relationship with a senior manager. I then decided to do a parallel study of peer relationships and their role in supporting individual development. In this second study, my collaborators and I interviewed individuals at three different career stages in order to explore how peer relationships are affected by developmenal concerns that are unique in early, middle, or late career years. The open systems perspective brought to the research process illuminated the important influence of individuals' needs and developmental tasks in shaping relationship dynamics.

---

*This recruitment process forfeited the opportunity to assess how representative the final sample is of the general management population. This was an acceptable strategy based on the assumption that theoretical sampling is more important than statistical sampling in an exploratory qualitative study (Glaser & Strauss, 1967).

In this study of peer relationships we used a similar research methodology; the unit of analysis was the dyadic relationship, and through interviewing pairs in one organization, we were able to understand how individuals' needs and organizational circumstances shaped relationships with peers. Fifteen managers spanning the three age groups of 25–35, 36–45 and 46–65 were interviewed about their career histories and about relationships with colleagues that they felt supported their development. These individuals worked in a large Fortune 500 manufacturing firm. The liaison within the human resources department provided us with a list of names of potential participants from which we randomly drew a pool of fifteen. The requirements for this population were that they had been working for the organization for at least three years, that they were in professional or managerial jobs, that they were in one of our age categories, and that they might want to participate in an interview study.

In addition to the fifteen focal research participants, one or two significant others identified in the primary sample were interviewed about the relationships and about their career histories. Peers were identified by the focal research participants during the first interview of a two interview sequence. When they were asked which colleagues, friends at work, or peers had supported their development, they identified significant others who were similar in organizational rank or age. At the end of the initial interview, focal participants were asked to identify up to two important peer relationships. The majority identified two, while the remainder identified either one or no significant others (see Table 1–2).

Our final research sample consisted of twenty-five relationship pairs. More than half of the relationships involved individuals who were at the same organizational level. It appeared that the similarity in rank insured a variety of common experiences as well as a relative ease in initiating communication. Eight cases of "level" peers were of significantly different ages. These relationships took on qualities of a mentor relationship; that is, one person had more experience or knowledge and could coach his or her peer in some domains. Similarly, "age" peers, those of the same age but different organizational level, took on some qualities of a mentor relationship but were also peerlike in the sharing of personal dilemmas characteristic of their life stage.

The two research samples complemented each other well. The parallel interview sequences made it possible to compare data from the two studies. The range of developmental relationships became clearer as relationships between junior and senior colleagues were contrasted with relationships among peers. In addition, career histories of individuals at different career stages in both studies highlighted the functions of relationships at different points in a career. By combining the two samples we identified patterns in the developmental dilemmas unique to the female research participants and in the dynamics of cross-gender relationships. Finally, since the studies were conducted in two settings that differed in structural and process dimensions, we could measure how the organizational context shapes the course of developmental relationships.

Decisions about setting and sample involved some tradeoff. For example, while the small sample sizes permitted intensive interviews that resulted in understanding relationship dynamics and the individual and organizational forces that shape them, these also limited our ability to generalize the research findings. The theoretical sampling procedure facilitated generating theory and hypotheses; it did not let us study how frequently each type of relationship occurred. Similarly, while the functions of developmental relationships have been defined, and the benefits and limitations of these relationships clarified, further research is needed to determine to what extent different types of relationships are available to individuals at different career stages in different organizational contexts. Finally, while the two research sites offered some setting variety, cross-organizational studies are needed to see how organizational factors affect the phases of developmental relationships. However, the two samples of relationship pairs enabled a comprehensive study of ongoing relationships between junior and senior colleagues and among peers that enhance individual development. Our primary objective for the research program was achieved.

## DATA COLLECTION

In practice, data collection and data analysis cannot be separated in exploratory qualitative research. As interviews are conducted, insights emerge about the phenomenon being studied. These new insights influence the kinds of questions to ask in subsequent interviews. Thus, immediate analysis of interviews leads to revisions of the data collection method. Theory is generated through new hypotheses and research questions that emerge as data collection proceeds.

The structure of the interview evolved during the course of data collection; initially, pilot interviews and relevant literature shaped our general list of questions. As interviews were conducted and I learned more about developmental relationships, I refined questions to test emergent hypotheses. Thus, the final interviews were different from the initial ones; questions were more focused because I was a more knowledgeable investigator. In more controlled hypothesis-testing research this variation in interviews would cause concern. However, the evolutionary nature of data collection in exploratory research helps us understand the phenomenon.

## The Interview Process _____

Recruitment of research participants was facilitated by an introductory letter from the liaison individuals in the human resources staffs that endorsed the study and outlined its purpose and scope. These letters emphasized the voluntary nature of the study and presented the project as one designed to clarify the nature of relationships with senior colleagues (in the first study) or with peers (in the second study) that supported individuals' development and career advancement.

These introductory letters were followed by telephone calls which allowed potential research participants to ask questions about the nature of the study. Three individuals in both settings declined the invitation stating that recent participation in other studies made this current opportunity too demanding of their time and energy. In most instances, however, individuals were delighted to review their career histories with a trained interviewer who wanted to listen to their experiences.

Each study called for two two-hour interviews with each individual, although in some cases (particularly with significant others) only one session was necessary. At the end of the interview sequence, we requested permission from the focal person (the person being interviewed) to contact the senior manager or peer who was identified as contributing to the individual's development. This way we obtained relationship pairs for the primary research sample. In two instances managers would not allow us to contact the significant others; the relationships that were discussed during the interview process had become problematic, and they were concerned about the potential negative impact of inviting these individuals to participate in interviews about their relationships. In all other instances research participants agreed to let the significant others be contacted. It was clearly stated that none of what we discussed during the interview process would be shared with others. This contract reinforced the confidentiality of the interview and minimized the potential intervention consequences of the interview process for each developmental relationship.

I anticipated that the interview would be a potent experience for research participants because it was designed to have the individuals reflect intensively on their career histories and on relationships that had significantly influenced their development. Pilot interviews demonstrated that individuals felt the interview was a self-revealing experience in which new feelings and thoughts about one's career were discussed in different and unfamiliar ways. I wanted to make sure that individuals chose to participate in this process without feeling coerced. During the telephone conversations that preceded a confirmation of an interview time, the voluntary nature of the research was stressed. A primary goal was to insure that people had enough information to make an informed decision about participation.

**The Focal Person Interview Sequence.** The interview sequence with the focal research participants consisted of two sessions. During the first session we reviewed the individual's career history and explored relationships that had been important during his or her time in the organization. In the first study, junior managers focused on relationships with senior colleagues who were currently supporting their development. In the second study, individuals at three different career stages focused on relationships with colleagues, friends in the organization, or peers who were currently supporting their development. In every instance we jointly reconstructed the individual's career history and experiences with significant others. While a pre-established set of questions guided the discussion, it was important to observe the flow of the interview experience. How each individual chose to tell his or her story influenced which questions were best to ask.

During the second interview session we explored one or two relationships with significant others that had been important in the focal person's career. In the first study these were senior managers who provided a wide range of mentoring functions. In the second study these were age peers or level peers who provided a variety of developmental functions that supported the focal person's attempts to address important personal or professional challenges. We reconstructed significant events as the relationship unfolded and followed the thoughts and feelings of the focal person as she or he told the story. Again, while a set of questions guided us, it was important to observe the flow of the interview to develop a sense of which particular questions and responses elicited the most complete information.

In the first study of mentoring, the original intent was to identify one important relationship after a review of the individual's career history was completed. After five interviews, it became clear that in some instances more than one senior manager was equally important to the individual's development; this was the first indication that mentoring was not always embodied in one individual but that several might provide mentoring functions. The pivotal question to identify which relationship(s) would become the focus in the second interview was, "Is there anyone among those that you have mentioned today that you feel has taken a personal interest in you or your development?" Feelings about the various individuals expressed during the first interview guided the choices of relationships for further study.

**The Significant Other Interview Sequence.** The interview sequence with significant others generally consisted of two sessions. However, in several instances the exploration of the relationship and how the individual's own career history and needs influenced the relationship was accomplished in one session. This occurred more often in the second study of peer relationships, and may be related to variations in interviewer styles since two doctoral students conducted many of the second interviews. In both studies the contact with significant others began with a review of how he or she had been mentioned by the focal person as having contributed to his or her development. All significant others were quite willing to participate in the study. The first interview was parallel to the second focal person interview session; we jointly explored the history of the relationship and how the significant other experienced it.

The second session of this interview sequence explored the significant other's career history. The purpose here was to illuminate how the relationship fit into the senior manager's or the peer's career as well as how personal needs influenced the course of the relationship. In some instances these two major agenda, exploration of the relationship and exploration of the individual's career, were reversed in the interview sequence. This variation was introduced when the interviewer felt it would facilitate the process of inquiry.

During interviews with senior managers in the first study, I began to understand the reciprocity of developmental relationships and how these relationships between junior and senior colleagues meet complementary needs of both individuals. With this insight, later interviews with significant others were more focused since the relevant questions had been clarified. This fine tuning of interview questions continued throughout both studies as my understanding of relationship dynamics and individual and organizational influences progressed.

**Biographical Interviewing.** This interview method has several qualities that distinguish it from traditional research interviews. While the interview sequence began with a list of questions and topics to be covered, each was different from the others because particular questions were used in response to the individual's way of telling his or her story. This flexibility facilitated our joint exploration by enabling the interviewee to manage his or her personal exploration. The variations in the specific events across interviews make it impossible to compare data on specific questions; however, the richness gained through this process does make full appreciation of the personal experiences of each individual manager possible. In addition, comparisons across interviews are based on an integrated understanding of each relationship.

This interview method is similar to the biographical interviewing process that Levinson et al. (1978) describe in their study of adult male development.

A biographical interview combines aspects of a research interview, a clinical interview, and a conversation between friends. It is like a structured research interview in that certain topics must be covered, and the main purpose is research. As a clinical interview, the interviewer is sensitive to the feelings expressed, and follows the threads of meaning as they lead through diverse topics. Finally, as a conversation between friends, the relationship is equal and the interviewer is free to respond in terms of his own experiences. Yet each party has a defined role in a sustained work task, which imposes its own constraints.

What is involved is not simply an interviewing technique or procedure, but a relationship of some intimacy, intensity and duration. Significant work is involved in forming, maintaining, and terminating the relationship. The recruiting of participants, the negotiation of a research contract, and the course of the interviewing relationship are phases within a single, complex process. Understanding and managing this process is a crucial part of our research method. Managed with sensitivity and discretion, it is a valuable learning experience for the participant as well as the researcher. (p. 15)

As a research interview, the method required that a certain range of topics be covered during the interview sequence. Various aspects of each manager's career history, the essential characteristics of developmental relationships, and how features of the organizational context affected individuals were covered in all interviews. Additional topics were covered when they were relevant to understanding these essential foci of the research.

As a clinical interview, it was important to pay particular attention to the affect associated with accounts of significant events. Questions, responses, and probes were designed to uncover positive and negative feelings that characterized each manager's experiences (Sullivan, 1954). A continuous tension of the combined research/clinical interview method is created by obtaining both internal and external data; that is, questions had to elicit both the concrete events surrounding career and relationship histories as well as the internal experiences of these events.

Reluctance to answer particular questions and projections onto the significant other offered insights into the relationship processes of interest. For example, questions about male/female dynamics and sexuality were often responded to with laughter. I interpreted this as resistance to a threatening issue that was unresolved for individuals in cross-gender relationships. I interpreted fantasies about how the significant other experienced the relationship as a projection of the individual's experience. For example, the statement that the significant other valued competence reflected the young manager's experience of the relationship as self-enhancing and self-confirming. These clinical interpretations contributed to the descriptive theory that emerged.

As a clinical interviewer, my relationship with the interviewee was another source of data. For example, senior managers' responses suggested possible understandings of how they relate to younger adults. In addition, frequent empathy with junior managers' accounts helped me understand their feelings and experiences. Clearly my personal experience of the interview and my personal history provided a backdrop for a deeper understanding of the personal accounts that I listened to.

As a "conversation beween friends," the interview relationship became intimate. The management of this relationship involved particular sensitivity to building rapport and trust during the first phase of the relationship, responding authentically within the boundaries of my role as researcher during the interviewing sequence, and explicitly addressing the termination of the relationship at the end of the interview sequence. I shared my own experience when it would enhance our joint exploration while being careful not to influence the perspective of the interviewee in his or her own account. By the end of the interview sequence our joint exploration created a degree of intimacy that would end with the termination of the research task. Both the interviewer and the research participant felt appreciation and loss and sometimes surprise and confusion. It was important to complete the final interview with a thorough debriefing of the experience in order to achieve an end to the research relationship.

## The Interview as a Potential Intervention

This interview method raises an important ethical concern. How can we conduct research so as to minimize intervention into the lives of the participants and the relationships being studied? The degree of self-disclosure prompted by the interview process might leave individuals with new insights that could create new questions and concerns. At the same time, such self-disclosure was necessary for understanding developmental relationships and their meaning for individual managers. This dilemma required careful research management so that individuals controlled how much information they shared. I assumed responsibility for making sure that managers could address concerns raised during the interviews prior to ending our relationship.

For most managers, the interview provided new insights into their career histories and the relationships we explored. At the end of each interview I invited individuals to comment on how they felt as a result of our discussion in order to resolve any "unfinished business" that emerged during the self-reflection process. Those who were relatively satisfied with their current lives and relationships expressed a sense of closure and self-worth.

> It was the first time in a very long time that I spent that much time talking about myself to somebody. It made me reflective. I don't know, it felt kind of good in some respects to go over what happened. It made me think about all the good things that have happened to me here and how good several people were to me. It did make me stop and think. Normally when you talk to somebody, it is not an interview, so there is a lot of give and take, and I just don't talk about myself that much for that long. It is quite a treat having someone pay attention to me for that long. I learned a lot about why my relationship with Bob had been so important to me.

Those who faced conflict in their relationships expressed a sense of confusion or frustration.

> I am a bit depressed now . . . there are things that I'm going to have to think about as a result of our discussion. . . . Visiting some of those feelings, as they happened, you feel anger and frustration or whatever, and in the process of the very nature of the interview and how it was structured, in terms of looking at my life . . . visiting all those feelings all in a period of a few hours — it was, oh my God, that kind of thing, where you can reflect back at any given point in time and remember feeling a certain way. In small doses it's quite a different story than to have it happen all at once.

In this situation, and in other similar interviews, I helped the individual explore his or her feelings at the end of the interview. I wanted to make sure that when they left the last interview, they had as few unresolved concerns as possible. I at least wanted to insure that new problems had not been created by the intense self-disclosing experience. The tension between wanting to learn as much as possible and wanting to respect the privacy of the individual was real.

Often individuals thanked me and my colleagues at the end of the interview for helping them learn about themselves. This appreciation pointed out the positive intervention consequences of the research process. Generally, managers found the interview an important learning experience from which they derived greater self-awareness and new insights into their relationships at work.

The interview method also posed a possible intervention into the relationships that were studied. I minimized this possibility by insuring the confidentiality of each manager's accounts. Comments from several junior managers in response to my request for permission to interview their significant senior managers suggested some concern about how the interview might affect their relationships.

> I have some reservations about that. One, I guess, is I am at a different level than I was at before, and I don't know if Jack feels that he is a sponsor to me now or that he did anything special for me that he wouldn't have done for someone else—and then to be asked in so many words, "Did you take care of Frank or were you his godfather . . . " he may say no and then his actions from there on may be to try to be more impartial and to go to the opposite extreme in relations with me. . . .

I interpreted this kind of response in two ways. First, relationships might be characterized by some uncertainty or lack of trust or that the junior manager was unsure of his or her perceptions of its importance. The prospect of me contacting the senior manager presented a threat. I hypothesized that in the interview with the senior manager, I might discover unresolved tensions in the relationship. In addition, this was an important time to assure the young manager that I would not share the content of our discussion with the senior manager. In all but one instance my response to this concern alleviated the fear of negative consequences, and the young managers said I could contact the senior manager because they trusted my intentions and sensitivity to possible consequences. Generally, those who expressed concern were involved in developmental relationships characterized by conflict or tension.

Other individuals responded favorably to my contacting their significant others. This indicated a level of trust in these relationships which eliminated any concern about potential negative consequences.

> Sure you can talk to Bill. I feel totally open with him. I haven't said anything to you that he doesn't already know anyway . . . that's why we have been so successful together. I think he'll enjoy it, and I'd be curious to know what he has to say afterwards.

Most research participants responded to the request in this fashion. I learned in the interviews with their significant others that these relationships were characterized by mutual respect and caring. The interview process was a confirmation of the value of the relationship to both individuals, rather than a threat. At the conclusion of the first study I learned that, after the interviews were completed, managers talked with each other about the experience. The interview experiences prompted discussions that had not previously occurred. These managers told me that they discussed aspects of the relationship that they discovered in talking with me.

> I saw him last Monday and we talked about the interviews. He told me that he had talked with you and how much he enjoyed reflecting on our relationship. I agreed. I felt good that he had agreed to talk with you—obviously he wanted to help you but it was also, I think, a sign that he valued our relationship—that it was worth talking about . . . we spent an hour or so sharing our perceptions—some of the things we mentioned we had never talked about before.

Clearly, this research method has intervention consequences. My responsibility as a researcher was to insure that potential negative consequences were minimized. Careful debriefing at the end of each interview sequence, careful linking processes to the significant others, and an invitation in the feedback report to participants to contact me with questions and concerns, reflect my efforts to behave responsibly. It is not possible to implement a study that requires intensive self-disclosure without some intervention consequences; both individuals and relationships are affected by the interview process (Brown & Tandon, 1978). The positive consequences of increased self-awareness and new insights about significant relationships outweigh potential negative consequences. Most importantly, potential negative consequences can be prevented through careful management of the research process.

## The Interviewer as the
## Primary Research Tool

This interview method is greatly influenced by the personal characteristics of the researcher. How I managed the interviewer-interviewee relationship, how I interpreted various responses to me during the interview sequences, and how I analyzed the entire data collection effort relates to what I myself brought to the interview. My own history created opportunities to learn as well as potential threats to valid interpretation of the data. Throughout the research process I tried to capitalize on the benefits of my personal experience and to minimize potential blinders my experience could place on my interpretations.

My age provided both opportunities and obstacles in the research process. As a young adult I found it relatively easier to develop rapport with the individuals in early career. I empathized with their experience, having worked as a novice manager in a corporate setting and having experienced several developmental relationships. This capacity to empathize presented the possibility of interpreting personal accounts of young managers to fit my own experience. When I strongly empathized with a young manager's experience, I pushed myself to consider alternative interpretations in order to allow for discrepancies between their experiences and my own.

My age presented a different experience with senior managers. I often entered these relationships with some anxiety about my ability to develop enough empathy and rapport. These feelings reflected my own posture toward authority as well as the posture toward authority that young managers reflected to me in the interviews. I wondered if they would have time to talk with me, I wondered if they would perceive me as a competent professional, and I wondered if I would be able to understand their experiences. As I entered interviews with senior managers, I had to manage these concerns so that they would not interfere with the relationship-building process. I learned over the course of the data collection that my anxiety was related to relationships in my own life and to the empathy I developed with young managers. Once I was aware of the cause of my anxiety, I was able to contact the senior manager and establish sufficient rapport to complete the interview.

At first my age appeared to present a disadvantage in my interviews with senior managers, but I also found value in the age discrepancy. I hypothesized that the senior managers' responses to me reflected their styles of relating to younger managers. This allowed me to learn, firsthand, something about what the senior managers brought to their developmental relationships. In my interviews with senior managers in cross-gender relationships, responses to me frequently paralleled young female managers' accounts of the relationships. Sexual tensions and protective concern during the interview helped me understand their experiences of relationships with senior managers.

My gender influenced the quality of relationships with young managers as well. I empathized with young female managers to such an extent that I found it difficult to maintain the boundaries of my role as researcher. I was often tempted to abandon the primary task in order to explore particular concerns that I experienced in my own career. I had to continually check my personal agendas in order to insure that I only pursued these concerns when they directly contributed to the primary research questions.

With young male managers I had a different set of concerns. Sexual attraction influenced the course of the relationship-building process and sometimes made it more difficult to accomplish the research task. I had to manage my personal feelings carefully so that I would allow the mutual attraction to enhance rapport but not distract us from the primary task. In addition, I sometimes had an internal negative reaction to male young managers' comments about their female peers and female senior managers. Throughout the research process I tried to use these relationships to understand male-female and authority dynamics in developmental relationships.

If another individual conducted the research, it is likely that different problems would be encountered during the interviews. Individuals who embark on a qualitative research project must be aware of the effect of their personal histories on the interview and on the final descriptive analysis (Berg, 1979). This self-awareness, encompassing continual examination of one's needs, anxieties, and biases, is crucial to effective implementation. If the researcher is aware of the impact of personal history and demographic characteristics on the research process, the final product will be enhanced rather than diminished by personal needs and experiences.

## The Value of a Team of Researchers

The value of a team of researchers lies in the checks and balances provided by the varying perspectives and personal histories each member brings to the study. In the study of relationships with peers, I benefited from the assistance of two doctoral students who helped me design the study, collect the data, and complete the analysis. We were all about the same age, and one student was male and the other female. Thus the effects of gender differences on the interview process and on the interpretation of findings were clarified as we compared our views.

While collecting the data we acted as sounding boards for each other. This way initial working hypotheses could be tested, and we could separate our preconceptions and our own experiences from what the data itself suggested to us. For example, while I was quick to label developmental functions using the framework developed when studying mentor relationships, my colleagues urged me to consider alternative ways to categorize the dynamics of peer relationships. Similarly, our male colleague pushed us to suspend our inclination to label significant gender differences until we had sufficient evidence.

We could also further our understanding of the nature of peer and developmental relationships by examining our own dynamics and process issues. As age peers we shared common experiences and values that sparked our interests in working together. At the same time, I was in a position of authority as a faculty member with more experience in conducting qualitative research and more familiarity with Adult Development and Career Development perspectives. The individuals who joined the research team did so because they wanted to learn more about qualitative methodologies by working on this project.

These demographic characteristics helped us learn about the complexities of peer relationships. Issues of competition, competence, conflict, trust, and intimacy became important as our relationships evolved, just as they were evident in the personal accounts of the research participants. To the extent that we were able to explore our own relationship dynamics, we were more insightful about the meaning of the stories told to us during the interviews.

These parallel processes were, at times, a mixed blessing. Since a great deal of time, energy, and interpersonal skill are required to identify and manage complex relationship dynamics, we had to work hard to make our research team effective. And, given the history of this program of research as well as each of our personal histories, we had varying levels of commitment to this kind of effort. When team members do not share a strong commitment and investment in a project, process issues may interfere with the quality of data collection as well as with the completeness of the final analysis.

We frequently reached a synergistic level when we had discussions at various points during the data collection and analysis phases of the project. However, I sometimes sensed that we could have pushed our understanding even further if we had more fully examined our own relationship dynamics. We could have used additional insight into our own process to make sense of the interview data, and we might have enhanced our own relationships in order to enrich our individual and collaborative work as well.

A team of researchers can be extremely beneficial if effective relationship-building occurs and if members are committed to maintaining a supportive and synergistic working climate throughout the project. The potential to produce a rich understanding from the data is expanded when individuals with different skills and personal backgrounds come together to conduct research. This potential is limited only by the process losses that may occur if competition, ineffective conflict management, or concerns about competence interfere with managing relationships among team members.

In the absence of a research team, there are times during this kind of exploratory qualitative research that discussions with colleagues are very useful, if not essential. Colleagues who are not immersed in the project but who are familiar with the field or the dilemmas of qualitative research can provide a valuable sounding board. They can help distinguish between a researcher's projections and valid interpretations of interview data, and they can offer concepts and categories that can organize the data into an understandable framework. In my first study of mentoring, members of my dissertation committee provided this resource.

## ANALYSIS

Data analysis began during the data collection phase of each study. The primary method of analysis was an inductive process in which tentative hypotheses concerning the nature of developmental relationships were suggested and revised as data were collected (Levy, 1963). As the number of relationships in the sample increased, themes and categories emerged from recurring patterns in the data. As the patterns continued across interviews, these themes and categories became the basis for a descriptive theory. This inductive process is characterized by continuous movement between data and concepts until sufficient categories have been defined. This methodology is described by Glaser and Strauss (1967) as the "constant comparative method of analysis."

> Joint collection, coding, and analysis of the data is the underlying operation. The generation of theory, coupled with the notion of theory as process, requires that all three operations be done together as much as possible. They should blur and intertwine continually from the beginning of an investigation to its end. To be sure, in any investigation, the tendency is to do all three simultaneously; but in many (if not most) studies of description and verification, there is typically such a definite focus on one operation at a time that the others are slighted or ignored. This definite separation of each operation hinders generation of theory. For example, if data are being coded and a fresh analytic idea emerges that jolts the operation, the idea may be disregarded because of preestablished rules or plain routine—thus stifling at that moment the generation of theory (p. 43).

Throughout the data collection phase, there is a tension between a desire to find the answers and a desire to remain open to new concepts and ideas. For example, after the first few relationships had been studied through the two-session interview, we examined transcripts of the concepts and themes that could describe each relationship, its role in each manager's career history, and how the organization had influenced its development. These concepts were noted as possible categories for analysis at later stages of the study. However, it was important not to become locked into these categories as the final framework for the descriptive theory.

Throughout data collection, subsequent transcripts were reviewed in a similar manner. Hypotheses related to the primary research questions were generated between interviews and then tested in the second interview session. At the end of the interview with each relationship pair, we outlined case histories with critical events and themes that explained the nature of developmental relationships. By comparing themes across cases we isolated which themes described the relationship dynamics reported here.

This analytic process is messy, at best. Living with the data and tentative explanations throughout data collection is a difficult task that entails constant anxiety about whether or not one will make sense of the data at the end. The desire for closure must be tempered so that inconsistencies are viewed as opportunities for clarification rather than threats to tentative understanding.

For example, at the conclusion of data collection for the first study, I had a list of categories and themes that recurred across the eighteen relationships. These were put aside for a month while I immersed myself in an intuitive sorting process of the case histories. I grouped cases that seemed to be similar in some unarticulated way and then attempted to explain the similarity. Those dimensions that could simultaneously explain the similarities and differences became the foundation of the final analysis.

The primary research questions guided the choice of categories and concepts that were used in the final description of relationship dynamics. Since the most important question concerned understanding the relationship as the primary unit of analysis, I searched for concepts that would describe the interpersonal process that characterized a developmental relationship. The intuitive sorting process resulted in the identification of two different sets of concepts to describe the interpersonal relationship. *Relationship functions* described the interpersonal exchange (see Chapter 2), and *relationship phases* described how developmental relationships unfolded over time (see Chapter 3). These static and dynamic perspectives provided a conceptual schema for describing the developmental relationship.

The second primary research question concerned how developmental relationships fit into the life and career histories of both individuals. I tried to understand how each individual's personal history and current needs shaped the course of a relationship. The concept of *complementary developmental tasks* showed how each person's critical psychological concerns influenced relationship dynamics (see Chapter 4). This concept was stimulated, in part, by relevant theory on adult and career development (Levinson et al., 1978; Schein, 1978).

Finally, the third primary research question concerned how the organizational context influenced the kind of relationships observed. As individuals described the history of developmental relationships, I listened for clues about how they experienced various features of the organization as they built these relationships. In a review of the transcripts, I noted what organizational features led to recurring themes. These features became the categories of analysis for understanding the influence of the organizational context (see Chapter 7).

In the subsequent study of peer relationships, findings from the first study influenced what questions were asked as well as what concepts and themes were developed during the analysis phase. For example, transcripts were reviewed for patterns of relationship functions; this resulted in defining functions provided in peer relationships, as well as a continuum of different types of these developmental relationships (see Chapter 6). In addition, data on organizational features were compared with those from the first study to see how the context shaped relationships and what educational or structural interventions might result in conditions that encourage mentoring and peer alliances. Finally, data on individuals' career histories helped me understand how needs change throughout life, how gender affects relationship needs, and how both gender and developmental tasks shape developmental relationships.

During the analysis phase of this second study, it was critical to be open to unanticipated understandings and issues. The inclination to build on previous learnings posed a real threat to valid interpretation of new data. Here, the research team was an invaluable resource since my colleagues had not been part of the first study and did not have the same understanding I had developed earlier. The different perspectives that they brought to the project enabled them to consistently challenge interpretations that were derived from the earlier study and not sufficiently grounded in data from the new interviews about relationships with peers.

The final set of categories that make up the descriptive theory presented here was arrived at by continuously recycling the data until recurring themes could be systematically grouped into categories. Many of the concepts and themes appeared early in the data collection process. None, however, were incorporated into the theory until the data had been studied carefully and comprehensively at the end of each data collection. Staying grounded in the data was the only way to insure that tentative concepts and hypotheses were illustrative of the stories that were told.

Delineating the descriptive theory involved using illustrative quotations from the case material. A test of the usefulness and accuracy of the descriptive framework evolved during the development of the theory. When case material could not be used to illustrate a concept, I concluded that the concept was inadequate in some way. The more individuals' accounts could illustrate the descriptive theory, the more credence I developed in my conceptual understanding.

In retrospect, the analytic process that resulted in a descriptive theory of developmental relationships appears systematic. In practice, however, there were times when I was confused and uncertain about how to proceed. Living through the confusion was an important part of the analytic process; ideas emerged only after I read, reread, and reflected on the interviews. I began delineating the theory only when I reached a sense of closure about my understanding. Even then, writing involved intuitively sorting the case material, identifying the organizing concepts, and presenting the clear link between concepts and data.

## IMPLICATIONS

There are many opportunities for further research on relationships in organizations and their role in adult and career development (see Chapter 8). Investigating relationship dynamics, relationship constellations at successive career stages, or how developmental tasks shape relationships, requires a research methodology that incorporates elements of qualitative interview studies. Whenever individuals' subjective experiences are of interest and the primary task is to generate theory rather than to test it, this kind of approach will be essential.

Too often the ambiguity and "messiness" of qualitative research discourage investigators from considering methodological decisions carefully. The importance of making informed choices about how to proceed at each major point in a research program cannot be overemphasized. It is only in retrospect that I have clarified the consequences of successive decisions that we made in the two studies of developmental relationships. These suggest several guidelines that can insure more informed choices in future research.

First, during the design of the research strategy it is essential to assess whether qualitative methods are appropriate for the questions being asked, to articulate the researcher's assumptions and personal interests so that they do not bias the data collection, and to ground the primary research questions in relevant theoretical perspectives (Isabella, 1983). Then, one can define the level of analysis for the study, establish the pivotal interview questions, and identify the consequences of the chosen boundaries and scope.

All of these tasks were completed in the studies of developmental relationships. However, the impact of my personal history and interests on the data were not clarified until the second study. This appears to be the most difficult guideline to follow, since it requires considerable self-analysis. In contrast, the consequences of the other decisions became clear quite early as we proceeded with the data collection and analysis phases of each project.

Second, during the data collection phase it is essential to insure that data are collected in a manner that helps the researchers make sense of the participants' personal accounts. A variety of methods are available to make this happen, including taping interviews, using a team of researchers, periodic discussions with uninvolved but knowledgeable colleagues, and ongoing assessment of how the researcher's own biases affect the data collection process.

In the study of peer relationships, a team of researchers was invaluable and highlighted the need for ongoing discussion and consultation during a qualitative research project. While the interview transcripts insure that no raw data are lost, interaction with knowledgeable colleagues insures that personal biases and blind spots do not interfere with valid data collection and analysis.

Third, during the analysis phase it is essential to employ methods which insure valid interpretation of the data (Isabella, 1983). The researcher must systematically review the data, move between data and theory as hypotheses are generated, and carefully consider those cases that do not seem to fit emerging categories and themes. These steps will insure that the final results are both comprehensive and compelling. The most difficult part of this phase is the ambiguity that the researcher has to live with until the appropriate categories and concepts are clearly defined.

The desire for closure and the pressures of other commitments consistently threatened valid analysis in both studies of developmental relationships. With experience I learned that premature conclusions can significantly limit the depth of understanding. The most difficult task at this stage is to manage the inherent ambiguity and complexity of the analytic process so that a complete and compelling framework can be discovered.

Finally, throughout every stage of the research process, ethical responsibilities must be recognized and managed (Isabella, 1983). Researchers must minimize the intervention consequences inherent in qualitative research of this kind, establish confidentiality and trust during data collection, and conduct careful debriefing sessions at the end of interviews. They must also allow research participants to manage their self-disclosure and exploration and summarize major results of the study for participants.

The ethical dimension of my research work only became apparent after the first study of mentoring had begun. As I talked to potential research participants, the importance of rapport-building, confidentiality, and specific procedures for assuring participants' learning as well as my own became clear. Neither study would have produced valid and useful insights about developmental relationships if I had not considered these issues.

If these guidelines are used to establish and implement a qualitative research strategy, the data collection and analysis procedures should support the investigator's objectives. The first step, however, is to determine whether this methodology is the most appropriate for the questions at hand. If comparative studies in several organizations are contemplated, or if evaluation of intervention strategies are of primary concern, other methods of inquiry, such as questionnaires and participant observation techniques, should be considered.

# References

Adams, J. *Women on Top: Success Patterns and Personal Growth*. New York: Hawthorn Books, 1979.

Alderfer, C. P. "Boundary Relations and Organizational Diagnosis," L. Meltzer and F. Wichet (eds.), *Humanizing Organizational Behavior*, Springfield, IL: Charles C. Thomas, 1976, 109–133.

— — —. "Change Processes in Organizations," *Handbook of Industrial and Organizational Psychology*, Marvin D. Dunnette (ed.), Rand McNally, 1976, 1591–1638.

— — —. "Group and Intergroup Relations," *Improving Life at Work*, J. R. Hackman and J. Lloyd Suttle (eds.), Santa Monica: Goodyear, 1977, 227–296.

Alderfer, C. P., and Brown, L. David. *Learning from Changing: Organizational Diagnosis and Development*. Beverly Hills, CA: Sage, 1975.

Alderfer, C. P., and Smith, K. "Studying Intergroup Relations Embedded in Organizations," *Administrative Sciences Quarterly*, 1982, 36–65.

Alleman, E. "Mentoring Relationships in Organizations: Behavior, Personality Characteristics, and Interpersonal Perceptions," unpublished doctoral dissertation, University of Akron, 1982.

"An 'Old Girl Network' Is Born." *Business Week*, November 20, 1978, 154–156.

Argyris, C. *Intervention Theory and Method: A Behavioral Science View.* Reading, MA: Addison-Wesley, 1970.

Atkinson et al. "Management Development Roles: Coach, Sponsor, and Mentor," *Personnel Journal*, 1980, *59*, 918–921.

Babad, E. Y., Birnbaum, M., and Benne, K. D. *The Social Self.* Beverly Hills, CA: Sage Publications, 1983.

Bailyn, L. "Accommodation of Work to Family: An Analysis of Couples with Two Careers," Rapaport, R. and R. N. (eds.), *Working Couples,* New York: Harper & Row, 1978, 159–179.

Baird, L., and Kram, K. "Career Dynamics: Managing the Superior-Subordinate Relationship," *Organizational Dynamics*, Summer 1983, 46–64.

Baker-Miller, J. *Towards A New Psychology of Women.* Boston: Beacon Press, 1976.

Bardwick, J. M. *Psychology of Women: A Study of Biocultural Conflicts.* New York: Harper & Row, 1971.

Baron, A. "Separate Training Sessions for Women?" *Training and Developmental Journal*, December 1979, 47–50.

Bartolome, F., and Evans, P. *Must Success Cost So Much?* New York: Basic Books, 1980.

— — —. "Professional Lives vs. Private Lives—Shifting Patterns of Managerial Commitment," *Organizational Dynamics*, Spring 1979, 2–29.

Bass, B. M., and Vaughn, J. A. *Training in Industry: The Management of Learning.* Belmont, CA: Wadsworth, 1966.

Beckhard, R. *Organization Development: Strategies and Models.* Reading, MA: Addison-Wesley, 1969.

Beckhard, R., and Harris, R. *Organizational Transitions.* Reading, MA: Addison-Wesley, 1977.

Beer, M. *Organizational Change and Development: A System View.* Santa Monica: Goodyear, 1980.

"Bendix Abuzz: Agee Shakes Up His Company." *Time*, October 6, 1980, 83.

Berg, D. N. "Developing Clinical Field Skills: An Apprenticeship Model," Alderfer, C. P., and Cooper, C. (eds.), *Advances in Experimental Social Processes, 2*, New York: Wiley, 1979, 143–164.

Berlew, D. E., and Hall, D. T. "The Socialization of Managers: Effects of Expectations on Performance," *Administrative Science Quarterly*, 1966, *11*, 207–223.

Bird, C. *The Two Paycheck Marriage.* New York: Pocket Books, 1979.

Bolton, B. "A Conceptual Analysis of the Mentor Relationship in the Career Development of Women," *Adult Evaluation*, 1980, *30*, 195–207.

Bowen, Donald D. "Identification Is to Mentoring as Infatuation Is to Love," address presented at the National Academy of Management Meetings, Dallas, TX, August 1983.

Bradford, David L., Sargent, Alice G., and Sprague, Melinda S. "The Executive Man and Woman: The Issue of Sexuality," *Sexuality in Organizations*, D. A. Neugarten and J. M. Shafrite (eds.), Oak Park, IL: Moore, 1980, 17–28.

Bray, D., Campbell, R., and Grant, D. *Formulative Years in Business: A Long Term Study of Management Lives.* New York: Wiley, 1974.

Brown, L. D., and Tandon, R. "Interviews as Catalysts in a Community Setting," *Journal of Applied Psychology*, 1978, *63*, 197–205.

Bunker, B., and Seashone, E. W. "Power, Collusion: Intimacy-Sexuality Support," Alice Sargent (ed.), *Beyond Sex Roles*, St. Paul: West, 1977, 356–370.

Burton, A. "The Mentoring Dynamic in the Therapeutic Transformation," *American Journal of Psychoanalysis*, 1977, *37*, 115–122.

Clawson, J. "Mentoring in Managerial Careers," *Work, Family and the Career*, C. Brooklyn Derr (ed.), New York: Praeger, 1980, 144–165.

– – –. *Superior-Subordinate Relationships for Managerial Development*, Doctoral Dissertation, Harvard Business School, 1979.

Collin, A. "Notes on Some Typologies of Management Development and the Role of Mentor in the Process of Adaptation of the Individual to the Organization," *Personnel Review*, 1979, *8*, 10–14.

Collins, E., and Scott, P. "Everyone Who Makes It Has A Mentor," in *Harvard Business Review*, July-August 1978, 89–101.

Cook, M. F. "Is the Mentor Relationship Primarily a Male Experience?" *Personnel Administrator*, November 1979, 82–85.

Dalton, G., Thompson, P., and Price, R. "The Four Stages of Professional Careers—A New Look at Performance by Professionals," *Organizational Dynamics*, Summer 1977, 19–42.

Dalton, M. *Men Who Manage.* New York: Wiley, 1959.

Davis, R. L., and Garrison, P. A. "Mentoring: In Search of a Taxonomy," Masters Thesis, MIT Sloan School of Business, 1979.

Deal, T. E., and Kennedy, A. A. *Comparable Cultures: The Rites and Rituals of Corporate Life.* Reading, MA: Addison-Wesley, 1982.

Derr, C. B. (ed.) *Work, Family and the Career.* New York: Praeger, 1980.

Digman, L. A. "How Well Managed Organizations Develop through Executives," *Organizational Dynamics*, Autumn 1978, 63–80.

Dowling, C. *The Cinderella Complex.* New York: Summit Books, 1981.

Epstein, C. F. "Encountering the Male Establishment: Sex-Status Limits on Women's Careers in the Professions," *American Journal of Sociology*, May 1970, *75*, 965–982.

— — —. *Woman's Place: Options and Limits in Professional Careers*. Berkeley: Univ. of California Press, 1970.

Erickson, E. (ed.) *Adulthood*. New York: W. W. Norton, 1980.

— — —. *Childhood and Society*. New York: W. W. Norton, 1963.

— — —. *Identity, Youth and Crisis*. New York: W. W. Norton, 1968.

Evered, R., and Louis, M. "Alternative Perspectives in the Organizational Sciences: Inquiry From the Inside and Inquiry From the Outside," *Academy of Management Review*, 1981, *6*, 385–95.

Filestead, W. *Qualitative Methodology*. Chicago: Markham, 1970.

Feurer, L. S. *The Conflict of Generations*. New York: Basic Books, 1969.

Flamholtz, E. G. *Human Resource Accounting*. Encino: Dickinson, 1974.

Garelick, J. "Academia's Reluctant Heroines," *Change*, 1980, *12*, 17–20.

George, P., and Kummerow, J. "Mentoring for Career Women," *Training, HRD*, February 1981, 44–49.

Gilligan, C. *In a Different Voice*. Cambridge, MA: Harvard Univ. Press, 1982.

Glaser, B. G., Strauss, A. L. *The Discovery of Granded Theory: Strategies for Qualitative Research*. Chicago: Aldine, 1967.

Goldstein, E. "Effects of Same-Sex and Cross-Sex Role Models on the Subsequent Academic Productivity of Scholars," *American Psychologist*, 1979, *34*, 407–410.

Goldstein, P. J., and Sorensen, J. "Becoming the Executive You'd Like to Be: A Program for Female Middle Managers," *S.A.M. Advanced Management Journal*, Fall 1979, *42*, 41–49.

Gordon, F. E., Stroeber, M. H. (eds.), *Bringing Women Into Management*. New York: McGraw-Hill, 1975.

Gould, R. *Transformations: Growth and Change in Adult Life*. New York: Simon & Schuster, 1978.

— — —. "The Phases of Adult Life: A Study in Development Psychology," *The American Journal of Psychology*, November 1972, *129*, 5.

Gabarro, J. "Socializations at the Top — How CCO's and Subordinates Evolve Interpersonal Contacts," *Organizational Dynamics*, Winter 1979, 2–23.

Hackman, J. R., and Oldham, G. R. *Work Redesign*. New York: Addison-Wesley, 1980.

Hackman, J. R., Oldham, G. R., Jansen, K., and Purdy, K. "A New Strategy for Job Enrichment," *California Management Review*, Summer 1975, 57–71.

Hackman, J. R., and Suttle, J. L. *Improving Life at Work*. Santa Monica: Goodyear, 1977.

Halcomb, R. "Mentors and the Successful Women," *Across the Board*, 1980, *17*, 13–17.

Hall, D. T. *Careers in Organizations.* Pacific Palisades, CA: Goodyear, 1976.

— — —. "Socialization Process in Later Career Years: Can There Be Growth at the Terminal Level?" *Work, Family, and the Career*, C. Brooklyn Derr (ed.), New York: 1980, 219–233.

— — —. "A Theoretical Model of Career Sub-Identity," *OBHP*, 1971, *6*, 50–76.

Hall, D. T., and Berlew, D. E. "The Socialization of Managers: Effects of Expectations on Performance," *Administrative Science Quarterly*, 1966, *11*, 207–223.

Hall, D. T., and Kram, K. E. "Development in Midcareer," in Montross, D., and Skinkerman, C. (eds.), *Career Development in the 50's*, Springfield, IL: Charles C. Thomas Press, 1981.

Hall, D. T., and Nougaim, K. "An Examination of Maslow's Need Hierarchy in an Organizational Setting," *OBHP*, 1968, *3*, 12–35.

Harrison, R. "Choosing the Depth of Organizational Intervention," *Journal of Applied Behavioral Science*, 1970, *6*, 181–202.

Hanson, M. C. "Career Development Responsibilities of Managers," *Personnel Journal*, September 1977, 443–445.

Hennig, M., and Jardim, A. *The Managerial Woman.* Garden City, NY: Doubleday, 1977.

— — —. "Women Executives in the Old-Boy Network," *Psychology Today*, January 1977, 76–81.

Horner, M. "Achievement Related Conflicts in Women," *Journal of Social Issues*, 1972, *28*, 157–175.

"How Jewel Resets Its Crown," *Business Week*, October 27, 1980, 178–180.

"How Networks Work for Women," *Management Review*, August 1981, 43–45.

Hull, J. "The Uses of Instruments in Laboratory Training," *Training and Development Journal*, May 1970, *24*, 48–55.

Hunt, D. M., and Michael, C. "Mentorship: A Career Training and Development Tool," *Academy of Management Review*, July 1983, *8*, 475–485.

Isabella, L. "Evaluating Qualitative Research: Five Criteria," paper presented at the Academy of Management Meetings, August 1983.

— — —. "Core Consultation in the Thirties: Relationship Systems which Enhance Adult and Career Development," unpublished manuscript, Boston University, 1981.

Jacques, E. "Death and the Mid-Life Crisis," *International Journal of Psychoanalysis*, 1965, *46*, 502–514.

Jennings, E. E. *Routes to the Executive Suite.* New York: McGraw-Hill, 1971.

Jung, C. G. *Modern Man in Search of A Soul.* New York: Harcourt Brace, 1933.

Kanter, R. M. *Men and Women of the Corporation.* New York: Basic Books, 1977.

————. "Working in a New America," *Daedelus*, Winter, 1978, 47–78.

————. *Work and Family in the United States: A Critical Review and Agenda for Research and Policy.* Russell Sage Foundation, 1977.

Kaufman, D. R. "Associational Ties in Academe: Some Male and Female Differences," *Sex Roles*, 1978, *4*, 9–21.

Kessler, R. C., and McRae, J. A. "The Effect of Wives' Employment on the Mental Health of Married Men and Women," *American Sociological Review*, April 1982, *47*, 216–227.

Klauss, R. "Formalized Mentor Relationships for Management and Development Programs in the Federal Government," *Public Administration Review*, March 1979, 489–496.

————. "The Mentors," *Public Management*, March 1979, 2–16.

Kolb, D., and Frohman, A. "An Organization Development Approach to Consulting," *Sloan Management Review*, 1970, *12*, 51–65.

Kotter, J. P. "The Psychological Contract," *California Management Review*, Spring 1973, 91–99.

Kotter, J. P., and Schlesinger, L. A. "Choosing Strategies for Change," *Harvard Business Review*, March-April 1979, 106–114.

Kram, K. E. *Mentoring Processes at Work: Developmental Relationships in Managerial Careers*, Yale University Doctoral Dissertation, 1980.

————. "Creating Conditions That Encourage Mentoring In Organizations," *Enhancing Engineers Careers*, IEEE Catalog No. VH0158-6, Palo Alto, CA, 1983a.

————. "Phases of the Mentor Relationship." *Administrative Science Quarterly*, December 1983b, *26*.

Kram, K. E., and Isabella, L. "Mentoring Alternatives: The Role of Peer Relationships in Career Development" in press, *Academy of Management Journal*, March 1985.

Kram, K., and Jusela, G. "Anticipation and Realization: A Study of Retirement," unpublished research report, Yale University, 1978.

Lawler, E. E. "The Individual Organization Problems and Promise," *California Managerial Review*, Winter 1974, 31–39.

————. "Reward Systems," Hachman, J. R., and Subble, L. J. (eds.) *Improving Life at Work*, Santa Monica: Goodyear, 1977.

Lawrence, P., and Lorsch, J. *Developing Organizations: Diagnosis and Actions*, Reading, MA: Addison–Wesley, 1969.

Lean, E. "Cross-Gender Mentoring—Downright Upright and Good for Productivity," *Training and Development Journal*, May 1983, 60–65.

Levin, K. *Field Theory in Social Science.* New York: Harper and Row, 1951.

Levinson, D., et al. *Seasons of a Man's Life.* New York: Knopf, 1978.

Levinson, D., Darrow, D., Klein, E., Levinson, M., and McKee, B. "The Psychological Development of Men in Early Adulthood and the Mid-Life Transition," in D. F. Ricks, A. Thomas, and M. Roff (eds.) *Life History*

*Research in Psychopathology*, *3*, Minneapolis: Univ. of Minnesota Press, 1974, 224–260.

Levinson, H. *Executive Stress*, Harper & Row, 1969.

— — —. "Management By Whose Objectives?" *Harvard Business Review*, July-August 1970, 17–26.

— — —. "On Being A Middle-Aged Manager," *Harvard Business Review*, July-August 1969, 57-60.

— — —. *Organizational Diagnosis*. Cambridge, MA: Harvard University Press, 1972.

— — —. *Psychological Man*. Cambridge, MA: The Levinson Institute, 1976.

Levy, L. *Psychological Interpretation*. New York: Holt, Rinehart & Winston, 1963.

Lewis, A. "MOTEC Pilot Project in Career Development," unpublished report, June 1981–June 1982.

Lewis, Ann D. "Developing Technical Careers in Large Corporations: Where Do the Responsibilities Rest?" paper presented at the IEEE Careers Conference, Palo Alto, CA, October 1983.

Louis, M. R. "Managing Career Transition: A Missing Link in Career Development," *Organizational Dynamics*, Spring 1982, 68–74.

— — —. "Surprise and Sense Making: What New Comers Experience in Entering Unfamiliar Organizational Settings," *Administrative Science Quarterly*, June 1980, *25*, 226–251.

Maccoby, E. *The Psychology of Sex Differences*, Palo Alto, CA: Stanford University Press, 1974.

Metha, A. "Networking: A Model for Change," *Journal of the NAWDAC*, 1979, *24*, 31–34.

"Mary Cunningham's Ordeal," *Boston Globe*, October 2, 1980, 14.

McLane, H. J. *Selecting, Developing and Retaining Women Executives: A Corporate Strategy for the Eighties*. New York: Van Nostrand, 1980.

Meyer, H. H., Kay, E., and French, J. P. "Split-Roles in Performance Appraisal," *Harvard Business Review*, 1965, *43*, 123–129.

Miller, E. C., and Form, W. H. *Industrial Sociology*. New York: Harper, 1951.

Miller, J. B. *Towards A New Psychology of Women*. Boston: Beacon Press, 1976.

Missirian, A. K. *The Corporate Connection: Why Executive Women Need Mentors To Reach The Top*. Englewood Cliffs, NJ: Prentice-Hall, 1982.

— — —. *The Process of Mentoring in the Career Development of Female Managers*, unpublished doctoral dissertation, the University of Massachusetts, 1980.

Morgan, G., and Smircich, L. "The Case for Qualitative Research," *Academy of Management Review,* 1980, *5*, 491–500.

Nadler, D. *Feedback and Organizational Development*. Reading, MA: Addison-Wesley, 1977.

— — —. "Managing Organizational Change: An Integrative Perspective," *Journal of Applied Behavioral Science*, (April/May/June) 1981, *17*, 191–211.

Nadler, D., and Tushman, M. "A Model for Diagnosing Organizational Behavior: Applying a Congruence Perspective," *Organizational Dynamics*, Autumn 1980, 35–51.

Neugarten, B. L. *Middle Age and Aging: A Reader in Social Psychology*. Chicago: Univ. of Chicago Press, 1968.

— — —. *Personality in Middle and Late Life, Empirical Studies by Bernice L. Neugarten on Collaboration With Howard Berkowitz and Others*. New York: Atherton Press, 1964.

Neugarten, D. A., and Shafritz, J. M. *Sexuality in Organizations*, Oak Park, IL: Moore Publishing Company, 1980.

Nieva, V. F., and Gutek, B. A. *Women and Work*. New York: Praeger, 1981.

Orth, C. D., and Jacobs, F. "Women in Management: A Pattern for Change," *Harvard Business Review*, 1971, *49*, 139–147.

Ordione, G. S. *Management Decisions by Objectives*. Englewood Cliffs, NJ: Prentice-Hall, 1965.

Osherson, S. *Holding On Or Letting Go*. New York: The Free Press, 1980.

Papanek, H. "Men, Women, and Work: Reflections on the Two-Person Career," *American Journal of Sociology*, January 1973, *78*, 852–872.

Peters, J., and Waterman, R., Jr. *In Search of Excellence*. New York: Harper & Row, 1982.

Phillips, L. L. *Mentors and Proteges: A Study of the Career Development of Woman Managers and Executives in Business and Industry*. UCLA Dissertation, 1977, University Microfilms International.

— — —. "Women Finally Get Mentors of Their Own," *Business Week*, October 23, 1978, 74–80.

Phillips-Jones, L. "Establishing a Formalized Mentoring Program," *Training and Development Journal*, February 1983, 38–43.

— — —. *Mentors & Proteges*. New York: Arbor House, 1982.

Porter, L. W., Lawler, E. E., and Hackman, J. R. *Behavior in Organizations*. New York: McGraw-Hill, 1975.

Price, M. "Corporate Godfathers: By Appointment Only," *Industry Week*, June 1981, 71–73.

Quinn, B. J. C. "The Influence of Same-Sex and Cross-Sex Mentors on the Professional Development and Personality Characteristics of Women in Human Services," unpublished doctoral dissertation, Western Michigan University, 1980.

Rapaport, R., and Rapaport, R. N. "The Dual-Career Family: A Variant Pattern and Social Change," *Human Relations*, February 1969, *22*, 3–30.

— — —. "Further Considerations on the Dual Career Family," *Human Relations,* December 1971, *24,* 519–533.

— — —. "Work and Family in Contemporary Society," *American Sociological Review,* June 1965, *30,* 381–394.

Reinharz, S. *On Becoming A Social Scientist.* San Francisco: Jossey-Bass Publishers, 1979.

Rice, A. K., "Individual, Group and Intergroup Process," *Human Relations,* December 1969, *22,* 565–584.

Roche, G. R. "Much Ado About Mentors," *Harvard Business Review,* January/February 1979, 14–28.

Rowe, M. "Building Mentoring Frameworks for Women (and Men) as Part of an Effective Equal Opportunity Ecology," Boston: M.I.T., October 1980.

Sarason, S. *Work, Aging, and Social Change.* New York: Free Press, 1979.

Scarf, M. *Unfinished Business: Pressure Points in the Lives of Women.* New York: Doubleday, 1980.

Schein, E. H. *Career Dynamics: Matching Individual and Organizational Needs.* Reading, MA: Addison-Wesley, 1978.

— — —. "Increasing Organizational Effectiveness Through Better Human Resource Planning and Development," *Sloan Management Review,* Fall 1977, 1–19.

— — —. "The Individual, the Organization, and the Career: A Conceptual Scheme," *JABS,* 1971, *7,* 401–426.

— — —. "Organizational Socialization and the Profession of Management," *Industrial Management Review,* Winter 1968, 1–16.

Schein, E., and Bailyn, L. "Life/Career Considerations as Indicators of Quality of Employment," A. D. Biderman and T. F. Drury (eds.) *Measuring Work Quality for Social Reporting,* New York: Russell Sage, 1976, 15–168.

Schein, E., and Van Maanen, S. "Improving the Quality of Work Life: Career Development," *Improving Life at Work,* J. R. Hackman, and J. L. Suttle (eds.) Santa Monica: Goodyear, 1977.

Shapiro, E., Haseltine, F., and Rowe, M. "Moving Up: Role Models, Mentors, and the 'Patron System'," *Sloan Management Review,* Spring 1978, 51–58.

Sheehy, G. "The Mentor Connection: The Secret Link in the Successful Woman's Life," *New York Magazine,* April 1976, 33–39.

Sofer, C. *Men in Mid-Career.* London: Cambridge Univ. Press, 1970.

Spelman, D. H., and Crary, L. M. "Intimacy or Distance? A Case on Male-Female Relationships at Work" working paper, Bentley College, Waltham, MA, 1983.

Spiezer, J. J. "Role Models, Mentors and Sponsors: The Elusive Concepts," *Signs: Journal of Women in Culture and Society,* 1981, *6,* 692–712.

Steele, F. *Physical Settings and Organization Development*. Reading, MA: Addison-Wesley, 1973.

Steele, F., and Jenks, S. *The Feel of the Workplace: Understanding and Improving Organization Climate*. Reading, MA: Addison-Wesley, 1977.

Stewart, W. A. *A Psychosocial Study of the Formation of the Early Adult Life Structure in Women*, Ph.D. dissertation, Columbia University, 1976.

Super, D. E. *Occupational Psychology*. California: Wadsworth, 1970.

— — —. *The Psychology of Careers*. New York: Harper & Row, 1977.

— — —. *The Psychology of Careers, An Introduction to Vocational Development*. New York: Harper, 1957.

Sullivan, H. S. *The Psychiatric Interview*. New York: Norton Press, 1954.

Sweet, H. D. *A Mentor Program — Possibilities Unlimited*. 1980. (ERIC Document Reproduction Service No. EJ 238 853).

Thompson, J. "Patrons, Rabbis, Mentors — Whatever You Call Them, Women Need Them, Too," *MBA*, 1976, *10*, 27; 30; 35; 36.

Tichey, N. "Conversation with Edson W. Spencer," *Organizational Dynamics*, Summer 1983, 21–45.

Tushman, M. *Organizational Change: An Exploratory Study and Case History*. Ithaca, NY: New York State School of Individual and Labor Relations, Cornell University, 1974.

Vaillant, G. *Adaptation To Life*. Boston: Little, Brown, 1977.

— — —. "The Climb to Maturity: How the Best and the Brightest Came of Age," *Psychology Today*, September 1977, 34–40.

Van Maanen, J. "Breaking In: Socialization To Work," *Handbook of Work, Organization and Society*, R. Dubin (ed.), Chicago: Rand McNally, 1976.

— — — (ed.) *Organizational Careers: Some New Perspectives*. New York: Wiley, 1977.

— — —. "Reclaiming Qualitative Methods for Organizational Research," *Administrative Science Quarterly*, December 1979, 520–527.

Van Maanen, J., Bailyn, L., and Schein, E. H. "The Shape of Things to Come: A New Look at Organizational Careers," *Perspectives on Behavior in Organizations*, J. R. Hackman, E. E. Lawler, and L. W. Porter (eds.), New York: McGraw-Hill, 1977.

Van Maanen, J., Dubbs, J., Jr., and Faullner, R. *Varieties of Qualitative Research*. New York: Sage Publications, 1982.

Watson, G. "Resistance to Change," W. G. Bennis, K. F. Benae, and R. Chin (eds.) *The Planning of Change*, New York: Holt, Rinehart and Winston, 1969, 488–498.

Webber, R. "Career Problems of Young Managers," *California Management Review*, Summer 1976, *18*, 19–33.

Welch, M. S. *Networking: The Great New Way for Women to Get Ahead*. New York: Harcourt, 1980.

White, M. S. "Psychological and Social Barriers to Women in Science," *Science*, 1970, *170*, 413–417.

White, R. "Motivation Reconsidered: The Concepts of Competence," *Psychological Review*, 1959, *66*, 297–323.

"Women's Networks Help Them Get Ahead," *International Management*, October 1981, *36*, 41–47.

Woodlands Group, The, "Management Development Roles: Coach, Sponsor and Mentor," *Personnel Journal*, November 1980, 918–921.

Zalesnik, A. "Managers and Leaders: Are They Different?" *Harvard Business Review*, May-June 1977, *55*, 67–78.

Zalesnik, A., Dalton, G. W., and Burns, L. B. *Orientation and Conflict in Careers*. Harvard University, Division of Research, 1970.

Zaltman, G., and Duncan, R. *Strategies for Planned Change*. New York: Wiley, 1977.

# NAME INDEX

Alderfer, C. P., 167, 189, 193, 199, 205, 210, 211
Alleman, E., 172
Argyris, C., 171, 173, 210

Babad, 199, 205
Bailyn, L., 13
Baird, L., 77, 79, 100, 103, 156, 182
Baker-Miller, J., 106, 107, 114
Bardwick, J. M., 71, 114, 115, 116, 117
Bartolome, F., 79
Bass, B. M., 171
Beckhard, R., 131, 167, 173, 188, 193
Beer, M., 18, 131, 161, 163, 167, 171, 173, 177, 179, 181, 187, 189, 190, 191, 193
Benne, 190
Bennis, 190
Berg, D. N., 224
Berlew, D. E., 77, 203
Bowen, D. D., 119, 120
Bradford, 109, 110, 111
Brown, 223
Brown, L. D., 189, 211
Bunker, B., 106, 109, 117
Burns, L. B., 67

Chin, 190
Clawson, J., 3, 22, 24, 48, 106, 155, 160, 200
Collins, E., 165, 183
Crary, L. M., 129

Dalton, G., 3, 67, 89, 94, 143, 148, 155, 159, 160, 165, 168, 178, 195, 213
Dalton, M., 81
Davis, R. L., 22

Deal, T. E., 16, 131, 153, 160, 164, 197
Digman, L. A., 159, 161
Duncan, R., 179, 190

Epstein, C. F., 71, 106, 109, 115, 116, 117
Erickson, E., 68, 70, 82, 95
Evans, P., 79
Evered, 210

Filestead, W., 210
Flamholtz, E. G., 178
French, J. P., 18, 182

Garrison, P. A., 22
George, P., 129
Gilligan, 116, 205, 207
Glaser, B. G., 210, 212, 227
Gordon, F. E., 113
Gould, R., 13, 67, 68

Hackman, J. R., 17, 171, 180, 181
Hall, D. T., 13, 40, 67, 70, 74, 77, 82, 87, 94, 115, 117, 145, 146, 147, 155, 159, 160, 161, 168, 170, 171, 178, 195, 203, 212
Harris, R., 189, 193
Harrison, R., 190
Haseltine, F., 3, 24, 186, 200
Hennig, M., 81, 106, 114, 116, 203
Horner, M., 115
Hunt, 21, 204

Isabella, L., 149, 160, 230, 231

# SUBJECT INDEX